Anti-Muslim Racism on Trial

This book constitutes a critical engagement with debates on the possibilities and limits of fighting racism with the help of criminal law. With in-depth analyses of cases of anti-Muslim violence in Sweden—a mosque fire, hate speech and of a series of assaults—*Anti-Muslim Racism on Trial* sheds light on issues central for understanding the ways in which racism is approached in court. It also illustrates the different forms that Islamophobia can take. Departing from a definition of law as a knowledge regime that embodies the power to decide on the meaning of the acts on trial and to establish a valid version of these events, the author explores the possibility of justice and recognition in court. From within a post-Holocaust and post-colonial context, this book recounts the complex and ambiguous history of laws against racism, examining the ways in which racist practices change in a society where certain manifestations of racism have come to be treated as crimes. As such, it will appeal to scholars of sociology and criminology with interests in Islamophobia, race and ethnicity and violence.

Marta Kolankiewicz is an Associate Senior Lecturer in the Department of Gender Studies at Lund University, Sweden.

Routledge Research in Race and Ethnicity

The Body, Authenticity and Racism
Lindsey Garratt

Australia's New Migrants
International Students' Affective Encounters with the Border
Maria Elena Indelicato

Talking Race in Young Adulthood
Race and Everyday Life in Contemporary Britain
Bethan Harries

Gypsy Feminism
Intersectional Politics, Alliances, Gender and Queer Activism
Laura Corradi

The Intersections of Whiteness
Edited by Evangelia Kindinger and Mark Schmitt

A Nation Apart
The African-American Experience and White Nationalism
Arnold Birenbaum

Crisis and Coloniality at Europe's Margins
Creating Exotic Iceland
Kristín Loftsdóttir

Anti-Muslim Racism on Trial
Muslims, the Swedish Judiciary and the Possibility of Justice
Marta Kolankiewicz

For a full list of titles in this series, please visit https://www.routledge.com/sociology/series/RRRE

Anti-Muslim Racism on Trial
Muslims, the Swedish Judiciary and the Possibility of Justice

Marta Kolankiewicz

LONDON AND NEW YORK

First published 2019
by Routledge
2 Park Square, Milton Park, Abingdon, Oxon OX14 4RN

and by Routledge
52 Vanderbilt Avenue, New York, NY 10017

Routledge is an imprint of the Taylor & Francis Group, an informa business

© 2019 Marta Kolankiewicz

The right of Marta Kolankiewicz to be identified as author of this
work has been asserted by her in accordance with sections 77 and 78
of the Copyright, Designs and Patents Act 1988.

All rights reserved. No part of this book may be reprinted or
reproduced or utilised in any form or by any electronic, mechanical,
or other means, now known or hereafter invented, including
photocopying and recording, or in any information storage or
retrieval system, without permission in writing from the publishers.

Trademark notice: Product or corporate names may be trademarks
or registered trademarks, and are used only for identification and
explanation without intent to infringe.

British Library Cataloguing-in-Publication Data
A catalogue record for this book is available from the British Library

Library of Congress Cataloging-in-Publication Data
Names: Kolankiewicz, Marta, 1977- author.
Title: Anti-Muslim racism on trial : Muslims, the Swedish judiciary
and the possibility of justice / Marta Kolankiewicz.
Description: Abingdon, Oxon ; New York, NY : Routledge, 2019. |
Series: Routledge research in race and ethnicity ; volume 31 |
Based on author's thesis (doctoral - Lund University, Department of
Sociology, 2015) issued under title: Anti-muslim violence and the
possibility of justice, | Includes bibliographical references and index.
Identifiers: LCCN 2018060729 (print) | LCCN 2019006564 (ebook) |
ISBN 9781315107783 (Ebook) | ISBN 9781138091962
(hardback : alk. paper)
Subjects: LCSH: Hate crimes–Sweden. | Islamophobia–Sweden. |
Racism–Sweden.
Classification: LCC HV6773.55.S8 (ebook) | LCC HV6773.55.S8
K65 2019 (print) | DDC 364.15088/29709485–dc23
LC record available at https://lccn.loc.gov/2018060729

ISBN: 978-1-138-09196-2 (hbk)
ISBN: 978-1-315-10778-3 (ebk)

Typeset in Times New Roman
by Integra Software Services Pvt. Ltd.

Contents

	Acknowledgements	vi
1	Introduction	1
2	Anti-Muslim racism: scales and contexts	12
3	Meeting with the court documents: methodological reflections	33
4	Making racism a crime	53
5	On the politics and poetics of hate-crime statistics	80
6	In search of a racist subject	102
7	Hate speech, linguistic injury and language in court	123
8	On judging and responsibility	143
9	Conclusions	161
	Index	170

Acknowledgements

This book is based on a research project that was carried out during my PhD studies at the Department of Sociology at Lund University. I am grateful to the Department for funding the research and for supporting my work during those years. I want to particularly thank my supervisors—Johanna Esseveld and Tomas Brante—who guided me in the research process. Moreover, I am grateful to the participants of the Critical Studies seminars, who were an important community for me during my time at the Department of Sociology.

The transformation of my PhD thesis into this book was possible, thanks to the generous financial support of the Centre for Middle Eastern Studies at Lund University. I want to thank Dalia Abdelhady for her encouragements.

My work on the book would not be the same if it was not for the inspiring and supportive environment at the Department of Gender Studies that has become my academic home in the last years. I want to thank my colleagues and friends at the Department. I am particularly grateful to Maja Sager, with whom I have worked in the last couple of years on another project on courts and anti-racism and discussed many issues that are central to this book.

Different people have commented on the manuscript. I am grateful to Les Back, Ruth Sheldon, Anders Neergaard, Åsa Lundqvist, Jonas Otterbeck, Heléne Lööw, Diana Mulinari, Svante Lundberg, John Solomos, Niklas Selberg, David Wästerfors, Reza Banakar and Erik Havelius for their comments. I am also thankful to the participants of different seminars in which I presented my work throughout the years: the MIM seminar at Malmö University, the Gender Studies Seminar at Lund University, the Human Rights Seminar at Lund University, the seminar at the Centre for the Middle Eastern Studies at Lund University as well as the seminar at the Centre for Multidisciplinary Studies on Racism at Uppsala University.

I have greatly benefitted from some exceptional collaborative spaces in academia. During the years of my PhD research and after, I have been fortunate to be a member of the PhD collective Critical Methodologies. Thank you, Pouran Djampour, Eda Farsakoglu, Ina Knobblock, Ann Kristin Lassen,

Acknowledgements vii

Kristin Linderoth, Tove Lundberg, Vanna Nordling, Katrine Scott, Johanna Sixtensson, Emma Söderman and Maria Tonini! More recently, I have been part of an anti-colonial reading group and an anti-racist pedagogies' reading group. I am thankful to my colleagues and students, members of these groups, from whom I am learning so much.

I also want to thank the staff at Routledge. In particular, Alice Salt and Jordan Neil who have supported me in the process of preparing the text for the publication.

My gratitude goes to Lucy Edyvean who proofread and edited the text.

I would not have been able to write this book if it had not been for my family, both back in Poland and in Sweden. Dani deserves here special thanks: supporting and motivating, he was always there to discuss every detail of my research. With patience and dedication, he read different drafts of the book, helped me with translations and editing. Finally, I have to thank my little darlings, Laura and Leo, who are experts in distracting me from work in the most lovely ways!

1 Introduction

> DAMAGE: The car was scratched on the right side of the body. The scratches were approximately 1.5 m long. The scratches were so violent and deep that the white base varnish was visible.
>
> The word Muslim had been scratched on the rear left passenger door, these scratches were also very violent and deep, also here the base layer of varnish was visible. The word Muslim had been scratched in an approximately 10 cm long and 2 cm tall text.
>
> The word Muslim had also been scratched on the hood. The text was approximately 100 cm long and 40 cm tall. The scratches were violent and deep, the base layer of varnish was visible through the scratches.
>
> (Police report, Case 1)

One night in 2009, a car was vandalized in a Swedish city. This was reported to the police in the morning. The police classified the act as damage to property and the above detailed description of the state in which the car had been found was made. With much accuracy, the length and height of the scratches on the paint were measured and recorded; similarly, their depth was observed on several occasions. It was noted that the scratches on the rear left passenger door and on the bonnet spelled the word 'Muslim', but nothing in the police report indicated that attention was given to what it might have meant to scratch the word 'Muslim' on somebody's car.

The description of the damage to the car is symptomatic of the ways in which the police produce evidence of injury: the harm is measured in centimetres of scratched paint. How the police described and recorded the injury as well as the police's act of classifying it as possibly a crime of damage to property involved an act of establishing the meaning of the reported event. The materiality of the damage was the most prominent, if not the exclusive, dimension of the injury taken into account in the police report. Other possible meanings of the act of carving the word 'Muslim' on somebody's car remained occluded in the technical language in which the material evidence of the crime was captured, and with them other dimensions of the injury that the act could have entailed.

2 *Introduction*

As with a vast majority of reported crimes, this case was never taken to court. Therefore, it never received any treatment by the judiciary. The police report, however, had already been structured by the language of the legal system, classifying the act as a particular type of crime, presenting the evidence of the occurrence of this crime according to the rules of how such evidence should be collected and described, and fixing the meaning of the act, and thereby the extent and nature of the damage. Thus, the power of the judiciary had already been at work in the above fragment, organizing the text according to its logic, leading to a particular type of closure. This closure is one of the main mechanisms of the judiciary's work. It involves the establishment of the legal truth of an event, by endorsing an interpretation thereof according to legally relevant frames and in terms that are intelligible to the legal understanding of justice. In the process, other possible ways of describing and accounting for the acts in dispute remain concealed, other possible meanings indiscernible, and other possible injurious effects unrecognized.

Anti-Muslim Racism on Trial is concerned with acts, like the one described in the police report above, that involve violence of a particular character directed at Muslims or people perceived as Muslims. The point of access to these acts has been the official statistics of police reports from the period 2006–2009 compiled and classified by Brå—the Swedish National Board for Crime Prevention—as Islamophobic hate crimes, as well as court documents of the cases that were taken to court. Brå identified approximately one thousand such cases reported to the police in Sweden in those four years. They involve violence of very diverse types: slander hurled in the midst of a quarrel between neighbours; blows dealt out on the street by a stranger screaming that he will kill all Muslims; a veil torn off the head of a Muslim woman by a passer-by; letters with threats and insults; a pig's head thrown on the property of a Muslim association on which a mosque was to be built; graffiti sprayed on a train, reading that Muslims should leave Sweden; anonymous phone calls in the middle of the night; a broken window in a mosque; denied entrance to a nightclub; threats on the Internet; abusive taunts shouted in a park; and hundreds of others. Throughout the book, I will be using the term *anti-Muslim racism* to suggest that there might be a dimension to the acts that gives them a specific character and to name this character of these acts of violence. Although they are most frequently acts of violence against individuals, they simultaneously invoke violence against a group. What is at stake here is 'the *perception* of a group in the body of an individual' (Ahmed, 2004, p. 55). The acts are *anti-Muslim* as they target individuals because of this kind of perception. At the same time, they contribute to the construction of a Muslim subject that emerges as a result of the violence. Following some scholars (e.g. Fekete, 2004, 2009; Meer & Modood, 2010, pp. 69–84), I choose to use the concept of *anti-Muslim racism*, rather than Islamophobia, for three main reasons. First, to draw attention to the ways in which the idea of non-belonging—cultural,

Introduction 3

religious or other—continues to be linked in these acts to the idea of descent, and in particular to that of the immigrant as an alien. Thus, these acts are racist because those who are targeted are burdened with a type of heritage, one that is impossible to shake off. Second, by using the term 'racism', I want to underscore some continuities and similarities with the histories of oppression that have existed in the West based on the idea of race, but also on the idea of religion and culture. I will claim that the meaning of these acts is difficult, if not futile, to decipher without reference to these histories. Finally, the term 'racism' helps, I believe, to draw attention to the role that perceptions of the physicality of those attacked, although impossible to reduce to the classic biological idea of race, still play in these acts of violence.

As in the case of the vandalized car described in the opening of this chapter, these acts of violence, accessed through the police files and court documents, are registered through certain *filters*: the narratives of those affected and involved; police jargon; the technical legal terminology in which the events are captured, classified and described; the persuasive tone of the prosecutor; and, last but not least, the discourse of the judges responsible for dispensing justice in the few cases that went all the way to court. These filters reveal some stories in themselves. The acts are already named, classified, sometimes defined, other times interpreted, and, in some dozen cases, judged. *Anti-Muslim Racism on Trial* is about these ways of naming, classifying, defining, interpreting and judging—it aims at understanding *the idiom and logics of judiciary* when dealing with cases potentially involving anti-Muslim racism. In a way, this book took shape as a result of an encounter with police and court documents, an encounter that was unsettling and at the same time intriguing, as these documents bear witness to a sort of violence occurring in court. This violence is different from the type of violence described by the police; there is no blood involved, no raised voices, no scuffles. Still, the rigid and formal language of judges who categorically fixed the meanings of the acts they were adjudicating discloses a particular type of power over the experiences of those involved in trials: the power to make some stories visible, others invisible; some voices heard, others silenced; some injuries recognized, others denied. This book will attempt to decipher the judicial interpretations and to understand the rationale behind these cases in order to explore how anti-Muslim racism is understood and treated in court.

The power of the judiciary

Several scholars have described and analysed the particular nature of the power of the judiciary (e.g. Cover, 1986; Derrida, 1989). Judges do not only speak through their judgements; they do things with their words. Verdicts are performative utterances exercising power (Austin, 2011, p. 151). Through the words uttered by a judge, the law is *enforced*, which means

4   *Introduction*

applied by force, in a way that is deemed legitimate by society (Derrida, 1989, p. 927). Thereby, the judgement carries with it a very tangible and concrete violence:

> Legal interpretative acts signal and occasion the imposition of violence upon others. ... When interpreters have finished their work, they frequently leave behind victims whose lives have been torn apart by these organized, social practices of violence. Neither legal interpretation nor the violence it occasions may be properly understood apart from each other.
>
> (Cover, 1986, p. 1601)

Hence, the words uttered in the courtroom, by setting in motion a chain of institutional practices, perform violence by depriving certain persons of freedom or property, separating family members from each other and allowing the state to interfere in people's lives. This manner of understanding the force or violence of law stems from a classic conception of power as exercised by the state on its subjects within a sort of contract in which individuals transfer their own power, defined as rights, like commodities, to a sovereignty.

When I write that in this book I will be addressing the power of the judiciary, it is, however, not this type of violence that I have in mind. Rather, I refer to mechanisms through which the judiciary imposes a particular way of getting to and establishing a *true* interpretation of the events disputed in court. Thus, I am interested in the court's representational practices and its ways of recognizing some kind of injury, while keeping silent about other possible perspectives. I will explore in this book how, during trial, some experiences are made legitimate, while others are denied. I will also analyse the relation between the language, epistemology and ontology of legal knowledge, on the one hand, and the possibility of certain claims for justice being formulated and an injury claimed, on the other.

The questions that I pose here are informed by an understanding of power that links its exercise with a regime of knowledge that aims at the establishment of a certain truth. This is, essentially, the definition of power that Michel Foucault formulated in his works on madness, sexuality and discipline and that he linked to his understanding of discourse that orders and controls social life, acting multidirectionally, both in productive and destructive ways. As Foucault puts it:

> In the end, we are judged, condemned, classified, determined in our undertakings, destined to a certain mode of living or dying, as a function of the true discourses which are the bearers of the specific effects of power.
>
> (Foucault & Gordon, 1980)

Foucault thereby shifts focus from the sources of authoritative violence, whose power could be defined in a classic way as the oppression of

Introduction 5

sovereignty upon its subjects, to the domains in which the regimes of truth are produced and human bodies disciplined more subtly and imperceptibly, such as through medicine or psychiatry. While Foucault did not analyse law itself, which remained to him an instance of the vanishing classic authority, I will follow Foucauldian feminist analyses of law and the judiciary that claim that law can be seen as a regime of truth (Smart, 2002). Thus, my interest lies in violence that takes place in court and my approach is shaped by an understanding of the law and the judiciary, not so much as an *instrument of authoritative power*, but as an *interpretative power* in and of itself. This approach is inspired by Carol Smart's argument:

> If we accept that law, like science, makes a claim to truth and that this is indivisible from the experience of power, we can see that law exercises power not simply in its material effects (judgements) but also in its ability to disqualify other knowledges and experiences.
>
> (2002, p. 11)

Smart claims that there are parallels in the ways that law and science operate in terms of making claims to truth. She furthermore argues that, through its method and in its language, law produces knowledge of the reality that it examines and adjudicates. In this sense, law operates like science, but in an extreme way—its claims to truth and its verdicts are firm and final and thereby other interpretations are categorically disqualified as invalid; there is only one unambiguous version of the disputed events that the court must establish during the trial. Moreover, by defining the terms of reference in which acts are interpreted in court, and by providing the language in which an injury can be expressed, law lays down the possible frameworks for justice claims. As such, law exercises its power by defining the limits of what Judith Butler calls 'speakability' and 'unspeakability', that is, by establishing a discursive field in which things can be expressed and zones of silence where experiences that cannot be expressed are retained (Butler, 1997, p. 136).

With this theoretical framework, I will explore how the knowledge about the acts involving anti-Muslim racism is produced and legitimized in court. In particular, I am interested in exploring the definitions and interpretations of racism made by the judiciary: Which meanings of a violent act targeting Muslims or people perceived as Muslims become legitimized in Swedish courts, and which meanings are occluded in the process? What is the rationale behind the judgements? How is racism defined in law and in court? What is necessary for an act to be classified as racist? And, more indirectly: What kind of injury can be claimed in court?

Contextualizing the book: beyond 'Swedish exceptionalism'

To study the ways in which anti-Muslim racism is dealt with by the judiciary in Sweden is interesting for several reasons. For some time, an idea of

6 Introduction

'Swedish exceptionalism' has become quite commonplace both as a part of the Swedish national identity and a kind of international renown. As various scholars have noticed, until recently the country was treated as *the* model of a tolerant and egalitarian society, combining welfare with multiculturalism (Eliassi, 2017, p. 18; Schierup & Ålund, 2011, p. 47). This exceptionalism has been considered not only as a feature of an inclusive state system, but also as a characteristic inherent to Swedish society and manifested in widespread tolerance and openness. It reflects a political ideal that granted immigrants and minorities extensive rights and broad inclusion in the welfare system as well as freedom of choice regarding their identities. It is often assumed that this ideal also led to a number of legal measures targeting racism and discrimination. In Chapter 4, I describe the genealogies of different laws against racism introduced in Sweden in an attempt to create a more nuanced image of the dynamics that led to the criminalization of some forms of racism.

This image of Swedish exceptionalism has been questioned, however, by those who study the development of the Swedish migration regime and multiculturalism, as disregarding urban segregation, labour market discrimination, and other forms of discrimination, and many other ways in which minorities in Sweden may have been excluded (Schierup & Ålund, 2011). Moreover, in the context of the developments in the 1990s, it has been noticed that, despite the exceptional levels of general tolerance, members of minorities in Sweden were already being confronted with growing racism (Pred, 2000). In this context, the two mass murderers attacking specifically immigrants—the Laser Man (*Lasermannen*) in the 1990s and, more recently, Peter Mangs—were often mentioned as having a significant impact on the everyday experiences of belonging and safety among immigrants and racialized minorities (Gardell, 2011; Khosravi, 2010; Tamas, 2005). Despite these criticisms, Swedish exceptionalism persists both as an international perception and as an important part of the Swedish national identity.

In recent years, another image of Sweden has started to circulate: Sweden as a failed state (Eliassi, 2017). In this imaginary, Sweden is also defined as exceptional, but this time because of its naïve faith in the model of a multicultural welfare state. Pictures of suburbs with burning cars are here mixed with racializing discourses about migration and lack of integration. This image of Sweden is connected to the idea of Swedish exceptionalism in a specific way—as if it were its negative: the Swedish multicultural model is portrayed as the source of the failure of the system, the openness is criticized as leading to uncontrollable demographic shifts, and it is claimed that tolerance needs some limits and constraints in order for Swedish society to remain gender-equal and for the welfare state to remain efficient. This image of Sweden as failed, or threatened by collapse, has its different variants. The most vulgar versions originated from and were spread by the far-right, most notably the Sweden Democrats, a party with roots in the White Power movement that entered the Swedish Parliament for the first time in 2010 and in 2014 became the third-largest party in the country (Elgenius & Rydgren, 2017; Rydgren, 2005). In a more moderate version, this image has been developed in a mainstream criticism of Swedish multiculturalism. In both versions, this dystopic image of Sweden has thrived, internally in Sweden and internationally, reflecting different kinds of ideological tensions and contentions. What is particularly significant, in the context of this book, is that certain ideas about Muslims and Islam have played a central role in this image of Sweden. Muslims and Islam have been repeatedly identified as a site and a source of threat to the Swedish nation or welfare state (Elgenius & Rydgren, 2017; Schierup, Ålund & Neergaard, 2018). In Chapter 2, I describe these discourses and imaginaries about Muslims and Islam in more detail.

Because of the ways in which these conflicting, albeit intertwined, images of Sweden have circulated and gained an almost paradigmatic significance, the case of Sweden is interesting in its singularity. To look at how the Swedish state, through its judiciary, is dealing with cases of anti-Muslim racism is interesting in this context for several reasons. It can be a way to go beyond such simplistic accounts of Swedish exceptionalism and to offer an analysis that, by being grounded in case studies, can bring us closer to the complexities and ambivalences of the ways in which anti-Muslim racism is articulated and treated by the Swedish state. It can be interesting also because it helps us to understand how racism in general, and anti-Muslim racism in particular, transforms and adapts to a context in which until recently there has been little space for blatantly racist expression. Particularly worthy of analysis here will be the reciprocal influence of racism and the law and, more exactly, an analysis of how the criminalization of certain forms of racism transforms and influences the ways that racism can be articulated.

Overview of the book

The book opens with Chapter 2 that introduces the contexts of anti-Muslim racism today. It proposes an understanding of acts reported to the police and gathered in Brå's statistics of Islamophobic hate crimes in a broader context of anti-Muslim racism in Sweden, Europe and the West in the last few decades. It uses the concept of scales and rescaling to show how we need to understand European and national scales to be able to attend to the meanings, workings and effects of these concrete acts of violence. The chapter discusses the Mohammed cartoons controversies, veil affairs and the 'war on terror' as significant for articulations of anti-Muslim racism. It also shows how the issues of migration and integration become central to how Muslims are defined in some nationalistic projects and in the emergence of a specific European project—the European Union. One of the points made is that acts of anti-Muslim racism interpellate some bodies and some subjects in particular ways. Apart from introducing these contexts, the chapter also aims at presenting the kind of reading of the material that will be developed in this book.

8   *Introduction*

Chapter 3 offers a reflection on the research process. By focusing on disruptive moments, abandoned perspectives and unsettling emotions, I try to explore the methodological and theoretical choices that I have made in this book. I see these as a result of an intersection of the institutional settings in which the knowledge that I produce is located and my personal struggles with the material that I analyse. I claim that my examination of, but also a certain interaction with, police records and court documents shaped my approach, influencing the choice of methodological tools and theoretical frameworks. In this sense, these were not merely preselected and applied to the material but they emerged *in the process* of my reading, reacting to and struggling with the documents that I was to analyse. I discuss here how the epistemological, ontological, terminological and political issues related to my project became evident and pressing as I explored the ways in which these issues are inherent in the workings and dynamics of the judiciary. In this way, the methodological reflections become an opportunity for me to present and analyse the court as a site of knowledge production, governed by specific epistemological and methodological logics.

The following two chapters introduce some crucial contexts relevant to the understanding of the case studies: Chapter 4 is dedicated to a historical overview of the Swedish legislation against racism and Chapter 5 provides a description and analysis of the statistical data on hate crimes produced by Brå.

More specifically, in Chapter 4, I explore the preliminary works that led to the adoption in Sweden of legal instruments against racism. The aim is to describe how some types of racist acts have been criminalized and how, in this process, the Swedish nation has been imagined as tolerant, open and diverse. My ambition is to historically contextualize the legal texts and to show how these are embedded in social dynamics related to the shame of racism, dynamics that could enable such laws to be enacted, although, at the same time, they often included a denial of racism. The chapter is designed to fulfil two functions: to introduce the laws relevant to the cases that I analyse later in my book, and to analyse the particular dynamics that shaped the ways in which racism is addressed in Sweden.

Chapter 5 is devoted to a description and analysis of the statistical data on hate crimes produced by Brå. The main reason for me to look more closely at how these data are collected and how hate crime is defined, classified, described and treated in Swedish national reports is the fact that my own material was accessed through these statistics. To critically examine how the knowledge about this type of act is produced is thus essential for my understanding of what kind of cases I have at hand. At the same time, this analysis sheds some light on what underlies such knowledge and how the institutional and political settings in which the statistics are collected, as well as the methodological choices of the state agencies responsible for these data, influence the very form of this knowledge. Here, I also describe how a particular category of Islamophobic hate crimes was singled out from

Introduction 9

and then absorbed back into other categories in the statistics. In a way, this chapter also continues the historical account initiated in Chapter 4, by addressing the changes in the ways some kinds of racist practices—now under the name of 'hate crime'—have been officially addressed in Sweden in recent decades.

The subsequent three chapters gathered present an analysis of selected cases that were adjudicated in court. In these chapters, I analyse the ways in which justice was meted out and explore the rationale behind the judgements. The choice of the cases was governed by an attempt to understand how courts proceed to identify racism. In this sense, these cases are somehow emblematic or particularly illustrative of some aspects of the court's understanding of racism.

In Chapter 6, where I examine a case of a mosque fire, I try to understand why the judges did not classify the case as racist and thus did not apply the penalty enhancement provision. I claim that the main focus in this case was on the defendant's *intentions* and *motivations* for the act of setting the mosque on fire. I suggest that the court looked for a particular *racist subject*—defined as ideologically explicit, cognizant of and open about their motives. In this case, however, the act had been performed by a person whose motivations remained opaque and whose relation to racist ideology was unclear and ambivalent, and this is why, I suggest, the court had difficulties in taking into consideration the possibility of a racist nature of the act of violence. I argue that it is this unrecognized meaning of the event that was claimed to be the core of the injury by the representatives of the Muslim community who reported the incident to the police and later testified in court. I discuss, moreover, how in their accounts they unsuccessfully tried to express a particular type of harm that the act of setting the mosque on fire and taking and throwing around the sacred books involved. I try to understand why this type of harm remains unnoticed and thus unrecognized in court. Chapter 6 also provides an analysis of a trial as a particular *scene of address* which shapes the possible accounts of those involved.

Chapter 7 approaches another kind of difficulty related to achieving justice in cases involving racism. This time it has to do with how verbal abuse, and language more generally, is treated in court. I analyse a case of offensive emails sent to a Muslim black female, a local politician. I try to understand the court's difficulties in perceiving the racist message of these letters. I argue that these difficulties are partly related to a particular approach to language endorsed by the court that strictly separates form from message. I explore this approach and show how it leads to a conception of racist speech as located in an inadequate form and thus defined as 'impolite', as a result of which racism is viewed as violating a certain type of civility. I suggest that such an approach defines racist speech as a property of some social classes. While identifying and trying to explain the court's approach to language, my method in analysing the case consists in deconstructing the language of the documents. Looking at how the judgement is rhetorically

10 *Introduction*

built, I claim that the process of dispensing justice cannot be limited to the *message* that is being communicated in the document, that is, the verdict; it already resides in the *form* of this document. I argue that the court's *practice* of language, how the form and message of the judgement are involved in the process of creating a meaning in this judicial speech act, contrasts with the explicit approach to language applied to adjudicate the offensiveness of the speech on trial.

In Chapter 8, two cases involving the same defendant and his very similar acts of physical and verbal violence against two taxi drivers are analysed. The point of departure is a bewilderment by the difference in how the cases unfolded and how this, in turn, resulted in very different treatment by the courts. This difference lay not so much in the verdicts in the two cases as in the rhetorical framing in the judgements: while the first case was approached, explained and adjudicated as a case of racist violence, in the second one, any reference to this possible dimension of the acts was missing. One of the factors that contributed to this outcome was how the acts on trial were understood by the injured parties. My argument is that it is important to see the agency of those involved in trials in order to understand the outcomes thereof. This also applies to how the judges interpret the law. The chapter is thereby an attempt to develop a more dynamic model of the judiciary, in which the laws are steadily transformed through the interpretative practice of those who judge.

In the concluding Chapter 9, I sum up the results of my study. Here I develop an understanding of racism based on insights gained throughout my analysis of the cases. Moreover, I develop an argument about the significance of the meeting between racist acts and law, and about how the context in which racism is forbidden by the law influences the character of racist acts. Finally, I re-examine the judgements, in particular exploring the nature of the silence around the possibility that the acts of violence on trial represent racism, and formulate a claim that the treatment of the cases by the judiciary involved a particular type of unrecognition.

Bibliography

Ahmed, S. (2004). *The Cultural Politics of Emotion*. Edinburgh: Edinburgh University Press.

Austin, J. (2011). *How to Do Things with Words*. Oxford: Oxford University Press.

Butler, J. (1997). *Excitable Speech: A Politics of the Performative*. New York; London: Routledge.

Cover, R. (1986). 'Violence and the Word.' *The Yale Law Journal*, *95*(8), 1601–1629.

Derrida, J. (1989). 'Force of Law: The "Mystical Foudation of Authority".' *Cardozo Law Review, 920*(11), 920–1046.

Elgenius, G. & Rydgren, J. (2017). 'The Sweden Democrats and the Ethno-Nationalist Rhetoric of Decay and Betrayal.' *Sociologisk forskning*, *54*(4), 353–358.

Eliassi, B. (2017). 'Conceptions of Immigrant Integration and Racism among Social Workers in Sweden.' *Journal of Progressive Human Services, 28*(1), 6–35.

Introduction   11

Fekete, L. (2004). 'Anti-Muslim Racism and the European Security State.' *Race & Class*, *46*(1), 3–29.

Fekete, L. (2009). *A Suitable Enemy: Racism, Migration and Islamophobia in Europe.* London: Pluto.

Foucault, M. & Gordon, C. (Eds.). (1980). *Power/Knowledge: Selected Interviews and Other Writings 1972–1977.* Brighton: Harvester Press.

Gardell, M. (2011). *Islamofobi* (2nd edn.). Stockholm: Leopard.

Khosravi, S. (2010). *'Illegal' Traveller: An Auto-Ethnography of Borders.* New York, NY: Springer eBooks.

Meer, N. & Modood, T. (2010). 'Islamophobia as Cultural Racism? Martin Amis and the Racialization of Muslims.' In A. Sayyid (Ed.), *Thinking through Islamophobia.* London: Hurst & Co., pp. 69–83.

Pred, A. (2000). *Even in Sweden: Racisms, Racialized Spaces, and the Popular Geographical Imagination.* Berkeley: University of California Press.

Rydgren, J. (2005). *Från Skattemissnöje till etnisk nationalism: högerpopulism och parlamentarisk högerextremism i Sverige.* Lund: Studentlitteratur.

Schierup, C.-U. & Ålund, A. (2011). 'The End of Swedish Exceptionalism?: Citizenship, Neo-Liberalism and Politics of Exclusion.' *Race & Class*, *53*(1), 45–64.

Schierup, C.-U., Ålund, A. & Neergaard, A. (2018). '"Race" and the Upsurge of Antagonistic Popular Movements in Sweden.' *Ethnic and Racial Studies*, *41*(10), 1837–1854.

Smart, C. (2002). *Feminism and the Power of Law.* London: Routledge.

Tamas, G. (2005). *Lasermannen: en berättelse om Sverige.* Stockholm: Ordfront.

2 Anti-Muslim racism
Scales and contexts

The Assistant Principal at a high school in Rönnstad left a letter at the police station in Rönnstad that was addressed to a pupil and contained offensive and racist elements.

CRIME

An unknown perpetrator is guilty of MOLESTATION by other reckless conduct molesting the injured party. This through a letter addressed to the person concerned with content in which the injured party is cursed, called a whore, with written text 'Muslims go home', 'all terrorists out' and 'Swedes first'.

INCIDENT

An unknown sender has mailed a letter addressed to the secondary school in Rönnstad and to the student Laila Farsi who is in the 3rd grade. The letter landed in the post-office box of one of the teachers. The teacher passed the unopened letter to Laila Farsi.

The letter contained images of Mohammed cartoons and a newspaper article in which Laila Farsi is in a picture. On the paper with the cartoons, someone has written 'Muslims go home', 'all terrorists out' and 'Swedes first'. On the newspaper article, someone has crossed over Laila Farsi's picture and written 'WHORE' and 'GO HOME'.

Leila Farsi has no idea who could have done this against her.

(Police report, Case 2)[1,2]

This chapter offers an overview of anti-Muslim discourses and imaginaries circulating in Sweden, and, more broadly, in Europe and the West. One of the purposes of this kind of contextualization of anti-Muslim racism is to provide a frame of reference essential to understanding the dynamics and nature of the acts of violence described in the police and court documents that constitute the material of this book. I try to show how these acts, rather than just being treated as manifestations of absurd outbursts or generic violence, can become intelligible and understood as deeply interconnected with the construction of Muslims as racialized subjects. Thus, this

Anti-Muslim racism 13

chapter is aimed at introducing particular ways of seeing and recognizing anti-Muslim racism. It has been guided by the following questions: What kind of contextisation is necessary in order to understand the message and injurious effects of acts like the one described in Laila Farsi's case that opens this chapter? What kind of histories, discourses and imaginaries have been recirculated in articulations of anti-Muslim racism in Sweden and Europe in the last couple of decades? What kind of established modes of offence does this type of acts utilize? And in what vocabularies is the offence expressed?

The method used to structure the overview of the relevant anti-Muslim discourses and imaginaries has consisted in identification of some tropes and motifs that have been recurring in the police reports from the years 2006–2009 over the cases that had been classified by Brå as Islamophobic hate crimes. In this sense, in this chapter, I begin to read my material. Rather than offering a complete analysis, however, this first reading helps me, on the one hand, to identify the sites of anti-Muslim racism in tropes and motifs as belonging to certain Islamophobic repertoires circulating in defined places and times, and, on the other, to provide illustrations thereof. My knowledge of these repertoires is, at the same time, based on the important emerging scholarship describing and analysing Islamophobia in the West (Berg, 1998; Bobako, 2017; European Centre on Racism and Xenophobia, 2006; Fekete, 2009; Gardell, 2011; Malm, 2009; Matthis, 2005; Meer & Modood, 2010a, 2010b; Morgan & Poynting, 2012; Said, 2003; Sayyid, 2010; Scott, 2007). Thus, my method consists in a constant movement back and forth between my empirical material and relevant literature on Islamophobia, and other literature that helps us understand articulations of anti-Muslim racism in Sweden and Europe today.

One claim made in this chapter is that it is useful to think about the workings of anti-Muslim racism in terms of *scales* (Richa et al., 2002). This means that, while the examples of acts of violence used in this chapter illustrate how anti-Muslim racism is articulated in everyday interactions and thus can be seen on *the scale of body and subject*, its understanding requires a kind of *rescaling* (Back & Sinha, 2018, pp. 39–40). Such a rescaling involves shifting the focus from the scene in which the concrete acts of violence take place to broader contexts in which contents, forms and modes of articulating anti-Muslim racism become intelligible. In this chapter, I explore mainly two such larger scales: the *national scale* on which the context of the Swedish nation-state is central and the *regional scale* on which the context of Europe and sometimes 'the West' are central.[3] In this approach, the scales cannot be reduced to discrete levels of circulation of anti-Muslim discourses, practices and representations. Instead, they are treated as different sites and aspects with specific dynamics shaping the very core of anti-Muslim racism.

While rescaling transforms our ways of understanding the *location and spatial relations* of anti-Muslim racism, pointing to the embeddedness of single acts of violence in broader anti-Muslim discourses, it also forces us to rethink *temporal frames* in which we see these acts. And thus, rather than

14 *Anti-Muslim racism*

limit our vision by a kind of presentism (Back & Sinha, 2018, pp. 39–40), the aim is to see them as historical and as recirculating different imaginaries that develop and shift over time. The temporal frames are important here in order to see anti-Muslim racism as a dynamic phenomenon constantly evolving and adjusting to new circumstances that needs to be analysed in its diverse temporal contexts, rather than as an ahistorical or trans-historical phenomenon of marginalization of Muslims (Sayyid, 2010, p. 16). The overview presented in this chapter will trace specific genealogies of anti-Muslim racism, paying special attention to its dynamics in the 2000s, the time of the occurrence of the cases presented in this study. I will, however, also briefly sketch the developments of the 2010s that have had an impact on articulations of anti-Muslim racism today showing their changing nature.

The Mohammed cartoons controversy and staging the clash of civilizations

The case of the letter received by Laila Farsi is not the only act of threat and insult reported to the police in Sweden in the aftermath of the Mohammed cartoon controversy.[4] Similar letters have been sent to individuals and organizations somehow related to Muslim communities. For instance, several pages including Mohammed cartoons from *Jyllands-Posten* were sent to a diplomatic institution with a handwritten message saying:

> Bombs will be placed in mosques and Muslim restaurants in the near future. Hurrah for freedom of the press! Throw the leeches out of the Swedish welfare society! Take Islam with you and go home!
>
> (Police report, Case 3)

Likewise, somebody sent a letter to a women's organization with two pages of Mohammed cartoons. On the back of one of the pages they had written 'Copy' and 'Spread'. These examples of the recirculation of Mohammed cartoons help us to see how certain events may have had an impact on articulations of anti-Muslim racism. Research has been done on how the Mohammed cartoon controversy has led to eruptions of violence towards people perceived as Muslims and deeply transformed the lives of Muslim communities (Högfeldt, Sander & Larsson, 2008). A similar impact has been observed in the United States and Europe in the aftermath of 9/11 and 7/7 (see, e.g., Peek, 2011; Seidler, 2007). What the examples above suggest, however, is that it is necessary to understand the role of the Mohammed cartoon controversy beyond simple triggers for violence. To this end, it may be useful to explore the nature and workings of the recirculation of the cartoons.

The anonymous sender of the letter to Laila Farsi used the cartoons as a means of molestation, along with other invectives. This suggests that the cartoons potentially bear a violent message similar to that of other insults

Anti-Muslim racism 15

contained in the letter. As is the case of other hate speech, such a reuse builds on a kind of repetition of the offence that the Mohammed cartoons originally instantiated (Butler, 1997, pp. 34–36).

However, this quote from the repertoire of anti-Muslim insult does something more than simply repeat an offence. The exclamation 'Hurrah for freedom of the press!' can be understood in the context in which the cartoons were framed as a performance of freedom of speech during the controversy and, at the same time, instituted as a value intrinsic to Western democracies. Legitimacy of the cartoons was claimed by situating the right to offend in the realm of European or Western civilization. Moreover, the imagined Western community, symbolized by the ideal of freedom of speech, was juxtaposed with an imagined Muslim community that was unable to tolerate an offence and thereby to adhere to Western values. In this Orientalist move, Islam was constructed as opposed to the West and not belonging to it. In light of this, the letters, by including the imperative 'Go home', seem to mobilize the imaginaries, by suggesting that Muslims and Islam do not belong in Sweden. In this sense, the employment of the Mohammed cartoons in the anonymous letters needs to be understood in the context of established ways of defining Islam and Europe as clashing.

The idea of a clash between Islam and the West, that has been influential in the last decades, was developed by scholars and taken over by politicians during the 1990s. It gained most attention after the publication of Samuel Huntington's article and then book *Clash of Civilisations* (Huntington, 1993, 2002). The clash-of-civilization thesis draws on an idea of civilizations— among others, the West and Islam—as monolithic, static and fundamentally different from each other, and uses this idea to diagnose the present and predict the future as being reducible to clashes. In its presentation of both the West and Islam, Huntington's thesis is highly Orientalist in that, similarly to Orientalist representations, it presents the two civilizations as a binary opposition, in which the Orient serves as an antithesis of the Occident (Said, 2003). The Mohammed cartoon controversy re-enacted the idea of clash of civilizations as a spectacle, fixing the identities of Muslims as fanatical, irrational and religious and of the West as democratic, rational and secular. Freedom of speech played a crucial role in these enactments, both as a core value attached to the West and as a mode of producing the controversy.

While the Mohammed cartoon controversy and other similar affairs taking place both before and after it drew on these broader frames, they would also activate specific national and local anxieties, shifting accents depending on context.[5] Sweden had an affair of its own—the Lars Vilks Mohammed drawings controversy—that began in 2007 with an art gallery refusing to exhibit Vilks's drawings and unfolded in the following years with several developments, including protests, threats and attacks against Vilks, as well as his participation in various public events. This controversy followed a very different scenario from the Danish one: from the refusal of the

16 *Anti-Muslim racism*

art gallery to exhibit the drawings, through reactions of both Swedish authorities and the art world to the cartoons, to much more divided opinions about Vilks's cartoons. In a way, the controversy developed also in relation to—and, to a certain degree, in opposition to—the Danish Mohammed cartoon controversy, exposing certain tensions between the countries' dominant ways of relating to the issues of migration, multiculturalism and freedom of speech. In this sense, the controversies represented an occasion to construct two different national projects in opposition to each other. In these, Sweden would stand for tolerance and political correctness, while Denmark would stand for liberalism and freedom of speech (for an analysis of Lars Vilks's controversy, see Orrenius, 2017).

Independent of these variations, what the different controversies have had in common is that they all have re-established offences as a conventional way of interpellating Muslims in Europe. As a result, insult has gradually become one of the dominating modes of addressing Muslims. While cartoons have become one of the most usual instances of such interpellation, it can also be found in other kinds of utterances. Oriana Fallaci's bestseller *The Rage and the Pride* (2002) had played a central role in this development (Bobako, 2017). The book has been interpreted as belonging to a specific genre, 'characterized not by truth or falsity, but by a concrete, ritual meaning': the slur. As such, 'it does not so much say something about reality, but rather institutes one of its own' (Tokarska-Bakir, quoted in Bobako, 2017, p. 54, my translation). In a similar way, the Mohammed cartoons and other representations of Muslims circulating in the European public space have instituted Muslims as subjects embodying a particular type of identity.

Veil affairs and the gendered nature of anti-Muslim racism

> Huda met a girl and a boy on the escalator. She was on her way down to the train station and the couple on their way up. The boy shouts very loudly at Huda that she should take off her veil because she is in Sweden and that she is a 'whore'. He shouts many things to her that Huda did not catch. When she came down to the platform, there were several people standing there and laughing at her/him.
>
> (Police report, Case 4)

The verbal attack on Huda illustrates the centrality of the veil as a device of identification and stigmatization of Muslim women. The significance of the imperative to 'unveil', by which Huda was addressed, can be grasped in the context of the use of 'unveiling' in the recurrent veil affairs in Europe. So, too, can the ways in which the attack seems to establish veiling as not belonging to Sweden, when we observe how the imperative to unveil is followed by the argument 'because she is in Sweden'. The attack on Huda seems to reveal a sort of tension in relation to the sexuality of Muslim women that has been present in the veil affairs. This can be sensed in the ways the insult mixes the idea of the veil as out of place in Sweden—something that in the veil affairs was often backed by an interpretation of the veil as a symbol of a woman's submission to her religion—with the sexualized slander 'whore'.

Huda's case is one of many gathered by Brå in which Muslim women are attacked. The veil seems to be one of the main markers to identify Muslim women and one of the main sites around which acts of anti-Muslim racism are performed. Veiled women are insulted, spat upon, molested and assaulted, and the veil is torn from their heads.[6] The veil also points to the gendered nature of anti-Muslim racism. Thus, in order to understand the attack on Huda and similar attacks, we need to explore the frames of reference that make these acts intelligible in a broader context of contestations around the veil: we need to understand the genealogies and nature of the veil affairs.

Throughout the last decade of the twentieth century and the first two of the twenty-first, the dynamics and intensity of different veil affairs changed considerably in Europe. From an issue that was present mostly in the French context, it became almost all over Europe a subject of intense debates and struggles. The veil has also become one of the attributes of Muslims that has been most subject to regulation, both in policies and laws, across Europe. When, in the late 1990s, the first attempts to restrict the use of the veil by Muslim girls and young women in French schools were made, it was still difficult to imagine that these kinds of regulations would within two decades be in force on national or local levels throughout most of the European Union[7] (Open Society Foundation, 2018). Moreover, this development has been further legitimized, at least in the domain of the labour market, by the EU Court of Justice in its decisions from 2017, in which the Court decided that it was not discrimination for an employer to have rules that prohibit the use of veils at work (Bougnaoui v Micropole SA case and Achbita v G4S). Still, this shift has taken place not without opposition and resistance: laws prohibiting Muslim female clothing have been questioned and rejected, like in the case of the Swedish local bans or the French 'burkini' ban (Open Society Foundation, 2018). What is important is that this development has created a growing mobilization around the veil among Muslim women, leading to struggles over definitions and interpretations of the practice of veiling, in some respects resembling the dynamics described by Frantz Fanon in his essay 'Algeria Unveiled' that explores struggles over the veil in colonial Algeria (Fanon, 1989).

Again, similarly to the Mohammed cartoon controversies described above, in order to fully comprehend the character and the stakes of the different veil affairs, one needs to take into consideration the European dynamics as well as the national and local contexts. The most paradigmatic case here still remains the French one, revolving initially and mainly around a ban on veils in schools, but later also including an attempt to ban the burkini. What is most striking in the French veil affairs—*affaires du foulard*—is how they are implicated in the context of the French colonial past that is

18 *Anti-Muslim racism*

echoed in the present politics towards immigrants. They also encapsulate a specific idea of national identity based on belonging to the *République*, with its distinctive ways of dealing with cultural differences and its focus on a particular vision of secularism—*laïcité*. Yet, to understand the impact of the French case on how the veil has come to be treated throughout Europe, it is important to note that the French veil affairs drew on and firmly established a Western objectification of Islam as incompatible with secularism (Scott, 2007, p. 9). In her analysis of the French *affaires du foulard*, Jaon Scott underlines these different factors feeding into French representations of the Muslim veil; in particular, she explores how the affairs were shaped by a specific idea of sexuality. She argues that: 'Islam's insistence on recognizing the difficulties posed by sexuality revealed more than republicans wanted to see about the limits of their own system' (2007, p. 154), pointing to how both what she calls 'the covered' and 'the open system' can be sexist. This realization would become particularly explicit in the burkini affair: when in 2016 the French police started to execute the local provision banning the use of the covering swimsuits used by Muslim women on the beaches in southern France, an Internet meme circulated in social media putting together a picture from 2016 of a male police officer forcing a women to undress, with a picture from 1925 of a man measuring the length of a woman's swimsuit, both pictures taken on French beaches. Hence, the veil affairs have troubled the French and the Western idea of liberation from sexism as an easy move from veiling to unveiling, suggesting that both practices can be implicated in the masculine gaze (Bobako, 2017; Delphy, 2015; Fanon, 1989; Scott, 2007).[8]

One of the most relevant features of the veil affairs across Europe is that they established a particular vocabulary to talk about Islam and Muslims. Remarkably, this vocabulary did not originate from the extremist right or the growing populist movements—although those too have used the veil in their anti-Muslim rhetorics—but from mainstream liberalism and, in some cases, even left-wing feminism. This means that anti-Muslim imaginaries cannot be reduced to the field of extremism, but have to be recognized as a part of the European mainstream. They constitute what Monika Bobako (2017, p. 221) calls 'progressivist Islamophobia' that inscribes itself in the conceptual framework of modernity and progress. Here, the Mohammed cartoon controversies and veil affairs meet each other, in that they both encapsulate ideas about a clash between Islam and the West, defined through the ideas of modernity, secularism, liberalism and individual emancipation as well as through a specific conception of human rights and freedoms. Moreover, what the veil affairs reveal is a complicity in creating these kinds of anti-Muslim imaginaries of some variants of feminism, especially those that stress emancipation from religion as a central part of women's liberation. In many respects, the experiences of Muslim women have become one of the points of contention and rupture in the feminist movements in the West, making splits between liberal and post-colonial feminists more visible.[9]

Anti-Muslim racism 19

In Sweden, the veil has only recently become an important site for this type of contention. In the period from which the police reports and court cases analysed in this book come, that is, from 2006 to 2009, the veil seemed still not to have entered the public debates to the extent that it had in France. The first attempt to ban the veil was presented in 2009, followed by several other attempts to ban either the veil or the burqa. All these attempts have failed, however. Motions have been tabled both by the far-right party, the Sweden Democrats, and the mainstream right and centre parties, following the above-described European trend of the veil as an issue for mainstream liberal parties (Open Society Foundation, 2018, p. 75). Until recently, probably the most notorious use of a representation of veiled women was in an election advertisement produced by the Sweden Democrats before the 2010 elections. It showed women dressed in burqas pushing prams in a race to collect welfare money, against an elderly white woman pushing a walking frame. The advertisement reproduced an idea of Muslim women as abusing the welfare system, at the same time as in its aesthetics it demonized veiled women as a threat, by playing with an image of demographic invasion, often present in Islamophobic conspiracy theories (Malm, 2009). Thus, the veil has been framed as problematic both in mainstream and far-right discourses in Sweden.

The accusation of terrorism and the 'war on terror'

> An unknown perpetrator committed an act of unlawful discrimination by saying to the injured party 'you fucking wog', 'you are a terrorist', 'fucking Muslims', 'fucking Arabs', *'fuck you'*, 'go to hell' and other things. The perpetrator also yelled to the other people on the train 'do not get on the train. He is a terrorist!'
>
> Malik Haddad works as a ticket controller for the local train company. He asked the perpetrator to show his ticket or to pay for the trip. The perpetrator said that he would get off the train at the central station and he thus would not pay. At the central station Malik Haddad asked the perpetrator to get off. He started then to scream and molest Malik Haddad. The perpetrator was under the influence of alcohol.
>
> (Police report, Case 5)

As discussed above, insult has become one of the central modes of inter-pellating Muslims in Europe. In the cases reported to the police that I analyse, the insult is often also conflated with accusations, casting suspicion on people perceived as Muslims. One of the central tropes is the accusation of terrorism. This kind of accusation is made in different contexts and situations. One example of such an insult is the situation reported by Malik Haddad. Another one was reported by a father whose son with roots in the Middle East was asked during a language class in school what he wanted to be when he grew up and responded that he

20 *Anti-Muslim racism*

wanted to be a pilot. To this he heard from his teacher: 'So that you can fly into the World Trade Center again?'

When pronounced in public spaces and, in particular, on public transport, like in the case above, such accusations play with what Vic Seidler calls 'landscapes of fear' that have emerged in many places in Europe in the aftermath of different terrorist attacks (Seidler, 2007). In these cases, those on whom suspicion is cast become exposed in complex ways to a situation in which fears and tensions might easily get out of control. The ways in which Muslims are *framed* as terrorists—and 'framed' here, following Judith Butler, is understood not only as 'perceived through an interpretative scheme', but also as 'falsely incriminated' (2009, p. 8)—need to be understood in the context of a repeated backlash, landscapes of fear and popular anger. Both traditional and social media representations of different terrorist attacks in the West have resulted in an identification of some audiences with the distant 'suffering other', producing the West as an imagined political and cultural community (Chouliaraki, 2006, pp. 157–160). How this kind of identification, combined with a growing fear, can work has been described by scholars writing about the experiences of Muslims in times of backlash (Peek, 2011).

What is, however, special about the type of vulnerability that the accusation of terrorism produces is that it is not only about Muslim communities being confronted with 'popular anger', but, in the words of Moustafa Bayoumi, about being subject to 'religious and national-origin profiling' (2011, p. 16). In this sense, an accusation of terrorism in a public space may also result in an intervention from those who represent the state. This kind of vulnerability needs to be understood in the broader context of the 'war on terror' that has had implications for the emergence of different variations of what Giorgio Agamben calls a 'state of exception' producing 'bare lives' (2005, pp. 87–88). In her analysis of the 'war on terror', Judith Butler draws on Agamben's concept to explore how some lives are defined as ungrievable and become the target of the 'war on terror'—both internationally and domestically in the United States—having their fundamental rights, usually treated as a core of Western democracies, suspended. In its extreme articulations, the culture of suspicion and of accusations of terrorism targeting some racialized subjects and communities can cost them their lives or freedom. Control of borders, surveillance of certain communities, policing of certain bodies—all these forms of governability constitute regimes in which securitization is a driving force, deeply transforming the very conditions of existence of some subjects and communities.[10] In the aftermath of the 2015 Paris attacks, Butler discussed how the introduction of a state of emergency in France had been intertwined with the practice of collective mourning (Butler, 2015). More exactly, she explores the links between the emergence of certain forms of precariousness and the affect circulating in Western societies after the terrorist attacks. The accusation of terrorism thrown on a train against a person whose body is racializable, by putting in motion particular kinds of affects, enacts this type of vulnerability.

Migration, nation, Europe

CRIME

Assault—hitting the injured party in the chest with a clenched fist causing pain and knocking the injured party to the floor. In connection with this the perpetrator reportedly screamed *'fuck you'* and *'go home'*. He reportedly also screamed derogatory things about Islam.

(Police report, Case 6)

Similarly to the above case, in which a mother reported the attack on her son to the police upon his arrival at the emergency department, *'Go home'* is a common imperative accompanying different acts of violence in Brå's statistics about Islamophobic hate crime. Moreover, it often figures independently as an utterance addressed to persons perceived as Muslims or to Muslim organizations. It could be graffiti, such as that sprayed on the building of a Muslim association reading: *'Muslims go home!* Muslims you are not welcome here', or it could be an email, like the one received by Adam, in which letters cut out from a newspaper formed the text: 'Out now! For an immigrant-free Sweden! Swedes first!' It could be a man yelling at his Muslim neighbour, 'You have to speak Swedish in Sweden' or a threatening letter sent to a Muslim association saying: 'Deport Muslims'.

All these cases illustrate a kind of everyday work of bordering that reproduces invisible borders (Djampour, 2018; Khosravi, 2010, p. 75). These acts define a type of imagined community, based on visions of national identity that have been growing in Sweden and in Europe. They reveal something about the ways in which nationalism and racism—in these cases anti-Muslim racism—are interconnected. For example, one person reported to the police that he had received a letter with threats: 'You and your children can never become real Swedes, because there are no Swedish Muslims. You are a Muslim and will remain a Muslim'. In another case, a person received a letter at work saying: 'Go home! You fucking Arab ape. We hate Arabs–Muslims … [signed:] The Swedish people. Stop any financial aid to Muslim countries!' One case concerned graffiti on a wall that read: 'Sweden for the Swedes, no mosques in Sweden'. The language of abuse in these acts reveals a particular intersection of racist imaginaries, brought in by invectives such as 'fucking Arab ape', and a notion of a community defined through religion understood as an inalterable attribute of a person, mimicking the biological idea of race, as expressed in the judgement: 'You are a Muslim and will remain a Muslim'. It also suggests that anti-Muslim racism needs to be understood in relation to the growing anti-immigration climate.

These imperatives appear in a context in which Muslims have increasingly been defined as not belonging to the nation-state. Anti-Muslim racism in

22 Anti-Muslim racism

Europe has, in the last decades, manifested itself in an anti-immigration rhetoric, and, conversely, migration has often been described as a movement of Muslims to Europe or, in more conspiratorialist versions, as a Muslim invasion (Malm, 2009, pp. 21–60). Thus, the issue of immigration has been framed in the vocabulary of 'immigration threat', which often conflates the figure of immigrant with that of Muslim (Halliday, 2002, p. 110). The issue of immigration has, however, been articulated differently in different countries, often depending on models of citizenship, common imaginaries about national identity, as well as legal, political and economic settings that regulate migration and integration (Bobako, 2017, p. 117). Last but not least, it also has to do with different colonial and post-colonial histories that not only have an impact on the forms and the character of immigration in these countries, but have also provided scripts according to which migrants and their descendants are defined and sometimes define themselves. All these factors have been influential in how certain post-colonial imaginaries and histories can be mobilized in anti-Muslim racism, shaping both the violence and the resistance to it.

The conflation of the immigrant subject with the Muslim subject can be seen as a result of parallel processes of the securitization of migration in Europe, of the emergence of racialized migration regimes and of the proliferation of anti-terrorist legislation across the continent as part of the 'war on terror'. As a result, Islamophobic discourses have started to intertwine with anti-immigrant ones (Fekete, 2009). These processes have also been matched by a gradual salience of religious identity as central for individuals and communities that had previously been identified and identified themselves in other ways, often coming from secularized contexts in which religion had not played an important role (Bobako, 2017, pp. 96–101; Yilmaz, 2016).

In Sweden, as in other European countries, it is thus interesting to trace how the dynamics of and shifts in anti-Muslim racism have been interconnected with a shift in the approaches to immigration, in articulations of hegemonic and alternative definitions of the Swedish national community. This can also help us understand how Muslims as a group were gradually singled out and received a certain social attention.

The history of Swedish Muslims is a relatively recent one. Although representations of Muslims and Islam embedded in the broader history of European colonialism and Orientalism had existed in Sweden for a long time, Sweden, unlike France and the United Kingdom that had colonies in countries with a significant Muslim population, had no colonies that could influence the character of Muslim immigration to the country. The migration to the country can, however, be characterized by relations produced in the context of what has often been called the country's 'complicity with colonialism' (Keskinen, 2009). Only recently have Islam and Muslims been identified as part of Swedish society. Hence, in the population census carried out in 1930, the category 'Mohammedans and others' was included among other religious denominations, and 11 persons declared that they belonged to this category (Otterbeck, 2014, January 24). It was not until the 1960s that the first larger Muslim group came to Sweden, mostly from Turkey as labour immigrants, and since the 1970s these have been joined by their families through the Family Reunification policy. Until 1980, immigrants from Turkey constituted the single largest Muslim group and were treated by many as *the* Muslims (Sander, 2004, p. 220). At the time, their Muslim identity was not regarded as relevant and they were considered predominantly worker migrants. This was partly related to the character of migration in Sweden, which was driven by the needs of the Swedish labour market, with labour migration reaching its peak in 1970 (Svanberg & Tydén, 2005, p. 337). After this, the labour migration gradually gave way to other forms of immigration, most importantly family reunification and migration of asylum seekers (Svanberg & Tydén, 2005, p. 338). As a consequence, since the 1970s, many of the asylum seekers who came to Sweden, mostly because of wars and conflicts in their countries of birth, would eventually often be identified as Muslims or as coming from countries or regions somehow related to Islam. Among them were Kurds from Iraq fleeing the Iran–Iraq war in the late 1970s, refugees from Lebanon, as well as Palestinians and Iranians arriving in the early 1980s. As a result of political tensions and conflicts, refugees from Somalia and Ethiopia came in the second half of the 1980s. In the 1990s, a large Bosnian population escaped the war in ex-Yugoslavia, followed by Kosovar Albanian refugees (Larsson, 2009, pp. 218–222; Sander, 2004). Most recently, refugees from Iraq, Syria and Afghanistan have been arriving in Sweden. Due to these diverse migratory histories, today's Swedish Muslims are probably one of the most heterogeneous Muslim populations[11] in Western Europe, with different linguistic, cultural, ethnic, political, economic and class backgrounds (Sander, 2004, p. 218). These communities also have different histories in Sweden, having arrived in the country at different periods and under different conditions and terms. Some are relatively new to the country, while others are well established, with several generations born in Sweden.[12]

A temporal frame is necessary to understand how these conditions shaping migration have changed in Sweden. What had widely been understood as a generous asylum policy was already starting to change by the end of the 1980s. With the Lucia Decision in 1989, the government introduced some restrictions on the refugee policy, claiming a lack of welfare resources, and thus linking the issues of immigration to those of welfare. It sent the signal that it was possible to limit immigration because of an alleged negative impact on the Swedish welfare system, an argument often put forward by those critical of generous immigration policies (Borevi, 2012, pp. 49–50). Since the beginning of the 1990s, Swedish migration policies, following a broader European trend, became more and more restrictive, a process that has occurred in the context of significant transformation in the welfare state and an expansion of neoliberalism both globally and in Sweden (Sager,

24 *Anti-Muslim racism*

Holgersson & Öberg, 2016, pp. 28–29). The drastic change came in 2015, in the midst of the so-called 'migration crisis', when borders were closed and migration regimes reformulated. A migration law reform was passed that considerably changed the legal framework and political and social conditions, transforming immigrants' possibilities of entering Swedish society, shifting asylum politics from human rights-oriented to labour market-oriented and establishing 'a continuum of deportability' as a permanent condition for those arriving in Sweden (Sager & Öberg, 2017, p. 6). The call for deportation, which in the 2000s was still an expression of far-right politics, has in recent years become audible in the political salons and mainstream media, and, as a consequence, the condition of deportability (De Genova, 2005) has become more and more a reality for many people living in Sweden.

Parallel to the transformations in the immigration policies, there has been a change in the institutional and political frames governing the definition of the place of immigrants in Swedish society. While in the first period after World War II immigration issues were left to the labour market,[13] from the mid-1960s, the state began to actively engage in immigration policy (Hammar, 1985, p. 11), as a result of which a basis for Swedish multiculturalism was laid. The main principles of the Swedish multicultural model were defined as: equality, freedom of choice and cooperation (*jämlikhet, valfrihet och samverkan*) (Prop. 1975:26, p. 1). According to these principles, immigrants were to gain the same rights and the same possibilities to enjoy these rights as Swedes, while, at the same time, they were left with a choice regarding their identity.[14] However, already by the early 1990s, it was clear that the model was not without flaws:

> Critical disjunctures between ideology and practice have taken the form of proscribed 'equality' versus discrimination and a hierarchic ethnic division of labour, 'freedom of choice' versus exclusiveness and segregation, 'partnership' versus bureaucratic control and techno-scientific monitoring.
>
> (Ålund, 1991, p. 4)

Hence, despite formal and legal ambitions, the position of immigrants in Sweden could be characterized as one of 'subordinated inclusion' (Mulinari & Neergaard, quoted in Keskinen, 2009, p. 23). At the same time, a backlash against the model was taking place as part of the process that I define as a 'crisis' in Chapter 4, with a growing critique of the principle of freedom of choice, as a result of which the government started to reformulate its policy towards immigrants. Rather than engaging in the debate about multiculturalism, it reoriented its policies regarding immigrants by identifying integration as the main aim. These shifts were also reflected in the vocabularies used: for instance, the less controversial term 'diversity' (*mångfald*) substituted the term 'multiculturalism' (*mångkultur*) (Borevi, 1998, pp. 176–179). Thereby, the emergence of the new migration regime was accompanied by transformations in the integration policies.

These transformations in the immigration and integration policies have been paralleled by the growth of the far-right movement in Sweden. As I describe in Chapter 4, already by the 1990s, this development had shattered the Swedish political scene and public life. More recently, however, another wave of far-right revival has taken place, with the Sweden Democrats entering the Swedish Parliament and becoming the country's third-largest political party. The advance of this party, which has roots in the White Power movement, in a country like Sweden, could at least partly be explained by the Sweden Democrats' strategy of adopting a so-called 'zero-tolerance of racism' policy and of coding its messages in more politically accepted vocabularies. At the same time, the party's political agenda has from the beginning revolved around the issue of migration and singled out Islam and alleged Islamisation as the biggest threat to the country.

Thus, on the national scale, Muslims, conflated with immigrants, have been portrayed as a threat both to the idea of the nation as defined in far-right imaginaries and as a threat to the welfare system in more mainstream political discourses. Acts of anti-Muslim racism can be better understood not only against the background of the above-described histories of shifting immigration policies, a challenged Swedish multicultural model and a Swedish welfare system under transformation, but also in the context of different, and often conflicting, visions of the Swedish nation. At the same time, it is important to locate rearticulations of nationalism in Sweden in the broader developments in Europe. Thus, different manifestations of anti-Muslim racism can be analysed in relation to the transformations and adaptations of a variety of nationalisms in the context of European integration—the result of which has been the creation and gradual enlargement of the European Union—and, most recently, also its partial disintegration. The 'Muslim question' in Europe is thus not just about the similarities of patterns of migration and migration regimes and their links to colonial experiences, nor just about the growing power of nationalism, but is also an issue at the core of the European project. Oliver Roy describes how two different identity politics have been relevant in practices of Westernization: Christianization and secularization (Roy, 2007). These are central to the two competing ways in which the project of the European Union becomes defined through is positioning towards Islam. While the former underlines the Christian (or in some versions, Judeo-Christian) origins of the European community, the latter draws on the imagined common experience of secularization as a European experience. These two different traditions meet in their opposition towards Islam:

> The critique of Islam is today a rallying-point for two intellectual families that have been opposed to each other so far: those who think that the West is first and foremost Christian (and who, not that long time ago, considered that the Jews could hardly be assimilated) and those

26 *Anti-Muslim racism*

who think that the West is primarily secular and democratic. In other words, the Christian Right and the secular Left are today united in their criticism of Islam.

(Roy, 2007, p. ix)

Conclusions

The main aim of this chapter has been to introduce the context relevant to the understanding of anti-Muslim racism in Sweden and more broadly in Europe and the West. With the help of cases from my material of attacks on people perceived as Muslims, I identified some central sites of anti-Muslim racism. I have described how certain of these acts can be better understood if situated in the context of the Mohammed cartoon controversies, veil affairs and the 'war on terror'. I have also claimed that these acts should be seen against the background of nationalist projects and European (dis)integration and their relation to restrictive migration regimes. I have suggested that only by bringing in and attending to these broader frames of reference can we make sense of the message, workings and effects of individual acts of violence.

My approach has been based on an idea that analytical rescaling can show how broader discourses as well as legal, political and social framings are related to everyday acts of violence. Zooming in on such interactions enables us to realize how some bodies and some subjects are framed, constructed and affected by anti-Muslim racism. So, my claim about the usefulness of thinking about anti-Muslim racism in terms of scales also works in another direction: it suggests that without attending to *the scales of body and subjectivity*, we will not be able to fully understand the phenomenon of anti-Muslim racism. The acts of violence described in the police files that I have quoted in this chapter interpellate some people as Muslims, thereby constructing a Muslim subject. Drawing on Altusser's concept, Judith Butler develops a theory of interpellation as a speech act that 'seeks to introduce a reality rather than report on an existing one' (Butler, 1997, p. 33) and that it does so through a citation of existing conventions. Butler also refers to Matsuda, who analysed how such interpellative acts work in cases of hate speech, by fixing some subjects in subordinate social positions and reinforcing structural domination (Matsuda, quoted in Butler, 1997, p. 18). She, however, recognizes how language carries with it a double function: it is both constitutive of the body and the subject and threatening to their existence. In light of this, anti-Muslim racism can be seen as contributing to the establishment of a particular Muslim subject and deeply shaping certain communities.

Notes

1 All the names of people, places and the like as well as some details in the cases, I refer to, have been changed in order to ensure the anonymity of those involved.

Anti-Muslim racism   27

I describe the process of anonymization in this study in a chapter entitled 'The Ethics of Renaming. On challenges and dilemmas of anonymization in a study of anti-Muslim racism' in the forthcoming volume *The Politics and Ethics of Representation in Qualitative Research. Addressing Moments of Discomfort.*

2 Some authors writing on racist language do not spell out racist slurs 'in a personal effort to avoid harm to others, and to prevent desensitization to harmful words' (Matsuda, 1989, p. 2329; cf. Essed, 1997, p. 149). In this book, however, I decided to spell out all racist slurs. I share and develop the argument that these words have offensive meanings embedded in them and that by repeating them, one actually recalls the history of oppression that they carry. Nevertheless, I also believe that there exists a possibility—albeit never completely riskless—of quoting these words in a subversive way and for critical purposes. Moreover, confronted with strategies to conceal racist slander by spelling out only some of its letters used by the defendant in the case I analyse in Chapter 7, I notice how this avoidance of spelling out the racist insult has become a new way of offending.

3 The relevance of understanding of this regional scale of Islamophobia has been discussed in the literature. Sayyid, for instance, has defined Islamophobia

> as a response to attempts to erode the West and the non-West framework. Islamophobia can perhaps be defined as the disciplining of Muslims by reference to an antagonistic Western horizon…. The distinctiveness of Islamophobia has to be related to the contemporary developments in the world. As such, it is structured by a post-colonial and post-Caliphate logic. The post-colonial logic raises doubts about the future of the world as being decipherable as an upscaled version of Western history…. What Islamophobia seeks to discipline is the possibility of Muslim autonomy, that is an affirmation of Muslim political identity as a legitimate historical subject.
>
> (Sayyid, 2010, pp. 15–17)

From this perspective, Islamophobia is conceived as a reaction to a loss of the European or Western hegemonies as a result of post-colonial transformations in the global order, and to questioning the idea of modernization and development. It is also related to migrations and the emergence of transnational communities in the West, among them communities affirming Muslim political identities. What is important to note is that the West is not necessarily understood in geographical or cultural terms, but rather as 'the idea of a Western telos towards which non-Western but Westernizing societies can orient, … a concession to tropes that are hegemonically articulated with a particular reading of Western history—e.g. modernity' (Sayyid, 2010, pp. 15–16).

4 The Mohammed cartoon controversy took place after the publication in 2005 of twelve cartoons featuring the Prophet Mohammed by a Danish newspaper, *Jyllands-Posten*. The cartoons were first protested against by Danish Muslim communities, but the Danish authorities announced that they would not intervene in the case. The controversy quickly went global, with boycotts and demonstrations spreading across countries both with Muslim majority populations and with significant Muslim minorities (Klausen, 2009). While this controversy has probably received most attention, similar 'affairs' have taken place in several countries both before and after the Danish controversy.

5 An antecedent of this type of controversy had been the Rushdie affair. However, the controversies that seem to be most relevant are those which took place at the beginning of the twenty-first century in different countries in Europe. Each of them, although similar, illustrates some important national variations. The

28 *Anti-Muslim racism*

Danish Mohammed cartoon controversy can be seen as a part of a transformation in the Danish political scene, with the growing influence of a far-right party openly critical of Muslim minorities. At the same time, it used more liberal ideas about humour as central to the Danish national identity. In the Netherlands, Theo van Gogh and Ayaan Hirsi Ali's film *Submission*, the subsequent assassination of van Gogh and the ways in which it was interpreted, encapsulated what Ron Eyerman calls the 'dilemma for the Dutch' that is 'the disparity between a commitment to religious tolerance and their relations with the Muslims living in their midst' (2008, p. 159). Still other dynamics would operate in France around the cartoons published by the magazine *Charlie Hebdo* and the subsequent attack.

6 My material is in this respect consistent with other research on Muslim women's experiences of discrimination and racism, both in Sweden (cf. Abdullahi, 2016; Listerborn, 2015; Sixtensson, 2009) and in other countries in Europe (FRA, 2017).

7 As of April 2018, six countries had national bans, five had local bans, in eight countries, bans were ongoing and in twenty-two, there had been failed attempts to introduce bans. Only in six countries in the EU had there been no discussions on banning the veil (Open Society Foundation, 2018).

8 Scott makes another important point in her book:

> The strong stand taken against headscarves was, in fact, a sign of the impotence and/or unwillingness of the government to address the problem it shares with many other European nations: how to adjust national institutions and ideologies that assume or seek to produce homogeneity to the heterogeneity of their current populations.
>
> (Scott, 2007, p. 40)

9 Again, the ways in which feminist movements in Europe have positioned themselves in relation to the issues of the veil often have to do with the local and national contexts, including the role of religion and secularism in the political sphere. A good example here is that of Poland, where critical views on Islam among feminists can partly be related to the ways in which the struggle with the Catholic Church over reproduction rights and gender equality has dominated the field of the contemporary feminism (Bobako, 2017, p. 263).

10 In Sweden, an Anti-Terrorism Act was introduced in 2013. Although the law does not directly target Muslims, until 2015, all indicted under this law were Muslims (Open Society Foundation, 2018). The law was strongly criticized by Muslim organizations (Sabuni, 2013).

11 It is impossible to establish the exact estimate of the Muslim population in Sweden since there are no official statistics in Sweden for religious affiliation. The numbers for the first decade of 2000 varied both according to the source and to how Muslims are actually defined, ranging from approximately 100,000, estimated by the Swedish Commission for State Grants to Religious Communities, to about 400,000; the latter estimate being almost 5% of the Swedish population (Bevelander & Otterbeck, 2010, p. 404). These numbers have changed in the last years due to the considerable migration from Syria and Afghanistan. In 2017, the Swedish Commission for State Grants to Religious Communities gave the number as over 150,000 members of different Muslim religious communities. It can also be assumed that the numbers of those who do not belong to a Muslim congregation but can be defined as Muslims also increased. While the most conservative estimates build on membership of Muslim religious organizations, the most liberal ones identify Muslims as belonging to some traditions or

Anti-Muslim racism 29

environments or having their roots in predominantly or largely Muslim countries. In other words, the definitions range from strictly religious definitions of a Muslim as a person professing certain beliefs and participating in religious practices, to those that identify Muslims through the concepts of culture or descent (Sander, 2004, pp. 213–215). Irrespective of the definition, however, in terms of numbers, Islam today is considered to be Sweden's second most significant religion, after Christianity.

12 This diversity is also reflected in the different ways in which Islam is practiced in Sweden. During the last decades of the twentieth century, Islam began to take root and become institutionalized in Sweden. This process has been framed, to a large degree, by the terms decided by the Swedish state, in which the welfare system, the gradual retreat of the Swedish Protestant Church from the public sphere, and the growing emphasis on secularism have played an important role. This, together with a generational shift, has led to the emergence of what some scholars have called—referring to the Swedish flag—the 'blue–yellow Islam' (*blågul Islam*) (Svanberg & Westerlund, 1999, p. 9).

13 The Swedish post-war immigration policy was first formulated in the 1960s and 1970s. In the official language, the term 'foreigner' (*utlänning*) was replaced by 'immigrant' (*invandrare*) (Hammar, 1985, p. 20), a shift that reflected a change in the way of thinking about those who were coming to the country. Now the immigrants' adaptation to their new country was emphasized (Svanberg & Tydén, 2005, p. 334).

14 Immigrants were guaranteed free Swedish language education during working hours; the children of immigrants were also granted a right to 'home language' classes supported by the Swedish state (Svanberg & Tydén, 2005, p. 335). Moreover, and in line with this policy, the state financially supported immigrant associations. Finally, the policy promoted cooperation between the majority population and the immigrants, by supporting immigrants' participation in political life, with the introduction in 1975 of non-citizens' right to vote and to be elected in local elections (Borevi, 1998, p. 171).

Bibliography

Abdullahi, M. (2016). *Forgotten Women: The Impact of Islamophobia on Muslim Women in Sweden*. Retrieved from Brussels: www.enar-eu.org/IMG/pdf/forgotten_women_report_sweden_-_final-3.pdf

Agamben, G. (2005). *State of Exception*. Chicago, IL; London: University of Chicago Press.

Back, L. & Sinha, S. (2018). *Migrant City*. New York: Routledge.

Bayoumi, M. (2011). 'Between Acceptance and Rejection: Muslim Americans and the Legacies of September 11.' *OAH Magazine of History*, *25*(3), 15–19.

Berg, M. (1998). *Hudud: ett resonemang om populärorientalismens bruksvärde och världsbild*. Stockholm: Carlsson.

Bevelander, P. & Otterbeck, J. (2010). 'Young people's attitudes towards Muslims in Sweden.' *Ethnic & Racial Studies*, *33*(3), 404–425.

Bobako, M. (2017). *Islamofobia jako technologia wladzy. Studium z antropologii politycznej*. Krakow: Universitas.

Borevi, K. (1998). 'Svensk invandrarpolitik under (om)fromulering.' *Politica*, *30*(2), 168–183.

Borevi, K. (2012). 'Sweden: The Flagship of Multiculturalism.' In G. Hagelund (Ed.), *Immigration Policy and the Scandinavian Welfare State 1945–2010*. Basingstoke: Palgrave Macmillan, pp. 25–96.

30 Anti-Muslim racism

Butler, J. (1997). *Excitable Speech: A Politics of the Performative.* New York; London: Routledge.

Butler, J. (2009). *Frames of War: When Is Life Grievable?* London; New York: Verso.

Butler, J. (2015). 'Mourning Becomes the Law.' Judith Butler from Paris at the Verso website.

Chouliaraki, L. (2006). *The Spectatorship of Suffering.* London; Thousand Oaks, CA: Sage.

De Genova, N. (2005). *Working the Boundaries: Race, Space, and "Illegality" in Mexican Chicago.* Durham, NC: Duke University Press.

Delphy, C. Trans. Broder, D. (2015). *Separate and Dominate: Feminism and Racism after the War on Terror.* London: Verso.

Djampour, P. (2018). *Borders Crossing Bodies: The Stories of Eight Youth with Experience of Migrating.* (PhD). Malmö: Malmö universitet.

Essed, P. (1997). 'Racial Intimidation: Sociopolitical Implications of the Usage of Racist Slurs.' In S. H. Riggins (Ed.), *The Language and Politics of Exclusion: Others in Discourse.* London: Sage, pp. 131–152.

European Centre on Racism and Xenophobia. (2006). *Muslims in the European Union: Discrimination and Islamophobia.* Retrieved from Vienna: http://fra.europa.eu/en/publication/2012/muslims-european-union-discrimination-and-islamophobia

Eyerman, R. (2008). *The Assassination of Theo van Gogh: From Social Drama to Cultural Trauma.* Durham, NC: Duke University Press.

Fallaci, O. (2002). *The Rage and the Pride.* New York: Rizzoli.

Fanon, F. (1989). *Studies in a Dying Colonialism.* London: Earthscan.

Fekete, L. (2009). *A Suitable Enemy: Racism, Migration and Islamophobia in Europe.* London: Pluto.

FRA. (2017). *EU-MIDIS II. Second European Union Minorities and Discrimination Survey. Muslims—Selected Findings.* Retrieved from Luxemburg: http://fra.europa.eu/en/publication/2017/second-european-union-minorities-and-discrimination-survey-eu-midis-ii-muslims

Gardell, M. (2011). *Islamofobi* (2nd edn.). Stockholm: Leopard (Falun: Scand Book).

Gilroy, P. (2002). *"There Ain't No Black in the Union Jack": The Cultural Politics of Race and Nation* (3rd edn.). London: Routledge.

Halliday, F. (2002). *Two Hours that Shook the World: September 11, 2001—Causes and Consequences.* London: Saqi.

Hammar, T. (1985). *European Immigration Policy.* Cambridge: Cambridge University Press.

Högfeldt, K., Sander, Å. & Larsson, G. (2008). *Muhammed-karikatyrer och rondellhundar: reaktioner, bakgrund och sammanhang.* Göteborg: Social resursförvaltning, Göteborgsstad: Göteborgsuniversitet.

Huntington, S. (1993). 'The Clash of Civilizations?' *Foreign Affairs, 72*(3), 22–50.

Huntington, S. (2002). *The Clash of Civilizations and the Remaking of World Order* (New edn.). London: Free Press.

Keskinen, S. (2009). *Complying with Colonialism: Gender, Race and Ethnicity in the Nordic Region.* Farnham, England; Burlington, VT: Ashgate.

Khosravi, S. (2010). *'Illegal' Traveller: An Auto-Ethnography of Borders.* New York: Springer eBooks.

Klausen, J. (2009). *The Cartoons that Shook the World.* New Haven, CT; London: Yale University Press.

Larsson, G. (2009).'Sweden.' In G. Larsson (Ed.), *Islam in the Nordic and Baltic Countries*. London; New York: Routledge, pp. 56–75.

Listerborn, C. (2015). 'Geographies of the Veil: Violent Encounters in Urban Public Spaces in Malmö, Sweden.' *Social & Cultural Geography, 16*(1), 95–115.

Malm, A. (2009). *Hatet mot muslimer*. Stockholm: Atlas.

Matsuda, M. J. (1989). 'Public Response to Acist Speech: Considering the Victim's Story.' *Michigan Law Review, 87*(8), 2320–2381.

Matthis, M. (2005). *Orientalism på svenska*. Stockholm: Ordfront i samarbete med Re: orient.

Meer, N. & Modood, T. (2010a). 'Islamophobia as Cultural Racism? Martin Amis and the Racialization of Muslims.' In S. Sayyid & A. Vakil (Eds.), *Thinking through Islamophobia: Global Perspectives*. London: Hurst & Co., pp. 69–83.

Meer, N. & Modood, T. (2010b). 'The Racialisation of Muslims.' In S. Sayyid & A. Vakil (Eds.), *Thinking through Islamophobia: Global Perspectives*. London: Hurst & Co., pp. 69–84.

Morgan, G. & Poynting, S. (2012). *Global Islamophobia: Muslims and Moral Panic in the West*. Farnham, Surrey; Burlington, VT: Ashgate.

Open Society Foundation. (2018). *Restrictions on Muslim Women's Dress in the 28 EU Member States: Current Law, Recent Legal Developments, and the State of Play*. Retrieved from New York: www.opensocietyfoundations.org/reports/restrictions-muslim-women-s-dress-28-eu-member-states

Orrenius, N. (2017). *Skotten i Köpenhamn: ett reportage om Lars Vilks, extremism och yttrandefrihetens gränser*. Stockholm: Bonnier Pocket.

Otterbeck, J. (2014, January 24). *De femton—eller hur många muslimer fanns det i Sverige 1930?* Retrieved from http://religionsvetenskapligakommentarer.blogspot.se/2014/01/de-femton-eller-hur-manga-muslimer.html

Peek, L. (2011). *Behind the Backlash: Muslim Americans After 9/11*. Philadelphia, PA: Temple University Press.

Richa, N., Victoria, L., Linda, M. & Susan, H. (2002). 'Locating Globalization: Feminist (Re)readings of the Subjects and Spaces of Globalization.' *Economic Geography, 78*(3), 257–284.

Roy, O. (2007). *Secularism Confronts Islam*. New York: Columbia University Press.

Runnymede Trust. (1997). 'Islamophobia: A Challenge for Us All.' Retrieved from www.runnymedetrust.org/companies/17/74/Islamophobia-A-Challenge-for-Us-All.html

Sabuni, K. (2013). *Swedish Muslims in Cooperation Network Alternative Report*. Retrieved from Stockholm: https://tbinternet.ohchr.org/Treaties/CERD/Shared%20Documents/SWE/INT_CERD_NGO_SWE_30871_E.pdf

Sager, M., Holgersson, H., & Öberg, K. (2016). 'Introduktion: Irreguljär migration i Sverige.' In M. Sager, H. Holgersson, & K. Öberg (Eds.), *Irreguljär migration i Sverige. Rättigheter, vardagserfarenheter, motstånd och statliga kategoriseringar*. Göteborg: Daidalos (pp. 7–48).

Sager, M., & Öberg, K. (2017). 'Articulations of deportability. Changing migration policies in Sweden 2015/2016.' *Refugee Review, III*, 2–14.

Said, E. (2003). *Orientalism*. London: Penguin.

Sander, Å. (2004). 'Muslims in Sweden.' In J. Anwar (Ed.), *State Policies towards Muslim Minorities: Sweden, Great Britain and Germany*. Berlin: Edition Parabolis, pp. 203–363.

32 Anti-Muslim racism

Sayyid, S. (2010). 'Out of the Devil's Dictionary.' In S. Sayyid & A. Vakil (Eds.), *Thinking Through Islamophobia*. London: Hurst & Co., pp. 5–18.

Sayyid, S. & Vakil, A. (2010). *Thinking through Islamophobia*. Oxford: Oxford University Press.

Scott, J. (2007). *The Politics of the Veil*. Princeton, NJ: Princeton University Press.

Seidler, V. (2007). *Urban Fears and Global Terrors: Citizenship, Multicultures and Belongings after 7/7*. London: Routledge.

Sixtensson, J. (2009). *Hemma och främmande i staden: kvinnor med slöja berättar*. Malmö: Institutionen för urbana studier, Malmö högskola (Malmö: Holmbergs).

Svanberg, I. & Tydén, M. (2005). *Tusen år av invandring: en svensk kulturhistoria*. Stockholm: Dialogos.

Svanberg, I. & Westerlund, D. (Eds.) (1999). *Blågul Islam?: Muslimer i Sverige*. Nora: Nya Doxa.

Yilmaz, F. (2016). *How the Workers Became Muslims. Immigration, Culture, and Hegemonic Transformation in Europe*. Ann Arbor, MI: University of Michigan Press.

3 Meeting with the court documents
Methodological reflections

In the middle of this research project, I participated in a seminar where I presented preliminary results of my research. I had a presentation with me. On slides, I displayed a table, a diagram and several quotes from the court judgements of the cases I was analysing. I gave an overview of my material. From the total number of hate crimes each year, I sectioned off the number of Islamophobic hate crimes and, from this, the number of those that went to court. Then I provided a classification where I identified different ways in which courts treated a possible nature of these crimes—what Brå was calling 'Islamophobic hate crimes'. I was able to establish that, in 60% of the cases that were resolved when the statistics were put together, the court did not consider the possibility that one of the motives for the crime was 'to aggrieve a person, an ethnic group or any other similar group of people by reason of race, colour, national or ethnic origin, religious belief or other similar circumstance', something that would make it possible to apply the penalty enhancement provision. In another 14%, the court took the penalty enhancement into consideration, but decided that it was not applicable. In only 19% of cases did the court recognize and acknowledge the kind of motive that made it possible to apply the penalty enhancement. The remaining 7% I categorized as ambivalent cases; the courts may, for instance, have applied a law against racism, but at the same time played down the racist nature of the acts in the judgement. The numbers spoke for themselves, displayed in a conventional pie chart, and the quotes were there to support my argument. The figures gave me confidence in my claims. I felt safe having them as *proof* that what I was talking about was a correct reflection of how Islamophobic hate crimes have been treated by the judiciary in Sweden.

At the beginning of the research project, I defined my aim as to conduct a qualitative study of acts of violence against Muslims in Sweden. The idea had been to look at how some experiences are recorded by the police and the judiciary and how their meaning is set through the processes of naming, describing and explaining them. A couple of years later, I was examining court documents in cases concerned with acts of violence against Muslims, opening my presentation with statistical data about Islamophobic hate crimes. Why would I need recourse to statistics if actually I was trying to

34 *Meeting with the court documents*

do a *qualitative* study and conduct textual analysis? What made me stick to figures, almost without noticing? And in what way did this tendency to fall back on a quantitative measurement of the subject I was studying influence what I was seeing and I was able to grasp?

In this chapter, I will describe the ways in which I have conducted my research. I will reflect here on the experience of meeting with the police and court documents, on the experience of working on the sensitive and politicized topic of racism, and the experience of producing knowledge in institutional settings of academia. The point of departure for these methodological reflections will be those moments in the research process that were somehow disturbing, messy and disruptive. I will take these moments as a starting point for my discussion on methods. I will also bring in perspectives, tools and ways of working that I used but eventually abandoned, as I believe they show that how and why we ask questions, gather data, treat material and conduct analyses is to some degree opaque for ourselves as researchers and that, by reflecting on them, we might be able to better understand what guides knowledge production in academia. Following some feminist and critical scholars, I will develop a claim that methodological and theoretical choices are not only inextricably intertwined, they are also deeply embedded in the institutional and social settings in which knowledge is produced, both those explicit in the rules of what good and acceptable science is and those inherent in the structures and politics that shape academia and its work (Collins, 2000; Haraway, 1988; Harding, 1992). At the same time, the methodological reflections presented in this chapter will help me to describe the logics and workings of knowledge production, not only in academia but also in the judiciary. They will be thus an opportunity to propose an understanding of epistemologies used in courts. Moreover, by describing the character, form and language of the police and court documents that I study, the form of knowledge produced in court will be explored.

Collecting evidence

Initially, I explained my tendency to rely on numbers in approaching and presenting my research by the fact that I had chosen to use the statistics collected by Brå to identify possible cases of acts of anti-Muslim racism in Sweden. I was aware of the constraints that this choice entailed. I was able to access only a fraction of such acts—those reported to the police. I knew from other types of research that crimes in general and what in the literature are called hate crimes are strongly underreported (FRA, 2009a, p. 8, 2009b, p. 50). I was also familiar with Brå's criteria and definitions that determined the range and nature of the data collected, something that I discuss in Chapter 5. Still, I assessed the main strength of the statistics to be in Brå's independence from the law enforcement system and judiciary: the definitions and criteria for the selection of hate crimes did not depend on classifications by the police, nor were they based on how the nature of these acts was approached in indictments or court judgements. In this sense, apart from providing access to acts of violence against Muslims, the material offered a unique opportunity to follow the cases and analyse how they were approached and treated by the judiciary. The decision to have as the point of departure the statistical data compiled by a national body meant that the primary material I received was of a quantitative character and, when it was not, it was ordered according to quantitative reasoning. At that point, I believed that the form in which I obtained the material—as tables compiled in statistical software—was responsible for my initial quantitative framework. I explained to myself that only by deciphering these data would I be able to access police reports and court files, which was my aim. Thus, the material that I received was predefined in two ways: it was not merely named 'Islamophobic hate crimes' and selected by specific criteria, but also delivered in a particular form—as statistical data in which acts that interested me were described with the help of variables.

I felt that I needed the statistics to be able to identify the cases that actually ended up in court, which would make it possible for me to discover how the judiciary treats such cases. In this way, I could get to the documents that would constitute the core of my study. Also, I had a feeling that by starting with such a large amount of material (four years of data from the entire country, almost 1,000 cases), I would acquire a systematic and complete overview of police reports concerning acts of anti-Muslim violence and would thereby be enabled to formulate some well-grounded arguments on how the judiciary deals with this type of racism. However, the idea was always to go beyond these quantitative frames and analyse the selected cases in a qualitative way. Thus, when I found myself time after time returning to statistics, I thought it was due to this origin of my material and to my own slowness in reframing it. Still, the more I immersed myself in the court documents, the more difficult I found it to abandon the figures, tables and diagrams. There was something disturbing and unsettling about the ways in which the acts were described and defined by the courts. I was still trying to identify what it was. In case after case, I was discovering that a different focus in the trials made a particular dimension of many of these cases muddled or invisible.

In one case, for example, a young man, Jonas Gustavsson, was wandering in a park. He was behaving aggressively, wielding a hammer, performing a Hitler salute and screaming '*Sieg Heil!*', '*Deutschland*' and 'Fucking Muslims!'. People in the park called the police. He was afterwards charged with agitation against a national or ethnic group and offence against the Knife Act. In the judgement, the court established that, considering the case law (*rättspraxis*) in cases of agitation against a national or ethnic group, performing Nazi gestures and screaming '*SiegHeil!*' in public should be considered a crime. However, the court decided that 'the utterances had a limited extent and were not spread to a larger number of people, the crime thus was considered to be minor'. Moreover, the court argued, 'Jonas Gustavsson does not seem to have Nazi or other racist sympathies, and the incident appears to

36 *Meeting with the court documents*

be an isolated occurrence among other things caused by intoxication' (Judgement, Case 7).

I was intrigued by the way the court defined the act and identified the site of harm. I was also struck by the explicit argument of the court, in which the causes of the occurrence were pinpointed with an astonishing certitude. Moreover, I wondered why the insult 'Fucking Muslims!' was left out of the court documents, although it was included in the police files together with Jonas Gustavsson's other shouts. All these things together added to an impression that important aspects of the crime had in fact gone unnoticed in court, or even that they became invisible *through* the legal process.

The more cases I discovered where courts turned out to be unable to recognize a type of harm caused by racism, the more I felt comfort in the statistical form of my argument. I believed that the figures in my tables and charts could actually prove that the injury had taken place; they could also attest to how the injury became invisible in the judicial process. In the end, I found myself caught up in collecting the evidence of the occurrence of this type of harm and started to understand that it was not accidental that I referred to figures to support my argument. I realized that there was a parallel between the ways I was producing knowledge and the ways that guided the court's strategies in deciding what a persuasive account was and how the reliability of evidence should be evaluated.

The evaluation of evidence in criminal trials in Sweden is guided by the general principle of free evaluation of evidence (*fribevisvärdering*), which means that judges should not be bound by legal rules, i.e. the rules defined by the law itself. However, according to the Code of Judicial Procedure, evaluation of evidence must not be arbitrary, intuitive or subjective. The process is greatly influenced by philosophy and behavioural sciences (Ekelöf, Edelstam & Heuman, 2009, p. 160). In practice, this means that judges are guided by rules defined in the doctrine that is part of legal training in Sweden. The doctrine, although questioned in recent decades, and shifting, partly as a result of the influence of psychological and cognitive methods, is still dominated by so-called 'probability-oriented methods' (Ekelöf et al., 2009, p. 161). In this sense, the reigning epistemology on which judges base their evaluation of evidence is one in which reality is measurable and knowledge about it is reached by means of statistics. So the two methods for evaluation of evidence most broadly discussed in Swedish legal textbooks consist in measuring the probability of a certain occurrence given the evidence presented in court and in measuring the probability of the occurrence being caused by a certain circumstance. The impact of statistics is also visible in formulas and terms used in manuals (e.g. the concepts of *ursprungssannolikhet* and *frekvenssatser*) that are intended to help explain how one should proceed to establish whether the evidence presented in court can support an account of particular acts and thus be treated as a basis for the legal truth about the occurrence of a crime (Ekelöf, analysed in Bladini, 2013, pp. 257–258). This applies also, albeit in a slightly different way, to the lay judges (*nämndemän*), who play a significant role in the Swedish judiciary, most importantly in the evaluation of evidence.[1] These judges do not have any legal training and are thus not familiar with the legal doctrine; however, they are supposed to follow the law in their judgements, which is introduced to them by the legally trained judge (*lagfarendomare*) who chairs the trial and the deliberations, and presents the lay judges with the legal rules relevant to the case (Lavén, 2013, p. 48).

As mentioned, the principle that the judges are not bound by any legal rules when they evaluate the evidence does not mean that they can do it in an arbitrary way. Instead, according to the law and the above-presented doctrine, the evaluation must be carried out objectively, which in turn is interpreted as being acceptable to other sensible people (cf. NJA II 1943, p. 445, quoted in Ekelöf et al., 2009, p. 162). The concept of sensibility can be understood as associated with reason and rationality. The rules that guide the ways in which knowledge is produced through a trial and a legal truth is reached date back to the first half of the twentieth century and reflect a very positivistic knowledge ideal (Bladini, 2013, p. 361). Moa Bladini, in her work on the ideal of objectivity and objectivity claims in the Swedish judiciary, identifies 'sensible people' as other judges and people of law and argues that the formulation reflects a positivistic ideal where the result of an investigation is valuable if it can be reproduced by any member of a knowledge-producing community. She further identifies this moment as one in which judges as individuals become invisible and interchangeable and thus the semblance of objectivity in court is created (2013, pp. 361–362). At the same time, the reference to sensibility, understood as reason and rationality, reflects a more general ideal of how reliable knowledge is produced, shaping the ways in which the evidence is presented in court, not only by lawyers but also by lay persons involved in trials.

When I write that my material was influencing the research process, I thus mean two things. First, the objective of my study was emerging in a confrontation with my material. In reaction to a silence around the type of injury caused by anti-Muslim racism that I discovered in the documents I was studying, I found myself eager to prove the existence of this kind of injury and of its unrecognition by the courts. Second, my material was influencing me in that I started to use the epistemological approach and methodological tools of the judiciary in order to produce a reliable account. My early attempts to analyse and present the material in a quantitative way were shaped by the ideal endorsed by the judiciary of what incontrovertible evidence is and how truth can be established and fixed. This was, I believed, the way to construct a convincing argument and claim an injury—the way to go if I wanted to prove my point.

Infected words

At the same time as I was framing my data as evidence, I was discovering that my vocabulary was anything but neutral. One of the frequent comments

38 *Meeting with the court documents*

I received in response to my research was whether I really needed to use the word 'racism'. The main argument provided by those responding in this way was that the word was very political and that using it in an academic text inhibited me from living up to the ideal of neutrality.

I was aware that '[r]acism is a problem word, a word with a great number of questions hung onto it and tied to it' (Taguieff, 2001, p. 36). Not only does it carry within it the histories of exploitation, persecution and extermination that were performed in the name of race or with race as an excuse, but from its very inception it was related to a particular kind of critique.[2] In this sense, it has been identified as an accusation. This is partly why, '[t]hroughout Europe, racism has become a category of abuse, a means of declaring one's political opponent an immoral and unworthy person' (Miles, 1993, p. 83), leading, also in academia, to a kind of political inflation. As I discuss in Chapter 4, in Sweden this kind of unease with the word 'racism' was additionally augmented by a specific history of the concept of 'race'.

It was suggested I should use more neutral language. I was, however, aware that the conceptual apparatus in different theories of racism and xenophobia varied a lot and that it was not easy to find a substitute for the term 'racism'. The two questions of how I define and conceptualize racism, on the one hand, and what vocabulary I choose to describe and analyse my subject, on the other, were actually closely related and equally infected. Thus, it was not only the words I was using that could be challenged and disputed. From scholars writing on the subject I learned that:

> In a very real sense the question of how to conceptualise racism has never been purely an academic matter. From its very origins the study of racism has been intimately connected to issues such as the rise of fascism, the holocaust, and the destructive consequences of racist political mobilisations.
>
> (Solomos & Back, 1996, p. 26)

Thus, replacing 'racism' with, for instance, 'xenophobia' was not merely a cosmetic change. Rather it entailed a reformulation of my theoretical approach towards a more universal explanation of the phenomenon. For the concept of 'xenophobia' is usually used to describe an inclination intrinsic to human communities, which can be explained either psychologically, as fear of the unknown or predilection for the familiar, or socially, as mechanisms of in- and out-group formations. Had I adopted such a conceptualization of the phenomenon, the contextual specificity and certain historical continuity that I was trying to highlight would have been erased. I recognized in this kind of suggestion to take away context and the political a particular kind of politics of science that Sandra Harding describes as institutional politics, working not through an intrusion on the science from outside, like political propaganda does, 'but through the dominant institutional structures, priorities, practices, and language of the sciences ... through the "depoliticisation" of science' (1992, pp. 567–568).

The fact that research on racism is such a sensitive matter shows that it is indeed very difficult to draw a clear line between conceptual, methodological and theoretical questions, on the one hand, and ideological ones, on the other. This is part of a larger issue of the relation between science and politics.

In the case of racism, however, academia's problems with recognizing these relations are additionally complicated by Western science's complicity in the history of racism. Historically, racist standpoints in natural and social science, literary and aesthetic expression, social language and perception have converged with political attitudes and activities (Goldberg, 1990, p. xiii). Science's role in the development of racist theories was twofold. On the one hand, scientific racism gained a very special kind of authority that enabled the theories of academic racism to flower, drawing its strength from the fact that the racist theories

> mimic scientific discursivity by basing themselves upon visible 'evidence' (whence the essential importance of the stigmata of race and in particular of bodily stigmata), or, more exactly, they mimic the way in which scientific discursivity articulates 'visible facts' to 'hidden cause' and thus connect up with a spontaneous process of theorization inherent in the racism of the masses.
>
> (Balibar, 1991a, p. 19)

In this sense, racism, by imitating scientific reasoning, gained a particular type of authority. On the other hand, racism became at one point a scientific theory that was studied, developed and spread through the institutional settings of science. As in many other places in Europe and in the United States, this was also the case in Sweden at the end of the nineteenth and the beginning of the twentieth century.

In this context, academia's uneasiness with the word 'racism' that I identified could be understood as a kind of uneasiness about its own history. Good intentions were mixed here with an ambiguity about the institutional past that bear embarrassing testament to universities' and science's complicity in establishing and spreading scientific racism. The ideal of neutrality is used to create a semblance of objectivity and detachment, while at the same time erasing a disturbing history.

Struggling with methodological nationalism

There was yet another thing that rendered my research sensitive. Other potentially inflammatory sites could be identified in the format of my research project. From the academic debates around the history and sociology of racism and anti-Semitism, I have learned that studies of racism were particularly sensitive when framed in national terms. The German *Historikerstreit* was an example that showed me how a seemingly neutral scientific debate could become closely related to the issue of national guilt

40   *Meeting with the court documents*

(Giesen, 2004, p. 134). From similar debates in my homeland of Poland, I have learned how universalistic and psychological explanations of racism, by drawing attention away from the historical and social contexts in which different articulations of racism emerged, were used by nationalists to avoid recognizing the harm done in the name of the nation (Tokarska-Bakir, 2004). In all these cases, the debates seemed to concern methodological and theoretical issues of studying historical events or social phenomena. Yet the strong emotions and great intensity of the controversies revealed that something more was at stake.

Studying the history of the Swedish legislation against racism, I discovered that the laws stemmed from dynamics in which international pressure was mixing with a shame of manifestations of racism. In Chapter 4, I describe how these dynamics can work in two directions: both to enable laws, such as the act on agitation against a national or ethnic group, and to attempt to suppress and deny the existence of racism. I started to understand that my own project was implicated in these histories and that the use of infected words like 'racism' could awaken similar affects, even in the seemingly dispassionate world of academia.

In this context, the idea of methodological nationalism acquired new meaning for me. It was not merely a criticism of a particular 'national gaze' that equates societies with nation-states, thereby disregarding both the local variations within national communities and the impact of globalization (Beck, 2003, pp. 454–456). Treating a particular society as delimited by the political frontiers of a nation-state in order to study racism bore the risk of constructing new kinds of generalizations, and seemed to meet resistance by affecting a particular national pride, thereby adding to the sensation of an accusation. The idea of 'Swedish exceptionalism', that I discussed in Chapter 1, complicated this kind of national framework even further.

Aware of the problems that the national framework of my research entailed, I nevertheless had some reasons for keeping it. First, the legal system and the judiciary, although never purely national, especially since World War II when they have been influenced by international and more recently European law, operate as a nationally coherent and relatively independent system. In Chapter 4, I problematize the simple dichotomies between the national and the international by showing how the emergence of Swedish laws against racism has been both linked to local events and influenced by global shifts and developments. I notice at the same time that, by being strictly connected with the apparatus of the nation-state, the Swedish legal system auto-defines and legitimates itself as related to a national community defined in political terms.

Second, by studying the history of legislation against racism, I discovered the role of the nation-state, with laws as an instrument, in producing and maintaining, or, alternatively, reversing and abolishing, racist structures. Through legal and political measures, the state defines who is classified as a citizen and how ethnic and national groups and other categories are determined, which 'in turn create the state, shape the state and transform the state' (Wallerstein, 1980, unpublished paper quoted in CCCS, 1982, p. 14). As some scholars analysing racism put it:

> This conception of the interplay between the state and the reproduction of ethnic/racial differences is important because it situates the operation of the international context within the complex reality of the political and economic forces in each national formation.
>
> (CCCS, 1982, p. 14)

Third, the material I was analysing reminded me about the role that a particular idea of the nation had in the acts of violence I was studying, something that I analysed in detail in Chapter 2. In many of the acts of violence described in the material, there was a clear convergence between articulations of racism and of nationalism. This could be understood in light of the theories that conceive of racism as a modern, European phenomenon, emerging in conjunction with the political order based on the nation-state (Balibar, 1991b, pp. 38–39). The relationship between racism and nationalism has often been described as a complex one: neither a simple derivation where racism emerges from nationalism, nor an antithetical relation, where the idea of nation is used as a means of inclusion and the idea of race as a means of exclusion (Miles, 1993, p. 59). Also, the distinction between biology and culture cuts through both racism and nationalism rather than constituting a borderline between the two, as racism has increasingly taken cultural difference as its central marker, while, at the same time, the idea of bloodline has been central to many nationalisms. Thus, in a time when racism has become disguised in cultural terms, the distinctive line between the biological determinism of racism and the cultural determinism of nationalism has become more blurred. Rather, as Miles claims, the difference between racism and nationalism lies in the latter's specification of 'an ideal political organization' that led to 'a specific political project' (1993, p. 61). Historically, racism and nationalism are thus intimately connected, which makes it difficult to properly understand contemporary racism in Europe without analytically relating it to specific nationalist projects.

So, while these theoretical issues informed my ways of conceptualizing racism and had impact on my methodological choices, I did not foresee that they would feed into the sensitivity of my subject. Only afterwards could I understand how the national perspective that I adopted, through the choice of material via the statistics collected on the national level and my focus on national legislation and the judiciary, could be perceived as a threat to a national community imagined through the ideals of tolerance and openness.[3]

Anger and anxiety

While I was discovering in my material how one particular character of the injury went unrecognized in courts, in my academic work, I was encountering a somewhat similar resistance and experiencing pressure to abandon my

42 *Meeting with the court documents*

vocabulary. Above, I have tried to describe how these processes were shaping the methodological choices and theoretical framework of my project in an inconspicuous, but persistent, way. They also made me grow stubborn. I do not remember when exactly I decided that to stick to words such as 'racism' and to defend the choices and stances would become an integral part of my project. I found myself endorsing what Les Back calls a 'hyper-political posture' (2004, p. 251). This froze my language and occluded my eye: I was unable to *read* the material in front of me, other than through categorical statements or through charts and tables.

The academic requirement that was imposed on me of living up to the Weberian ideal of value-free research met here with the legal tradition that divorces the judiciary from ethics, in which the Swedish legal system is rooted (see, for example, Hedenius, 1963). The pressure to suspend judgement in my research intersected strangely with the very tissue of my material. While the court documents that I studied were literally judgements—court decisions firmly establishing the *true* version of the events, delivering verdicts about the occurrence or non-occurrence of crimes, and fixing the causes thereof in neatly defined sites of responsibility—they were crafted in a very special way as if pronounced by the law itself and detached from the moral stands of the judges. This kind of judicial craft stems from the philosophical claim that law is independent of morals and ethics, and expresses itself in the narrative strategies adopted by judges writing the judgements. The subject speaking in the judgements uses what Moa Bladini calls the 'objectified voice' and the 'invisible voice' (2013, pp. 281–295), giving the impression that the act of judgement is performed by the judiciary and not by human actors. This appearance of independence—the independence of the legal text from ethics and the independence of an invisible and assumedly objective judging subject in court from their political ideas or moral values—creates an impression that judgements are value-free, although actually they assert the legality of and responsibility for the acts on trial.

Dealing with material in which the issue of judgement and responsibility, and therefore of ethics and politics, was so prominent yet still carefully concealed under the semblance of objectivity, the requirement of suspending my own judgement for the sake of research brought about the opposite effect, resulting in my adopting a militant tone and a stubborn posture. Discovering how a certain type of injury was being neglected or even obscured in court, I understood that there was no clear line between empowerment and confrontation in my research. And I was defining the *political* and *ethical* aims of my study as witness to a form of injustice that my material was revealing. At a certain point, however, I felt stuck in the categorical distinctions between racism and non-racism. Somehow my research started to resemble the clear-cut judgements of the courts I was studying: the crime had been committed or not, it had racist motives or not, the defendant was guilty or not. There was no grey zone, no place for ambiguity, no doubt.

It was when I started to deconstruct the court's definition of the racist subject, in a case that I analyse in Chapter 6, and thereby to identify the

Meeting with the court documents   43

sources of the failure to recognize a particular type of injury performed in this case, that my own crude black-and-white judgements were shattered. If my initial definition of racism was similar to the one endorsed by the court in this case, it was so not in its contents nor in its shape but in its categorical tone. This stiff posture, allowing no ambivalence, made it impossible for the court to notice the complex and opaque forms that racism could take. For me, it meant that I limited myself to proving that courts did not notice racism without trying to understand why this happened. Only later, when reading Les Back's reflections on his research of advocates of intolerance and racism (2004), I realized that my own hanging on to categorical vocabularies had its roots in an anxiety provoked by a threat of *understanding* racism that would entail nuance and ambiguity. It was the threat of losing the safe haven provided by a categorical anti-racist posture and moving into a grey zone of consciousness of which Les Back, drawing on Levi, writes. If racism could be identified not in realized intentions or explicit motives, but rather in those dimensions of actions that reproduce a particular imaginary and may exceed our own cognizance, as I claim in Chapter 6, or in the language we speak, as I discuss in Chapter 7, how could *I* stay totally clear of it? In attending to these affective dimensions that were shaping my research in ways that I had not foreseen, I began to open up to my material. I could now recognize the sense of disorientation about which Les Back writes when formulating his postulate for reflective engagement:

> It is precisely this sense of disorientation that I want to propose as an interpretative position from which ethnography—even of one's political enemies—should be conducted. ... The ethics of such an inquiry must confront the fact that bearing witness to whiteness also involves being placed on the spectrum of the grey zone. This can never and should never be resolved. It is the comfortless condition of looking into the face of racism and seeing a trace of oneself reflected in its eye.
>
> (2004, p. 261)

Learning to read the material: towards an understanding of court documents

And so I started to read the court documents anew. I redefined my aim as a wish to understand the rationale behind the judgements and, in particular, to understand what caused a peculiar silence around the possibility of the acts judged in court as having a racist nature. I let my investigation be guided by a certain unsettlement that I experienced in the meeting with the material. To some degree, this unsettlement and the questions that I started to formulate were inspired by the theoretical frameworks that shaped my own understanding of anti-Muslim racism. In this way, my reading of the court documents and the resulting analysis that I present in Chapters 6, 7, and 8 have been theoretically guided.

44 *Meeting with the court documents*

I began to interpret the silence around racism that I encountered in the material in the light of theories of cultural trauma (Caruth, 1996; Cohen, 2001; Eyerman, 2008; Felman, 2002; Giesen, 2004; LaCapra, 2001). These theories explain how societies deal with troubling events, histories and practices. Especially relevant to this study are those involving different articulation of racism. Cultural trauma theories helped me understand how some events or experiences leave a trace on cultural identities. They also display the centrality of the mechanisms of silencing, denial and abjection of the troubling past from collective memory.

I also investigated how my unsettlement was related to a gap between how I had learned to understand racism and how it was defined in the law and in courts. Exploring these differences now became one of the main objectives of my study. My understanding of racism was shaped by theoretical perspectives according to which racism emerged at a determined point in time, in certain social settings and unfolded in particular histories (e.g., Fredrickson, 2003; Rattansi, 2007). As such, it has been inseparable from the larger processes and events taking place in Europe and European colonies and deeply embedded in certain regimes of knowledge, in power relations and in economic systems. In other words, my approach to racism was historical and contextual.[4] Acts of racism could only be intelligible when read in relation to certain discourses and imaginaries. In Chapter 2, I introduced some such key anti-Muslim discourses and imaginaries and other relevant contexts crucial for understanding anti-Muslim racism in Sweden.

While these theories helped me to develop tools for identifying and understanding racism in my material, it became evident that my definition differed sharply from how the courts defined racism. My aim was to reconstruct and analyse the courts' definitions. The task was difficult partly because these remained implicit and unexpressed in most cases, and partly because of the nature of the material—court documents.

What is recorded from the trials, as well as the format of this record, is decided by the principles guiding the Swedish judiciary. Written texts of the judgements, together with concise notes from the trial, are the only official traces of what happens in court. As a result of reforms in 1996 and 2008 aimed at making trials simpler, more modern and more effective, several new rules were introduced in the Swedish courts, guiding the ways in which records are kept and judgements written. In most cases, including the ones that I studied, this has resulted in minutes from the trials being replaced by short notes and video or sound recordings of the interviews of witnesses, and the format of the judgement being simplified. The use of video and sound recordings was mainly designed to facilitate and make more effective the work of the courts of appeal (*hovrätterna*), which could now rely mainly on the evidence presented in district courts (*tingsrätter*) without having to hear the witnesses and parties again. The video material from the trial is kept only until the decision has been rendered final and binding, and it is then destroyed. Apart from concise notes from the trial and the written judgement, no other records of hearings or court proceedings are kept.

This limited amount of written records from trials is also a result of the principle of oral proceedings applied in criminal trials in Sweden (Justitie-departementet (1998, Chapter 43, Section 5 and Chapter 46, Section 5). The principle means that it is the parties' right to present their arguments and to be able to reply orally to accusations. The form of a trial is strongly influenced by this principle, which is visible in rules such as the one that no participants in the trial should read from notes, except if evidence is presented in written form. In theory at least, trials shall consist in the judges hearing the parties, the witnesses and others involved, and, based only on this hearing, decide on the guilt and the sanction. The decision is reached in closed deliberations of the judges taking place after the trial. The judgement is just a record of the decision and it is written afterwards.[5] Thus, the principle of oral proceedings, as well as the ideal of an effective, quick and modern trial, has considerably limited the amount of paper documents presented in court and produced during the trial.

The principles underlying the trial had an important influence on what my material looked like. Written judgements are my main entry to the trials. Apart from them, I had access to the free text (*fritext*), a descriptive part of the police report produced by police officers where they give an overview of the reported event. In order to get more insight into the cases on which I focus in my analysis, I requested and received documents from the police investigation, including photographs of the crime scene, minutes from the police interviews, memos written by police officers and prosecutors working with the case and other possible evidence gathered throughout the investigation. The police files I used as auxiliary material, while the written judgements remained the basis for my analysis.

The written document of the judgement is designed as follows. It opens with the name of the court as well as the place and time in which the decision is pronounced. Then the parties and their legal representatives or assistants are specified. Often the claimed crimes with the corresponding section of law are referred to. Thereafter comes the court's decision in the case. This is followed by a summary of the parties' testimonies and their description of the circumstances of the acts at trial. Next, the grounds for the court's decision are presented, stating what has been proven in the case. The document closes with information about how the decision can be appealed and the signature of the judge assigned to the case (Justitie-departementet (1998, Chapter 30, Section 5). The order of the document is unchangeable and decided by established rules for legal procedures, giving all the judgements a uniform design. The documents can, however, vary as to length, degree of details about the event as presented in court and extensiveness of the judges' explanation of their decision.

According to Bladini, the overture of the document—a heading displaying the court's seal and its name—is an expression of the objectifying voice of the court, which is aimed at establishing the document's legitimacy and authority to perform the speech act of judgement (2013, p. 285). The

46 *Meeting with the court documents*

character of the following two largest sections of the document, which constitute the core of the judgement, differs as to their function in relation to the act of judgement. While the first is the court's summary of the testimonies of the parties and other evidence presented in court, the second section consists of the court's justification of its decision. The accounts included in the two sections are assigned different status: the former is a report of how the events were presented in court; the latter constitutes the establishment of the official version of the acts on trial. However, in both parts, it is actually the court that is talking and it is through its voice that the trial and, indirectly, the acts disputed in the trial are conveyed to me. With my growing interest in the ways that courts define, frame and understand the acts they are judging, these documents provided me with an opportunity to read how the interpretative power of the judiciary—their power to firmly fix meanings of a polysemic social reality—is performed.

To grasp these workings of the judiciary I started by asking how courts proceed to identify racism. Most noticeable was the court's emphasis on motive as the criterion for an act to be treated as a racist crime, combined with a specific definition of what a motive is. This contrasted with the studies that problematized the idea of the individual's motive as the distinctive feature of racism, such as Hannah Arendt's analysis of the Eichmann trial (2006) or Kathleen M. Blee's analysis of women involved in the Ku Klux Klan and of white supremacist. Both Arendt and Blee are critical of overemphasis on perpetrators' intentions and motives in the conceptualizations of racism (Blee, 2005). Inspired by these discussions, I selected a case that I analyse in Chapter 6 in which the issue of intention and motive was central, although approached by the court in a concise and indirect way.

While reading this case, I was discovering the nature of the power of the judiciary. The law's and the court's impact on what could be said and how it could be framed went much deeper than to inform the ways in which justice was claimed or innocence pled, strongly shaping the *accounts* of those involved in the trials. Drawing on Judith Butler's work, I treated trials as *scenes of address* (Butler, 1997, 2005), where some injuries are being claimed, some motives are being defined and some subjects are being constructed *in relation to* the legal definitions of injury, motive and subject as well as in relation to the court's understanding of racism. From this perspective, it was possible to see a deep effect of the word of the law on the narratives of those involved in the case. At the same time, from the concise summaries of the testimonies of the witnesses, I tried to reclaim the narratives in which the events were being shaped as meaningful for those involved. My aim in the analysis was to recreate the polyphony of the voices present in court, which enabled me to reach a complex and deeper understanding of the dynamics of justice and recognition or the lack thereof.

My attempt to read what different participants in the trial were communicating was part of a broader project of making these voices audible and therefore of an attempt to reverse the symbolic violence of the court. This meant struggling through the impersonal summary of the testimonies to understand what those speaking had been trying to communicate while, at the same time, discovering what it means to have one's account narrated in the third person. This was the moment when the limitations resulting from my choice of material were the most discernible: I had not been present in court and had never met those involved in the trial. I had to rely on the court's voice in order to recover these stories. Cognizant of the parallels between the regimes of power embodied in court and in academia, I realized that this task was to some extent doomed to failure from the outset. Was not the authoritative voice of the court replaced by an authoritative research voice? How could I read these narratives from the court documents and write them into my academic text without exercising a type of symbolic violence similar to that of the judiciary, this time through an analytical work? Was there a method, a particular type of approach, which could lead me to an interpretation that was both empowering and understanding?

The choice of the second case, which I analyse in Chapter 7, was also both theoretically inspired and empirically grounded. This time, I found the case emblematic since it shed light on how insulting language was treated in court and, more specifically, on the court's ability to identify and read racist slur. Through my study of the history of legislation against racism in Sweden, I learned that verbal violence, in the form of insult or agitation against a national or ethnic group, has often been the form of racism easiest to address by the law. The main aim of Chapter 7 is to understand the court's philosophy of language in general and in particular its ways of identifying and defining injurious, racist language.

The choice of the last two cases, those presented in Chapter 8, was motivated partly by a sense of surprise: how similar acts performed by the same person could unfold into two very different cases. One of the cases seemed to present a counterexample to my argument developed in this book. The judgement focused on the racist nature of the acts on trial. This aspect of the injury was clearly recognized and remedied by the judge, who provided convincing grounds for his verdict based on relevant legislation and case law. This did not fit the idea that it was the legal reasoning that prohibited the possibility of racism being addressed in court. The case thereby represented a challenge to my critique of the judiciary. The challenge was appealing, and I decided to include this case in my book in order to expand my view of the judiciary.

Hence, the tools and points of entry to analyse my material were developing, at least partly, in the process of reading the court documents and as a response to their nature and character—the particular format of the judgement, the ways in which the voices of the court and the narratives of those involved in trials were shaped, the rhetorical workings of the language; they were also theoretically informed. There was yet another dimension to this relationship between the form of my research and the nature of the material I was studying. As I gradually realized the weight of the rhetorics in the

48   *Meeting with the court documents*

judicial process and devoted my analysis to how judges formulate their judgements, the issue of the rhetorics in my own writing became of central importance. I realized that whom and how I was to persuade or influence depended also on the way I would tell the story of how justice is dispensed in Swedish courts.

Conclusions

Ethnographers often claim that the knowledge produced through fieldwork or interviews is a fruit of a particular interaction, created in a dialogical relationality between the researcher and those who are being studied. This means that ethnographic practices involve not only learning about, but also learning from, research participants (Sheldon, 2016, p. 37). In this chapter, I have tried to explore whether similar dynamics can be identified when working with a very different type of material: written documents. I have asked myself to what extent my approach, method and type of analysis were the result of the interaction with the documents that I was reading.

I have suggested here that it was the nature of my material—the court documents—that shaped and transformed me. The research process was undertaken in parallel to how courts, by lending credence to some accounts and authenticating some evidence, establish legal truths and thereby produce knowledge about the acts and events disputed in a trial. I have discussed how at the outset of my research I was mimicking the courts, letting my project be dominated by *a collection of evidence* of anti-Muslim racism that went unrecognized in a court unable to address this particular dimension of the injury and take certain narratives into account. I have tried to connect these ways of producing knowledge to certain epistemological and ontological traditions in academia, the very site from where I myself was talking. I have located my research project in a broader institutional setting that was constantly exercising an impact on my vocabulary and thereby on the theories that I had at my disposal. I have also described how I attempted to extricate myself from the embrace of the kind of knowledge production that carries with it very particular powers of persuasion.

Much of the dynamics of the research process took place at the emotional level. I have described my anger in reaction to the injustice and unrecognition that I discovered in the court documents, but also in reaction to the strategies of distancing that academia was imposing on me through a requirement of strict separation of fact from value and through the attempts to depoliticize my language. I have tried to problematize these emotions by showing how they led me to embrace a rigid position and consequently froze my language and disabled my capacity to read. At the same time, I have tried to identify another source of my hyper-political posture—a kind of anxiety related to the study of a 'distasteful' subject. I started to learn how initial methodological strategies were indeed related to a desire to distance myself from this subject, as is often the case when researchers try to

Meeting with the court documents 49

understand people or phenomena towards which they feel repugnance (Esseveld & Eyerman, 1992, p. 222). Somehow distance provided a safe haven and closeness felt threatening. My struggle with these emotions has lasted throughout the entire research process, with a particular type of discomfort steadily shaping my research position.

By using my material as a source of knowledge, but also as a point of reference and site of contrast in issues regarding epistemology and ontology, I have become more aware of what kind of power an act of interpretation exerts. My discovery of the violence embedded in the courts' describing, defining and providing an understanding of the events on trial has served as a warning against a kind of responsibility that the production of knowledge, and above all the production of knowledge backed by the institutional authority of academia, entails. In this way, I have tried to develop an understanding of methodological strategies and analytical tools as deeply implicated in the ethics and politics of knowledge production.

Notes

1 Lay judges have significant power in deciding verdicts and penalties. In the district courts, lay judges participate mainly in criminal cases and some family suits. They constitute a majority as in each such case three lay judges with individual votes and one legally qualified judge take part. In the courts of appeal, there are three legally qualified judges and two lay judges in criminal cases and some family suits (Justitiedepartementet, 2013, p. 101).

2 For example, when the word 'racism' appeared for the first time in French dictionaries, between 1922 and 1930, it already sounded pejorative, designating a philosophy of history based on a primacy of biological factors and a system of prejudice and a conception of the world that was 'judged to be as false as harmful or dangerous, even scandalous or monstrous, and attributed to an enemy declared as such' (Taguieff, 2001, pp. 84–85). The invention of the word in French must be seen in the ideological and political context of French–German relations at the beginning of the twentieth century. Hence, the stigmatizing semantic field of the word lumps together 'the following pejorative nouns: racism/anti-Semitism/(pan-) Germanism/Nazism/fascism/extreme right/right' (Taguieff, 2001, p. 81). Similarly, in English, the word 'racism' appeared much later than the word 'race'. While the latter dates back to the early seventeenth century, the former entered the English language only in the third decade of the twentieth century. Indeed, as Fredrickson puts it: 'the concept of racism emerges only when the concept of race, at least some of its applications, begin to be questioned' (2003, p. 156). And just like in French, the appearance of the concept 'racism' was related to the criticism of the German National Socialist ideology. The word 'racism' first came to English from German in a translation of the book *Racism*, written by Magnus Hirschfeld, and was afterwards picked up by a number of authors, both British and American, who criticized the Nazi idea of race (Miles, 1993, pp. 28–29).

3 I was also aware of the risks of writing in English and thus potentially for an international public and keeping this national framework as a point of departure. I learned about it from, among others, the historians who studied the history of sterilization in Sweden and saw the results of their research being politicized and used abroad in an attack on the Swedish welfare state as a political system (see the Introduction to the 2005 edition of Broberg & Roll-Hansen).

50   *Meeting with the court documents*

4 In my interpretation, I followed in particular George M. Fredrickson's reconstruction of the historical trajectory of racism conceived as 'mainly, if not exclusively, a product of the West' (2003, p. 6), the climax of which took place in the overtly racist regimes of Nazi Germany, the Jim Crow segregation system in the United States and South African apartheid, but which 'originated in at least a prototypical form in the fourteenth and fifteenth centuries rather than in the eighteenth or nineteenth ... and was originally articulated in the idioms of religion more than in those of natural science' (2003, p. 6). This approach to the history of racism undermined the strict distinction between hard, biological racism—a product of eighteenth- and nineteenth-century science—and soft, cultural racism—often understood as a new, post-war phenomenon. By establishing a continuity between the elements of early prototypes of racism—such as the persecution of Jews and Muslims during and after the *reconquista*—and later formulations of anti-Semitism, this approach disclosed how the concepts of race and culture, or religion, have been conflated in these histories. It also highlighted how the idea of biological difference has been subjected to different metamorphoses, from the concept of 'blue blood' in the Middle Ages or the Spanish *limpieza de sangre* (Fredrickson, 2003, p. 33), through the scientific career of the concept of 'race' in the modern West, to allusions to 'origin' or 'stock' that still inform thinking about ethnicity and nationality (Fredrickson, 2003; see also Rattansi, 2007, p. 100). It showed how scientific racism, even though it focused on the concept of biological race, incorporated some earlier ideas about cultural properties of racial groups. In spite of the decline of scientific racism, some bodies have continued to be singled out and stigmatized for their biological attributes, such as skin colour, although usually in a somewhat covert manner. At the same time, culture and religion have been defined as almost natural and unchangeable properties of certain groups, inherited from one generation to another (Rattansi, 2007, pp. 104–105). In this context, the ideas of race and culture can be understood as often conflated and influencing one another, each forming a *perceived heritage*, either strictly biological, manifested in skin colour and other differences in appearance, or cultural, manifested in language, religion, customs, ways of life, and so on.

5 This form of judicial proceedings may represent a challenge to a study like the present one, concerned with the judicial process but with the empirical material based on written documents only. Had I observed the trials in the cases that I analyse, I might have been able to notice some more aspects of this process. My decision to focus on the judgements in the already concluded cases preselected by Brå, however, can be justified by a couple of considerations. First, as already mentioned, I took my starting point in the statistics on hate crimes produced by Brå. I believed that, by looking at the cases that were classified by an independent body as Islamophobic hate crimes, I could observe how this aspect of the crime was approached by the courts. Moreover, I had access to a large number of cases and followed them through the entire legal proceedings. Second, although the trial is based on the principle of oral proceedings, and it certainly provides a frame to the judicial process, the verdict itself is voiced in the form of a written document—the judgement. It is through this written document that the court's decision reaches the parties. This document is also central for understanding the court's rationale behind the judgement since the deliberations of the judges after the trial are held behind closed doors.

Bibliography

Arendt, H. (2006). *Eichmann in Jerusalem: A Report on the Banality of Evil*. New York: Penguin Books.

Meeting with the court documents 51

Back, L. (2004). 'Politics, Research and Understanding.' In C. Seale, G. Gobo, J. Gubrium & D. Silverman (Eds.), *Qualitative Research Practice*. London: Sage, pp. 249–265.

Balibar, É. (1991a). 'Is There a Neo-Racism?' In É. Balibar & I. Wallerstein (Eds.), *Race, Nation, Class: Ambiguous Identities*. London: Verso, pp. 17–28.

Balibar, É. (1991b). 'Racism and Nationalism.' In É. Balibar & I. Wallerstein (Eds.), *Race, Nation, Class: Ambiguous Identities*. London: Verso, pp. 37–68.

Beck, U. (2003). 'Toward a New Critical Theory with a Cosmopolitan Intent.' *Constellations: an International Journal of Critical & Democratic Theory*, 10(4), 453–468.

Bladini, M. (2013). *I objektivitetens sken—en kritisk granskning av objektivitetsideal, objektivitetsanspråk och legitimeringsstrategier i diskurser om dömande i brottmål.* Göteborg: Makadam.

Blee, K. (2005). 'Racial Violence in the United States.' *Ethnic and Racial Studies*, 28(4), 599–619.

Broberg, G. & Roll-Hansen, N. (Eds.). (2005). *Eugenics and the Welfare State: Sterilization Policy in Denmark, Sweden, Norway, and Finland.* East Lansing: Michigan State University Press.

Butler, J. (1997). *Excitable Speech: A Politics of the Performative.* New York; London: Routledge.

Butler, J. (2005). *Giving an Account of Oneself.* New York: Fordham University Press.

CCCS (Centre for Contemporary Cultural Studies). (1982; 1992). *The Empire Strikes Back: Race and Racism in 70s Britain.* London: Hutchinson; London: Routledge.

Collins, P. (2000). *Black Feminist Thought: Knowledge, Consciousness, and the Politics of Empowerment.* New York: Routledge.

Ekelöf, P., Edelstam, H. & Heuman, L. (2009). *Rättegång. H. 4.* Stockholm: Norstedt.

Esseveld, J. & Eyerman, R. (1992). 'Which Side are You On? Reflections on Methodological Issues in the Study of "Distasteful" Social Movements.' In M. Diani & R. Eyerman (Eds.), *Studying Collective Action*. London: Sage, pp. 217–237.

FRA. (2009a). *Data in Focus Report. Muslims.* Retrieved from: http://fra.europa.eu/en/publication/2010/eu-midis-data-focus-report-2-muslims

FRA. (2009b). *EU-MIDIS European Union Minorities and Discrimination Survey. Main Results Report.* Retrieved from: http://fra.europa.eu/en/publication/2012/european-union-minorities-and-discrimination-survey-main-results-report

Fredrickson, G. (2003). *Racism: A Short History.* Woodstock: Princeton University Press.

Giesen, B. (2004). 'The Trauma of Perpetrators: The Holocaust as the Traumatic Reference of German National Identity.' In R. Alexander, B. Giesen, N. Smelser & P. Sztompka (Eds.), *Cultural Trauma and Collective Identity*. Berkeley: University of California Press, pp. 112–154.

Goldberg, D. (1990). *Anatomy of Racism.* London: University of Minnesota Press.

Haraway, D. (1988). 'Situated Knowledges: The Science Question in Feminism and the Privilege of Partial Perspective.' *Feminist Studies*, 14(3), 575–599.

Harding, S. (1992). 'After the Neutrality Ideal: Science, Politics, and "Strong Objectivity".' *Social Research*, 59(3), 567–587.

Hedenius, I. (1963). *Om rätt och moral.* Stockholm: Wahlström & Widstrand.

Justitiedepartementet (1998). *The Swedish Code of Judicial Procedure (Ds1998:65).* Retrieved from: www.government.se/contentassets/a1be9e99a5c64d1bb93a96ce5d517e9c

52   Meeting with the court documents

Justitiedepartementet. (2013). *Nämndemannauppdraget—breddad rekrytering och kvalificerad medverkan (SOU 2013: 49)*. Stockholm: Fritzes.

Lavén, H. (2013). *Hur domstolar dömer i brottmål: om domare, rättegång, bevisning och påföljder* (1st edn.). Stockholm: Norstedts juridik.

Miles, R. (1993). *Racism after 'Race Relations'*. London: Routledge.

Sheldon, R. (2016). *Tragic Encounters and Ordinary Ethics: Palestine–Israel in British Universities*. Manchester: Manchester University Press.

Solomos, J. & Back, L. (1996). *Racism and Society*. London: MacMillan Press.

Taguieff, P.-A. (2001). *The Force of Prejudice. On Racism and Its Doubles*. London: University of Minnesota Press.

The Swedish Code of Judicial Procedure. (Ds 1998:000). Retrieved from: www.government.se/contentassets/a1be9e99a5c64d1bb93a96ce5d517e9c/the-swedish-code-of-judicial-procedure-ds-1998_65.pdf

Tokarska-Bakir, J. (2004). *Rzeczy mgliste*. Sejny: Pogranicze.

Wallerstein, I. (1980). Unpublished paper quoted in CCCS (1982).

4 Making racism a crime

It needs to be stated that the foremost weapon in the struggle against racism is an open debate. Opinions and attitudes that manifest themselves as racism can thereby be fundamentally influenced. It is thus important to defend fundamental democratic rights, such as free exchange of opinions, and to emphasize the respect for the equal value of every human being in every context. At the same time, it is important that every actual expression of racism is fought against forcefully, not just as a reaction to the individual events but also to show that these tendencies are unacceptable in a democratic society.

... A person that attacks or threatens people because they are from another country or from another culture should know that he or she is thereby diverting from the norms prevalent in Sweden and that the discriminatory motive is considered an aggravating circumstance when the act is judged in a Swedish court.

(Prop., 1993/94:101, pp. 15–16)

At the beginning of the 1990s, the Swedish Parliament (*Riksdagen*) voted for the introduction of penalty enhancement provision to the Swedish Penal Code, in cases where one of the motives for the crime was 'to aggrieve a person, ethnic group or some other similar group of people by reason of race, colour, national or ethnic origin, religious belief or other similar circumstance' (SFS, 1962:700, Chapter 29, Section 2(7)). The balanced tone of the government bill contrasted sharply with the sense of urgency present in Swedish society in reaction to manifestations of racism that had become more obtrusive in the previous decade. In the bill, the legal protection from racist violence and discrimination was carefully weighed against the fundamental democratic rights to freedom of speech and freedom of assembly. The above quote is expressive of this cautious rhetoric. It also reveals how the process of making racism a crime has been interwoven with the project of defining the norms that this crime violates, thereby constructing a national identity based on tolerance, diversity and openness.

The aim of this chapter is to present the Swedish legislation designed to address different forms of racism, with focus on criminal law. I study these

54 *Making racism a crime*

laws in the historical context in which they were introduced and seek to identify the rationale behind their introduction. To do this, I mainly analyse the preliminary works produced in the process of making these laws. Tracing the genealogy of the Swedish legislation against racism seems important here for two reasons. First, it illustrates how ways of speaking about the acts that I am interested in have changed over time in Sweden, making it possible to identify certain significant shifts in the official discourse and at the same time to notice continuities. Second, the historical documents that I analyse are used by courts as the main source for the interpretation of laws. Thus, my presentation of these documents is intended to prepare the ground for the case studies that constitute the core of this book.

My account of the history of the Swedish legislation against racism is done through a close reading of preliminary works,[1] mainly the Swedish Official Reports (*Statens offentliga utredningar—SOU*) and government bills (*Propositioner*) by the force of which these laws have been introduced.[2] I explore what kind of dynamics have shaped the ways in which laws against racism have been formulated, justified and expounded. In doing this, I also examine how some historical processes have led not only to the emergence of a new kind of crime but also to the definition of a norm. Through this historical account, I trace the emergence of a particular vision of national community. Finally, I shortly refer to a history of the term 'race' in legal texts in Sweden, arguing that it is significant for an understanding of the shame around racism and ways of dealing with it.

Although this chapter focuses on the Swedish context, it will soon become evident that the emergence and transformation of the Swedish legislation in this field have been closely related to some important global developments. In this sense, it is impossible to understand the genealogies and dynamics of the legislation against racism in Sweden without taking into consideration such events as the Holocaust, the Civil Rights movements or anti-colonial struggles that in different ways have led to the introduction of the relevant laws and international instruments. The account presented here will pay attention to and shed a light on these dynamics and will show how they have been intertwined with the developments in the Swedish context.

Recognition and denial: historical background of the legislation against racism in Sweden

In the shadow of the Holocaust: introducing the act on agitation against a national or ethnic group

In 1948, a new crime—agitation against a national or ethnic group (*hets mot folkgrupp*)[3]—was defined in Chapter 11 of the then Swedish Penal Code (*Strafflagen*). It was described as consisting in publicly threatening, libelling or defaming a people of a certain descent or creed. The preparatory works gave the following immediate reasons for the introduction of the act:

Making racism a crime 55

The need for a criminal provision to which anti-Semitic propaganda should belong was ... made more urgent by the fact that this kind of propaganda had started to be emitted from Sweden, which according to reports from Swedish diplomatic representations and consulates brings *an embarrassing attention* in large parts of the civilized world.

(Första lagutskottets utlåtande, 1948, nr 39, p. 31, my emphasis)

When the Swedish state for the first time decided to address the issue of racism in law, it was a sense of embarrassment caused by the propaganda produced by a notorious Swedish anti-Semite, Einar Åberg, which triggered this process. The problem of this type of propaganda was not new, nor was the idea that it should be addressed by law. Åberg himself had begun his activity back in the 1920s and had been sentenced several times for disorderly conduct in relation to this. Swedish lawmakers were also familiar with other cases of anti-Semitism that had been brought to trial in the 1940s: one of a person in a public place carrying a board with the words 'Jews are the authors and instigators of the war'; another of a shop displaying a notice 'No admittance for Jews and half-Jews' (Straffrättskommittén, 1945, p. 226). Moreover, already during the war, motions proposing legal measures were tabled but rejected (Straffrättskommittén, 1945, p. 194), and in 1944, a report on this topic was produced by the Penal Law Committee (Straffrättskommittén, 1945) recommending the introduction of an article on agitation against a national or ethnic group into the Penal Code. However, despite this recommendation, the dominant idea of the report was that anti-Semitism was an exception rather than the rule:

The phenomenon, which by request should be countered by a regulation of the aforementioned kind, namely anti-Semitic propaganda, has in our country only to a limited extent presented itself in such a way that it may qualify for criminal justice intervention.... Popular opinion has shown no sign of being affected either by manifestations of the propaganda that are already punishable or by those that could be targeted by criminal justice through an extension of the law. Judging from the present state of affairs, there is no reason to fear that the propaganda in the near future will take on too malignant forms.

(Straffrättskommittén, 1945, p. 226)

This was the official stand on the problem of anti-Semitism both during and after the war: as expressed by Christian Günter, the foreign minister at the time Åberg was discussed, there was no anti-Semitism in Sweden save for exceptional cases (SÄPO:s arkiv, RPS, Stockholm, quoted in: Lööw & Nilsson, 2001, p. 12).

However, the end of the war and the disclosure of the Nazi atrocities against Jews brought about a shift in the way anti-Semitism was treated. From that moment on, anti-Semitism could no longer be tolerated without

56 *Making racism a crime*

causing an international embarrassment. In Sweden, as in the rest of Europe, it would still take decades to fully recognize the Holocaust as an extreme instance of racism, to construct it as a symbol of the absolute evil (Alexander, 2009) and to work through problematic episodes of Swedish history in relation to the Nazi extermination of European Jews.[4] Still, already in the years after the war, the ghostly presence of the memory of the genocide was shaping, albeit in indirect and opaque ways, the processes that led to the creation of laws against racism. When, after the war, Åberg expanded his activity and started to spread anti-Semitic leaflets translated into different languages in several other countries (Berggren, 1999, p. 95), this provoked stark reactions abroad. One of the organizations that intervened was the American Jewish Committee in New York. As a result, the law was passed and Åberg became the first person to be sentenced for agitation against a national or ethnic group, which was why the law was initially referred to as *Lex Åberg* (Lööw & Nilsson, 2001, p. 11).

However, even though the immediate cause for the discussion of the introduction of the legal measures was the production of anti-Semitic propaganda in Sweden, the problem of anti-Semitism was still framed as something external, not existent in the country. At other times, it was reformulated so that Jews were not mentioned at all, and instead anti-Semitism was defined as tensions and conflicts between different unspecified groups:

> Our country is indeed fortunate in having eluded disruptive battles in modern times between different national, linguistic or religious groups, but this situation can change.
>
> (Prop., 1948:80, p. 443)

When anti-Semitism was named, it was often described as something exclusive to Nazism, an ideology alien to Swedish public opinion:

> Nothing in the teachings of the now defeated Nazism would therefore upset the Swedish opinion more than large groups of people being regarded as inferior in relation to a so-called master race and in the propaganda even being described as 'Untermenschen'.
>
> (Prop, 1948:80, p. 446)

This externalization of the problem of anti-Semitism was also achieved by claiming that anti-Semitic propaganda was 'in conflict with the foundations of *our* civilization that people should not be persecuted for their descent or religion' (Prop, 1948:80, p. 445, my emphasis) or 'in conflict with *Christianity's and a democratic society's* common basic beliefs' (Prop, 1948:80, p. 446, my emphasis). In this way, anti-Semitism was defined as both reprehensible and, as per definition, not belonging to 'our' (Christian and democratic) civilization.

Making racism a crime   57

Another frequent argument used in opposition to the introduction of the law on agitation against a national or ethnic group was that the proposed article would be counterproductive. One example of this argument being used was when, shortly after its introduction, the minister of justice attempted to exclude the proposed article on agitation against a national or ethnic group from the bill on changes to the Penal Code, by arguing:

> A regulation of the aforementioned content could nourish the claims that Jewish citizens or other minority groups in our country have been given a privileged position and that this could come to sharpen tensions within the population instead of promoting peaceful coexistence.
>
> (Prop, 1948:80, p. 444)

The argument that the criminalization of anti-Semitic propaganda could serve as a proof of the privileged position of Jews in Sweden dangerously resembled the claims of the propaganda that the law was targeting, namely the conspiracy theory that Jews had a particularly powerful position in the world. Nevertheless, the claim that the law would have the opposite effect, and lead to conflicts between different groups in society, became regarded as a legitimate argument opposing legislation against racism, significantly shaping the ways in which such laws would be worded and expounded in the future.

Sparked by the feeling of 'embarrassment', the discussions leading to the criminalization of racist propaganda in Sweden established a discourse in which racism would be talked about and addressed in law. I argue that this discourse was a result of an intersection of international pressure and internal transgressions, and, more importantly, that it was informed by a profound and ambivalent shame that manifestations of anti-Semitism were evoking in the post-Holocaust era. The shame worked in two opposite directions. While, on the one hand, it led to the introduction of progressive legislation against racism and, some decades later, to an acknowledgement of the necessity to work through troubling episodes of the past, on the other hand, it entailed silencing, denial, belittlement and externalization of the problem of anti-Semitism and other forms of racism.

In the decades afterwards, these dynamics manifested themselves mostly in a silence around the issues of racism and anti-Semitism and a very limited application of the new law almost exclusively to the cases of anti-Semitic propaganda (Helene Lööw, 2000, p. 115). Sporadically, the discussion about the law was taken up in response to particular events, as in the 1960s when an 'epidemic of swastika-painting'—a wave of anti-Semitic incidents—went through Sweden, following similar events in other European countries. These incidents led to the penalty for agitation against a national or ethnic group being toughened. Yet, when discussed in the parliament, the incidents were interpreted as pranks by youth, unconscious of what they were doing: 'Mainly, these were cases of pranks by meddlesome youngsters and other immature people, who were likely inspired by information in

58 Making racism a crime

newspaper articles, as well as in television and radio broadcasts about demonstrations in other countries' (II kamm. prot., 1960, nr 2, p. 257). Those arrested 'explained that they are neither anti-Semites, nor politically interested' (II kamm. prot., 1960, nr 2, p. 257). Also, this time the problem was externalized: even when anti-Semitism manifested itself in Sweden, it was attributed to foreign inspiration. Moreover, it was excused by ideological unawareness, which put the motive into question. Once again a warning was given: 'We should ... not exaggerate the situation.... There is a risk that people in and outside of Sweden are led to believe that we, here in Sweden, have a major Jewish question [*jude-fråga*]. This is fortunately not the case.' (II kamm. prot., 1960, nr 2, p. 264).

The impact of anti-racist mobilizations abroad: ratifying the International Convention on the Elimination of All Forms of Racial Discrimination

The issue of racism, often approached as discrimination, was taken up several times by the Swedish Parliament in the following years, in the majority of cases as a reaction to diverse incidents deemed somehow problematic.[5] Still, no legislative measures were taken. There were three recurring justifications for this. First, racism, it was claimed, did not exist in Sweden (JO:s ämbetsberättelse, 1965, p. 80, quoted in: Justitiedepartementet, 1968, p. 15). Second, it was argued that the best way of fighting racism was through education and enlightenment. The third argument went that this type of legislation would lead to a differential treatment of some groups and individuals, which would, in turn, inhibit their integration into society (Allmännaberedningsutskottetsuttalande, 1964: 27, in: Justitiedepartementet, 1968, p. 13). Thus, throughout the 1960s, there was still a strong resistance in Sweden to approaching the problem of racism with law. This was often accompanied by a denial of the existence of the problem.

A change came in the early 1970s, when the Swedish legislation was influenced by a global shift in the approach to racism. In 1971, Sweden ratified the International Convention on the Elimination of All Forms of Racial Discrimination (hereafter, 'the Convention'). The Convention was itself a watershed. Its adoption by the international community was not only a success of the diplomatic struggles of several African states (Egon, 1966, pp. 997–998), but also a sign of the global impact of an important anti-racist mobilization. Two struggles made up this mobilization: an anti-colonial struggle most prominent in Africa and Asia, and the Civil Rights movement in the United States. The two were 'deeply interconnected historically and conceptually, geopolitically and existentially' (Goldberg, 2004, p. 218). Together, they opened up the possibility of opposing racism also with resort to law.

The impact of anti-racist mobilization was also discernible in Sweden. The international involvement in solidarity work in the fight against colonialism was an important part of political and social movements in Sweden at this time. However, while the struggle against racism abroad was one of the central political slogans in the 1960s, it would take time before racism became framed as a significant problem to be faced at home.[6]

So, once again, the change in the Swedish law came mainly as a result of international influence, now understood not so much as diplomatic pressure, as it was in the case of anti-Semitic propaganda produced in Sweden, but as an impact of global anti-colonial and anti-racist mobilizations and as a sense of needing to live up to an emerging ideal of a tolerant state opposing racism. As a consequence, the existing law on agitation against a national or ethnic group was amended and a new act on unlawful discrimination was passed.

Only gradually did racism start to be considered a threat at home, and this happened in the context of the transformations occurring in Swedish society as a result of immigration. Paradoxically, while the concern with protecting immigrants in Sweden from racism was rising, it was often expressed in ambiguous terms: for instance, using the argument that one source of 'race problems and other minority problems' was 'the growing addition of a population of foreign origin and other habits and behaviours than ours' (Prop, 1970:87, p. 58).[7] The claim was based on the assumption of the existence of a homogeneous 'we' with uniform 'habits and behaviours'. Such an assumption, in the context of the debate on racial discrimination and minority protection, reveals how much the project of creating a modern nation-state entailed a homogenization of the population and assimilation of differences, not only embodied by the immigrants but also by the members of national minorities and indigenous peoples that had lived in the territory of Sweden for centuries. As a result, these groups were made invisible, as instantiated in this quote.[8]

At the time when the Convention was adopted, the recognition of racism as a problem faced at home and of a need for legal remedy began to be articulated more clearly. And thus the justification of the ratification of the Convention read:

> Already the fact that different forms of racial discrimination exist today in our country constitutes a sufficient reason to revise the current legislation on the protection against racial discrimination. The question of the need for such legislation must, however, not only be seen in the light of today's situation but must also be judged considering that Sweden will continue to be an immigrant country.
>
> (Prop, 1970:87, p. 58)

The legal measures, it was claimed, should not only address individual cases of racial discrimination but also 'have a normative effect' (Prop, 1970:87, p. 58).

The crisis and getting over it: adopting the penalty enhancement provision

Ten years later, in 1981, a new Swedish Official Report investigated whether the law had succeeded in achieving the intended 'normative effect'. And the answer was:

60　*Making racism a crime*

Reality contradicts it. Is this because the public simply does not know that the act described in the law is punishable? Is it because the penalty is too light? Is it because it has proven safe to express contempt as according to the law, since neither police, prosecutors nor courts have found 'agitation against a national or ethnic group' worth fighting?

(Arbetsmarknadsdepartementet, 1981, p. 20)

In what followed, the report expressed indignation about the fact that the law turned out to be ineffective in a case of 'leaflets with strongly derogatory opinions about immigrants in Sweden' (Arbetsmarknadsdepartementet, 1981, p. 11) and suggested that this was partly due to the police's and prosecutors' 'own attitudes and lack of empathy' (Arbetsmarknadsdepartementet, 1981, p. 21). The criticism not only revealed a recognition of the problem of racism in Sweden, in particular racism against immigrants, but also acknowledged the state's failure to deal with this problem: in the period between 1970 and 1980, only three cases of agitation against a national or ethnic group were tried. Even more importantly, racism within the judiciary was identified as one of the reasons for this failure. The most noticeable shift was in how racism, including institutional racism, was approached: openly acknowledged and fiercely criticized.

The recognition of the need to protect immigrants in Sweden from racism was translated into concrete measures. The law on agitation against a national or ethnic group was extended to protect this group. The report stated that Sweden was now a land of immigrants with a large number of ethnic minority groups (Arbetsmarknadsdepartementet, 1981, p. 53). The main aim of the amendment to existing legislation was to provide proper protection for these new groups in society. The ways in which the situation of immigrants was defined in the report were to a high degree informed by the discourse of the new immigration policy[9] that was formulated in that period:

The goal of freedom of choice proclaimed by the Government in the immigration policy is also a clear expression of society's opinion that immigrants in Sweden should themselves determine to what extent they want to keep or develop their own ethnic identity or merge into a Swedish cultural identity. For the great majority of first- and second-generation immigrants, this is, however, not a choice between two possible ethnic identities, but an identity development based both on the culture and norms of the country of origin and on those of the new homeland.

(Arbetsmarknadsdepartementet, 1981, pp. 55–56)

To refer to the aim of freedom of choice in the context of the fight against racism was symbolic of the redefinition of the question of identity in the new doctrine of multiculturalism. This doctrine was becoming important for the ways in which the increasing demographic diversity was framed and

Making racism a crime 61

regulated. In Sweden, the emergence of domestic multicultural policies towards immigrants coincided with broad, although not undisputed, solidarity engagement abroad—most importantly against apartheid—which in the 1980s was manifested both on the level of Sweden's international relations and on the level of social movements (Thörn, 2006, p. 191). David Theo Goldberg argues that even if the link between anti-apartheid and multiculturalism was indirect and complex, it did result, in some countries, in an anti-racist ideal beginning to permeate new culturally diverse societies in the form of multiculturalism opening up 'socio-cultural arrangements and institutional life to a more diverse set of habits and practices' (2004, p. 222).[10] This was the case in Sweden, where the legislation against racism started to be discussed in the 1980s and 1990s in these new frames and under the impact of global solidarity and the ideal of multiculturalism.

Despite these emerging frameworks of recognition, strategies of denial were still returning in the discussions about the introduction of legal measures. One particularly fragile issue was the criticism of not having banned racist organizations that Sweden received from the Committee on the Elimination of Racial Discrimination (CERD), the United Nations body monitoring the implementation and observance of the Convention. As a matter of fact, when discussed in Sweden, as in many other countries, the ban on racist organizations was most often portrayed as creating a tension between two ideals: the ideal of diversity and tolerance on the one hand, and a particular ideal of democracy, promoting freedom of expression and freedom of association on the other. The resistance to the implementation of the ban, however, would often be manifested in the denial of the need for such an act:

> [E]ven if taking into account isolated events that have occurred lately, it can be stated that there are hardly any significant groups with racial persecution on the agenda. Openly racist organizations have very few members, and they are internally divided and have no influence. Wherever they appear, they are met by strong reactions of disgust from others, which should, incidentally, be far more important and effective than legislation.
>
> (Prop, 1986/87:151, p. 111)

Yet such an open denial was becoming more and more difficult, especially because the end of the 1980s and the beginning of the 1990s witnessed some disturbing developments that were spelled out in a 1991 report:

> Furthermore, there are indications that organized racism may be gaining ground. Sweden is assessed to, at a slower pace, follow the same development as other Western European countries, where Nazi and other right-wing extremist ideas have gained a surprising foothold in recent years, and where racist violence in some cases have an extremely worrying spread. In Sweden, there has statistically been some kind of

62 *Making racism a crime*

attack on a refugee centre every three weeks in the last three years. There is no evidence that organized racists are behind the attacks. However, in some other cases a connection has been demonstrated between a specific group and committed crimes.

(Arbetsmarknadsdepartementet, 1991, pp. 14–15)

This time, the alarmist tone of the report reflected the social climate in Sweden, what I will call here a crisis. Attacks on refugee centres, cross-burnings, insurgence of the White Power movement, the referendum against a refugee centre in Sjöbo, the election of the xenophobic party *Ny demokrati* to the parliament, and what became known in the media as Laser Man's shootings at immigrants in Stockholm and Uppsala—all these gave the impression that racism was looming over the country and that something needed to be done. While this sense of urgency was embedded in the frameworks of the ideal of multiculturalism and tolerance, the discussion on possible legal measures was still impacted by different strategies to diminish these difficult issues.

It is in this context and in the same year that the Laser Man was brought to trial that the government eventually proposed a bill on penalty enhancement. The choice of a specific legal measure was once again following international practice. Similar acts had been widely adopted, especially in the US and the UK context in the 1980s and 1990s, and in the following decades proliferated in other countries (for the developments in the United Kingdom and the European Union, see Chakraborti & Garland, 2015; for the developments in the US, see Henry, 2009; Jenness & Grattet, 2001; Levin, 2009).[11] The disturbing events that put the issue on the agenda in the first place and led to the bill were referred in the preparatory work, albeit sporadically and in a rather enigmatic way:

A series of events in the last years shows that acts with racist or similar motives constitute a serious threat to the legal security that is the right of everyone in our society, regardless of background or origin.

(Prop, 1993/94:101, p. 21)

However, the nature of the 'events' was left unexplained. Racism was in this context presented as a threat, not so much to certain vulnerable groups as to democratic society and to European civilization:

Persons that actively propagate racist ideas often claim to be defending Swedish, European or Western culture. But this culture has been successful mostly because of the openness, diversity and tolerance that these persons are attacking. Civilization, among other things, means to learn to live with differences. As shown by the Nazi period in the history of the twentieth century, it was also ultimately the European civilization as such that the Nazi wanted to annihilate.

(Prop, 1993/94:101, p. 4)

Making racism a crime 63

Racists were here accused of misinterpreting Swedish, European and Western civilization. The bill attempted, in a way, to reclaim the terms 'Swedish culture' and 'European civilization' from the hands of nationalists and racists and redefine them as a project of Enlightenment characterized by tolerance and diversity. Yet this defence of European civilization and Swedish culture was at odds with the growing contemporary critique of the idea of European civilization. Such critique had been articulated from several different sites. Most importantly, it had been a contribution of anti-colonial movements and post-colonial scholarship that had reinterpreted the ideas of progress and universalism as lying at the core of the European colonial project (e.g. Said, 2003). It had been, at the same time, expressed in explanations of the Holocaust according to which the Holocaust, rather than being an aberration, was a result of a particular formation of European modernity and the European Enlightenment (e.g. Arendt, 2004; Bauman, 2000). This critique was also paralleled by a postmodern deconstruction of metanarratives of progress and emancipation underlying the idea of European civilization. These voices, often springing from outside of Europe or from its margins, had led to several debates that went on through the continent, in which an attempt was made—not without resistances—to come to terms with the dark sides of European history, most importantly colonialism and the Holocaust. The debates resulted in new substantive research on sensitive and often marginalized topics,[12] and significantly undermined the positive image of European civilization. In this context, the government's interpretation of twentieth-century history becomes even more revealing. Just like Nazism ultimately was seen as an attempt to annihilate European civilization (the Jewish victims of Nazism are just given a shadow of presence in this text in the word *förinta*, that in Swedish means 'annihilate', and in the nominalized form, *Förintelsen*, is used to denote the Holocaust), racism was redefined as a threat, not so much to groups and individuals singled out because of the colour of their skin, their religion or their origin, as to Swedish culture defined as democratic and tolerant.

The ambiguous dynamics of struggling with racism were once again working in two directions: towards recognizing and confronting diverse forms of racism on the one hand, and towards overcoming[13] and putting them in the past on the other. At the same moment when laws and policies were introduced that insisted upon formal equality and the value of diversity, opening up for shifts in discourses and practices towards immigrants and towards the problem of racism, this trend began to be undermined by resistance and a slow retreat. In the meantime, these two dynamics worked simultaneously, bringing about mixed and often contradictory effects.

As mentioned above, the penalty enhancement provision introduced at that time applied to a crime if one of the *motives* is to offend a person because of race, colour, national or ethnic origin, religious belief or other similar circumstance. The provision referred to the intent and, more specifically, the motive of the perpetrator. It was not an obvious way to go, most

64 Making racism a crime

importantly because motive is not a commonly used concept in the criminal law and is handled with difficulty by the judiciary. This had already been visible in relation to the law on agitation against a national or ethnic group. For instance, the following argument was formulated as early as 1952 as a line of defence during a police interrogation of Einar Åberg:

> His [Åberg's] inner conviction is that the Jews under the cloak of communism have the intention to conquer the world and thereby transfer all property into Jewish possession. Åberg wanted to stress that the writings distributed by him were spread *only for the purpose of illumination* in order to prevent the intention of Judaism in the aforementioned regard. *He has thus not had any intent* to create agitation against or persecution of Jews by spreading the writings.
>
> (Police interrogation record, Säpo archive, quoted in:
Berggren, 1999, p. 96, my emphasis)

Because of the awareness of difficulties with providing proof of motive, when the idea of the penalty enhancement was first drafted, it was proposed that, instead of talking about racist motives of an act, the law could talk about its racist features. Eventually, however, the bill limited the law to crimes with certain motives. The main reason given for this was that the law would otherwise 'become too general and lose precision' (Prop, 1993/94:101, p. 23).

Even though introduced with minorities in mind and as a reaction to an overt manifestation of racist violence, the penalty enhancement provision was designed in a way that made it applicable also in cases in which representatives of the majority population were victims, and this interpretation was explicitly expounded in the preliminary works:

> [T]he provision should, of course, be applicable also to other crimes committed with such discriminatory motives. This means that the provision may be applicable not just when, for instance, Swedish people attack immigrants, but also in the opposite situation, that is, when people with foreign origin attack a person or persons simply because they are Swedes.
>
> (Prop, 1993/94:101, p. 22)

This interpretation of the provision, despite its distinct genealogy, corresponded to demands made by the far-right that reverse racism should be recognized as a problem in Sweden (Motion 1993/94:A35, 1993/94:A36). It can, however, be better understood to reflect a general trend towards a neutral formulation and a broad applicability of the legal measures. It thereby illustrates how what might be seen as acts of justice for some historically vulnerable groups, when expressed in legal language, lose their historical and political specificity.

Developments in the field of labour law and civil law: anti-discrimination legislation

Since the late 1980s, and more clearly in the 1990s and 2000s, the issue of racism started to be framed as a problem of discrimination more than a problem of violence or organized extremism. This shift stemmed partly from international developments, most importantly the influence of the European Union[14] on the legislation of the member states. The first provisions against ethnic discrimination formulated under civil and not criminal law were introduced at the end of the 1990s (Lag 1999:139 om etnisk diskriminering) and the beginning of the 2000s (Lag 2001:1286 om likabehandling av studenter i högskolan). Initially, their aim was mostly to counter racial discrimination in the labour market, which in Sweden is traditionally regulated by civil and labour law. In the years to follow, anti-discrimination regulations proliferated, addressing different grounds for discrimination in different areas of social life, with the 2003 Discrimination Act as an important example. Thus, already at that time, a trend was discernible, both internationally and in Sweden, towards a general regulation against discrimination, one that would include, in principle, all areas of social life independent of the grounds of discrimination (Justitiedepartementet, 2001). This development partly materialized in the 2008 Discrimination Act.

As a consequence of this transformation, the problem of racism, along with other similar problems, was addressed by an act under civil law. Radical anti-racist claims to address some historical forms of social injustice were in this way translated into a language of protection of the universal human rights of every individual,[15] understood through individualism and universalism (Diskrimineringskommittén, 2006, p. 45; Prop., 1997/98:177, p. 19, 1999/2000:143, p. 27). This development is most visible in the neutral framing of the regulation that in practice disconnects the protection against discrimination from particular groups, instead extending it to all individuals with any kind of ethnic or religious identity. In this way, anti-discrimination legislation has been gradually decoupled from its original struggles for justice for historically disadvantaged groups towards a general protection for individuals treated as bearers of certain identities but detached from particular histories of social and structural injustice.

The transfer of anti-discrimination legislation from criminal law to civil law, partly motivated by developments in EU legislation and partly by the inefficiency of the criminal provision on unlawful discrimination, was accompanied by an attempt to decriminalize discrimination, by removing the act on unlawful discrimination from the Penal Code (Justitiedepartementet, 2001). It was argued that,

> the criminal provision on legal discrimination does not have a symbolic value of such weight that it alone could motivate preserving the provision. On the contrary, we believe that the negative consequences that

66 *Making racism a crime*

most likely will follow from the lack of efficiency that can be noted in the application of the provision should be considered most important in the coming deliberations concerning the design of the Swedish law on discrimination.

(Justitiedepartementet, 2001, p. 138)

In the end, however, the provision on unlawful discrimination was kept in the Penal Code, with the following arguments:

Decriminalization would, in our opinion, be inappropriate, both from the general preventive perspective and owing to the symbolic function of criminalization. The fact that the government uses what may be regarded as the strongest expression of dissension—criminalization—has a symbolic value and constitutes a means of emphasizing that the government in Sweden views this issue as a matter for common concern. As we see the matter, the government's responsibility and the resources that the government provides via the police and prosecutor service cannot be replaced by a system where work against discrimination is entirely transferred to the private sphere. An opposite stance, where discrimination would only be combated via damages in civil cases, could possibly be perceived to mean that the government has abandoned its interest in the issue of discrimination.

(Diskrimineringskommittén, 2006, p. 51)

In this statement, a particular, symbolic role was assigned to criminal law that not only punishes the wrongs done against the individual, but also defines these wrongs as harmful to society as a whole. This is in line with how the workings of criminal law have been understood internationally. An example can be seen in Hannah Arendt's discussion of the function of criminal law in the context of the Eichmann trial, when she wrote:

Criminal proceedings, since they are mandatory and thus initiated even if the victim would prefer to forgive and forget, rest on laws whose 'essence'—to quote Telford Taylor, writing in the *New York Times Magazine*—'is that a crime is not committed only against the victim but primarily against the community whose law is violated.' The wrongdoer is brought to justice because his act has disturbed and gravely endangered the community as a whole, and not because, as in civil suits, damage has been done to individuals who are entitled to reparation. The reparation effected in criminal cases is of an altogether different nature; it is the body politics itself that stands in need of being 'repaired,' and it is the general public order that has been thrown out of gear and must be restored, as it were. It is, in other words, the law, not the plaintiff, that must prevail.

(Arendt, 2006, p. 261)

This struggle concerning the way of approaching the issue of discrimination in the law, over what might seem to be technicalities and practicalities of legal solutions, reveals the symbolic nature of legal provisions and the state's role in addressing certain problems. The discussion about the elimination of an inefficient and, to a large degree, unused provision from the Penal Code sheds some light on the actual development in the area of the work against discrimination. The *de facto* transfer of the problem of discrimination from criminal law to civil law can be regarded as a gradual withdrawal of the state and a pushing of the problem into the private sphere.

Racism or other forms of social injustice, when defined as discrimination, draw attention to economic injustices. Basically, discrimination is about different ways in which some unprivileged groups' access to different types of resources is constrained. The relatively new legislation against discrimination is a way of making this dimension of racism visible. At the same time, the privatization of the problem of discrimination, through its treatment under civil law, is a sign of the state's withdrawal from this area. The social problem of economic inequality and marginalization of some groups becomes thereby a private issue of individuals who have a right to a lawsuit, provided they have resources to go to court. This is paralleled by a weakening of the state's role in redistribution of wealth and by the acceleration of economic globalization. The process can be better understood if seen in the broader context of a global decline of struggles that aim at countering distributive inequalities of resources and power (Fraser, 2000, p. 108).

To sum up, as a result of the ambiguous processes described above, Sweden has put in place a range of legal measures against racism. These processes have not only had a decisive impact on how norms and crimes were defined around a particular concept of racism, but have also reshaped racist practices and discourses in significant ways.

The rise and decline of the concept of 'race' in Sweden

In 2001, as a result of the parliament's statement that 'there is no scientific ground for applying the term "race" to human beings' (Justitiedepartementet, 2001, p. 187), the Swedish government carried out an official investigation into the occurrence of the word 'race' in Swedish law texts. This review of the law was followed by an in-depth overhaul of the dominant scientific positions on the issue of the existence of races as formulated by the Royal Swedish Academy of Science. The concept's historical background, its relation to the concept of 'ethnicity', its use in the common language and in the Swedish press were also analysed. Last but not least, some recommendations in regard to the use of the word were formulated: 'There are strong reasons for eliminating, or when applicable exchanging, the concept of race in the law, and this is also possible' (Justitiedepartementet, 2001, p. 220). This work was preceded by Sweden's international involvement in the struggle for elimination of the word 'race' from international legal instruments.

68 *Making racism a crime*

Despite the recommendations, the decision to completely eliminate the word 'race' from the provisions in question was postponed (Prop, 2001/02:59, p. 25) and later restricted (Diskrimineringskommittén, 2006, p. 52). This concern with erasing the word 'race' from legal and other official texts was not new in Sweden. In what follows, I will trace some earlier instances when the word was rejected and others when it reappeared in the law text, in order to illuminate some important features of how racism has been dealt with in Sweden.

During World War II, when the law on agitation against a national or ethnic group was first discussed, the groups that were to be protected by the law were referred to as 'groups of citizens of a certain creed or race' (Motions 1942, I:179, II:233, quoted in Straffrättskommittén, 1945, p. 222). The final text of the law, however, referred to 'peoples of a certain origin or creed' (Första lagutskottets utlåtande, 1948, nr 39, p. 33). While the substitution of 'groups of citizens' by 'peoples' was justified by the will to make the law more inclusive by covering propaganda against groups that are not Swedish citizens nor necessarily live in Sweden, no more elaborated argument for dropping the term 'race' can be found in the preliminary works. Yet the elimination of the term can be understood in the context of the larger discursive shift taking place at the time in Sweden.

This shift was most visible in transformations of the field of Swedish racial hygiene.[16] Until the 1930s, the branch of science called racial biology (*rasbiologi*) had had a well-established and influential position in Sweden, with the State Institute for Racial Biology founded in 1922 through a motion signed by representatives of all parties of the parliament. This broad consensus reflected the hegemonic position of scientific racism. The Institute was headed by Herman Lundborg, who was dedicated to racial biology and physical anthropology and in particular to racial biological investigations of the Sami people, which involved cranial measurements, photographic documentation and serological tests. These activities resulted in publications on the racial character of the Swedish nation. Scientific racism was furthermore popularized through, among other things, an exposition that went on tour in Sweden in 1919, presenting photographs of Swedish racial types (*folktyper*). However, at the onset of the rise of Nazism in Europe, there was a gradual shift, reflected in the Institute receiving a new director and thereby a new profile.

Gunnar Dahlberg, in contrast to his predecessor, condemned the Nazis' use of scientific racism and eugenics and moved towards more liberal eugenics. The concept of 'race' was slowly abandoned and replaced by the concept of heredity (*arv*). Dahlberg became a critic of the idea of race, and after the war he participated in a UNESCO research group that in 1950 presented a 'Statement on Race' (Broberg, 1995, p. 78). When the Swedish Commission on Population, in which Gunnar Myrdal played a major role, was set up to investigate the Swedish demographic crisis and to propose some solutions, racial ideas played a marginal role (Björkman, 2011,

Making racism a crime 69

p. 157). In the work of the Commission, the idea of degeneration was still in focus, but its definition was different. Degeneration was no longer (or at least not to such a degree) dependent on the presence of racially inferior elements in the population, but on the feebleminded (*sinnesslöa*) and other antisocial subjects. The main focus now shifted from racial heredity to social environment. The Commission's Racial Biology Delegation appointed to elaborate sterilization laws[17] was renamed the Hereditary Biology Delegation.

The gradual falling into disfavour of the term 'race' was thus a process that had already begun in Sweden in the 1930s and was related to a more general retreat of scientific racism.[18] As in other parts of the Western world where scientific racism had been a dominant doctrine in previous decades, in Sweden, this change involved a transition from biological determinism to theories of the environment as a factor determining variations in the human species. This shift was not purely scientific. Rather it resulted from a combination of political, social and scientific developments, where criticism of Nazism played a central role. Finally, just like in the United States and the United Kingdom, in Sweden, the criticism of scientific racism did not result in the complete and direct overthrow of the tradition, but rather its gradual softening (Jackson & Weidman, 2004, pp. 158–159).

In this context, the dropping of the word 'race' from the law on agitation against a national or ethnic group appears as part of a broader dissociation from the previously predominant scientific view of race; a dissociation important in the aftermath of World War II, especially since the law in question touched on the sensitive issue of anti-Semitism. The word 'race' reappeared, however, in a text of law in the 1970s, when the International Convention on the Elimination of All Forms of Racial Discrimination was ratified. The definition of the groups protected by the legislation was reformulated following the Convention. These were 'a certain people of a certain race, with a certain skin colour, of a certain national or ethnic origin, or of a certain creed' (Act on Agitation against a national or ethnic group, 1971–1981/82 version, quoted in Prop, 1981/82:58). This reformulation reflected the language of the international debate, where the concept of 'race' was taken up and reclaimed by some of the Civil Rights and Liberation movements and used in the fight against racism.[19] Following the text of the Convention, 'descent' (*härstamning*) was substituted by 'national or ethnic origin' (*nationell teller etnisk tursprung*), and the words 'race' and 'colour' were added.[20] This return of the concept of 'race' reflects the nature of the 1970 legislation that was a result of a process of transplantation and translation, rather than of Sweden's internal struggle against racism. The translation of the Convention's wording, with its focus on the issues of race and colour that shaped the anti-colonial and civil rights struggles, linked the Swedish legislation against racism to the global context. However, in considering the efforts to cut Sweden off from the legacy of scientific racism, the return of the term 'race' could be considered rather disturbing.

70 *Making racism a crime*

Soon this faithful translation was calibrated to enable dissociation from the idea of race, thus creating a distance from this value-laden and discredited word. The dissociation became visible in the 1981 substitution of the expression 'group of a certain race' by 'with reference to race' in the laws on unlawful discrimination and agitation against a national or ethnic group. At the same time, the fight against the very word 'race' became an element of debates on racism. Sweden's international engagement, mentioned at the start of this section, in the revision of the legal instruments aimed at erasing the word 'race', is just one example.

One of the reasons that the parliament eventually kept the word 'race' in some places in the legal texts was that total elimination of the word could lead to less protection of some groups targeted by racism (Justitiedepartementet, 2001, p. 19). When discussing the history of the concept of 'race', it was mentioned in the report that the Swedish word '*ras*' has a more narrow meaning than the English 'race' or the French '*race*'. It was claimed that:

> The use of the derivation 'racism' in English to all forms of hostility towards immigrants and ethnic conflict is therefore ... linguistically closer than doing the same in Swedish.... [T]he word 'racism' is more and more frequently used in the Swedish debate in a sense that seems to include almost all forms of xenophobia and hostility towards immigrants. Formerly, this meaning was generally restricted to beliefs that directly or indirectly alluded to innate, biologically determined differences in characteristics. This definition was considered to, without much trouble, cover the Nazi racial teaching as well as the North American and South African colour racism....
>
> [R]acism claims in particular that there is a difference in value between peoples based on biology, which means that one people is what it is by nature and cannot really become something else or better.
>
> (Justitiedepartementet, 2001, p. 210)

This discussion of the proper definition of the word 'racism' at the same time as the need for the word 'race' was re-evaluated shows how the two concepts were understood as interdependent. So, although the report's aim was to eliminate the word 'race' from legal texts when used in a manner considered problematic because of the assumptions of the existence of biological races, this entailed certain criticism of the use of the word 'racism' as well, as if the latter could not exist once the word 'race' had been eliminated. Although the issue was not further discussed, the report seems to propose a cautious use of the word 'racism'.

In a different context, a similar argument was put forward in a motion tabled at the beginning of the 1990s. Here it was proposed that the term 'organized ethnic persecution' (*organiserad etnisk förföljelse*) should be used instead of 'racism' for crimes, such as those committed at that time by the White Power organization White Arian Resistance (*Vitt Ariskt Motstånd*).

The following justification was given: 'It is important that the term racism is not unnecessarily given too wide a meaning' (Motion, 1993/94:A36).

In this sense, making the word 'race' taboo in Sweden seems to have contributed to the emergence of what Goldberg calls 'racelessness' (2001, p. 230). Goldberg claims that, when analytically distinguished, anti-racialism cannot be equated with anti-racism. While the former is a commitment to a struggle against racial doctrines, including the fight against the concept of 'race' and against racial categorization, the latter is a struggle for the end of racism understood as a historical set of imposed conditions of subjugation (2004, p. 217). So, although attitudes such as the one informing the Swedish rejection of the concept of 'race' have their roots in anti-racist consciousness, the rejection of the term might have an influence on the ways in which the problem of racism can be addressed in the future. This seems to have happened also when the use of the concept of 'racism' started to be questioned in this context. Thus, the concern with the erasure of the word 'race' might have had the side effect of making the task of addressing the legacy of racism difficult. Goldberg's illuminating interpretation of the distinct workings of anti-racism and anti-racialism can suggest some risks involved in official efforts in Sweden to get rid of the term 'race' in the legal context:

> Antiracism requires historical memory, recalling the conditions of racial degradation and relating contemporary to historical and local to global conditions. If antiracist commitment requires remembering and recalling, antiracialism suggests forgetting, getting over, moving on, whipping away the terms of reference, at best (or worst) a commercial memorializing rather than a recounting and redressing of the terms of humiliation and devaluation. Indeed, antiracialism seeks to wipe out the *terms of reference*, to wipe away the very *vocabulary* necessary to recall and recollect, to make a case, to make a claim.
>
> (2004, p. 225, my emphasis)

Conclusions

In this chapter, I have described the dynamics underlying the development of the Swedish legislation against racism. In these dynamics, immediate events have intersected with certain important shifts in the ways racism has been defined and treated; internal developments in Sweden have crossed with international struggles for justice and recognition originating in the colonial world and in civil rights movements; radical claims have been curbed by cautious words; and issues of historical and structural disadvantage of certain groups have been translated into the legal language of universalism and individualism.

I have attempted to show how the process of criminalizing racism consisted not only in defining it as a crime, but also in constructing racism as something shameful. At the same time, I have argued that it was only when

72 *Making racism a crime*

racism had become something, at least to some degree, 'embarrassing' on the international arena that the discussion about legal measures was taken up seriously. The history of criminalization of racism has been driven by contradictory dynamics in which, at the same time as a legal provision against racism was proposed and discussed, the significance or the scale of the problem of racism could be played down. Hence, the recognition of racism in law could be, strangely enough, combined with denial. These dynamics might be better understood if we try to see the recognition and denial as both originating from a kind of shame that has started to inform the perception of racism in the post-Holocaust and postcolonial era. In this sense, the documents that put the Swedish legislation against racism in place bear witness to the complexity and ambivalence of the process of making racism a crime, a process in which claims for justice were met with evasion and unrecognition. The criminalization of racism has had yet another effect: it helped to reaffirm that the norm is a society clear of racism, in this way contributing to the construction of a particular image of the collective identity.

In a sense, the work on legal measures against racism in Sweden has led to a recognition of racism as a problem, but this recognition bore an inherent paradox. What Sara Ahmed writes in relation to the developments in universities in the United Kingdom is illuminating also for this discussion:

> [S]aying 'we are racist' becomes a claim to have overcome the conditions (unseen racism) that require the speech act in the first place.... What is important here is that the admission converts swiftly into a declarative mode: the speech act, in its performance, is taken up as having shown that the institution has overcome what it is that the speech act admits to. Simply put, admissions of racism become readable as declarations of commitment to anti-racism.
>
> (2006, pp. 107–108)

This new way of framing racism as 'a memory of what is no longer' (Ahmed, 2012, p. 164) constitutes the historical context of this book. One of the questions that I will try to address in the chapters that follow is how this context influences the Swedish judiciary's treatment of racism against Muslims; in other words, how the fight against racism is actually *performed* in acts of justice and with the help of the legal instruments analysed here.

Notes

1 The Swedish legislation is a result of the following process: The matter to be addressed by a law is analysed by a commission or an inquiry committee and a report is produced; this report is published in the Swedish Official Reports series (*Statens offentliga utredningar—SOU*) and is referred for consideration to

Making racism a crime 73

relevant bodies that submit their comments. Based on the report and the comments from the referral bodies, the ministry in charge drafts a government bill (*proposition*) that is submitted to the Swedish Parliament. The bill is dealt with by one of the parliamentary committees and counter-proposals (*motioner*) may be tabled by any member of parliament. After deliberation by the committee, the bill is submitted to the parliament for approval. If adopted, the bill becomes a law. In this process, several documents are produced that are called the preparatory works (*förarbeten*). The most important of these are usually government bills. The preparatory works constitute one of the central sources of law in Sweden and are used by courts to interpret the law in question (cf. Sveriges Riksdag, 2018).

2 This approach has important consequences for the image that will emerge in this chapter. First of all, these documents, in particular the bills, are the fruits of a compromise. It might seem that there has been a universal consensus on the shape, meaning and objectives of these laws. This was often not the case. As such, this is the most important limitation of the research procedure I have adopted here. Had I followed the emergence of the legislation against racism through debates in the Swedish Parliament or with more attention dedicated to the comments of the referral bodies and motions submitted by the opposition parties, I would have been able to provide a more complex image of the history of this legislation. Similarly, it would be interesting to analyse the reports that never led to any changes in law and investigate the reasons for this. This would have allowed me to shed some light on potential limits of the use of legislation to counter racism. For instance, in the years 2004–2006, a series of reports was produced to address the problem of structural discrimination and these were not followed by the introduction of any laws (Justitiedepartementet, 2005a, 2005b, 2005c, 2006a, 2006b, 2006c, 2006d, 2006e, 2006f, 2006g, 2006h, 2006i). I decided, however, that this would go beyond the introductory character and scope of this chapter, which is to provide a background to the empirical study. Still, it is important to keep these limitations in mind.

3 The name of the crime, *hets mot folkgrupp*, has been translated in different ways into English: for instance, incitement to racial hatred (Lööw, 2000) and agitation against a national or ethnic group (Lööw & Nilsson, 2001, p. 49). The latter is also used in the official translation of the Swedish Penal Code and, since it seems to be the most established one in the literature, it has been adopted here.

4 As elsewhere in Western Europe, this collective work of confronting the history of the Holocaust began quite late: in the 1980s. As a result of intense debates about the history of World War II, substantial research was produced dealing with Sweden in the context of the Holocaust. Episodes from Sweden's history were brought to light and discussed, such as the restrictive immigration policy towards Jews before and during the war, the practice of stamping a 'J' in the passports of Austrian and German Jewish immigrants, introduced in 1939, as well as student protests in Uppsala and Lund against the arrival of some ten Jewish doctors to Sweden in 1939 (see e.g. Andersson & Tydén, 2007; Hammar, 1964; Svanberg & Tydén, 2005a).

5 Such as racial discrimination by Swedish United Nations soldiers in the Congo or cases of discrimination of 'Gypsies', as they were referred to at the time, in hotels and restaurants in Sweden (Justitiedepartementet, 1968).

6 In this context, the then minister of transport and communication and prime minister-to-be, Olof Palme, was still an exception, in the early 1960s, to raise the problem of prejudice against immigrants. In his speech given on Christmas of 1965 (*Tal till Utlandssvenskar*), Palme stated that: 'Democracy is firmly rooted in this country. We respect fundamental rights and freedoms. Murky racial

74 *Making racism a crime*

theories have never gained a foothold. We consider ourselves unprejudiced and tolerant, but it is not that simple.' And he added: 'Perhaps it is easier for people to feel indignation about great injustices in the world than to involve ourselves in the little problem in the next block' (Palme, 1965, p. 4).

7 This argument echoed one that was present in pre-World War II refugee debates: that Jewish immigrants brought with them anti-Semitism (Larsmo, 2007, pp. 193–228).

8 The project of creating a homogeneous modern state is particularly manifested in the histories of the policies towards Roma (called 'Gypsies' at that time) and Sami (called 'Lapps'). The Roma, officially forbidden to enter Sweden until 1954, were marginalized and excluded until the 1960s, at which point they became defined as a social problem and, after extensive debate, subject to 'modernization' (Svanberg & Tydén, 2005b, pp. 353–362). The Sami, on the other hand, the country's indigenous people, were subject to a colonial project. The law was an important tool in their colonization: they were not only deprived of the right to land, but also, until 1961, of the right to file lawsuits, which considerably limited their access to justice. During the 1970s, the debasing denomination 'Lapp' was replaced by 'Sami' (Lundmark, 2008, p. 223).

9 For more details about the history of the Swedish immigration policies, see Chapter 2.

10 Interestingly, the anti-apartheid movement, both in Sweden and elsewhere, rarely addressed the question of racism at home. When in the 1980s anti-racist movements became visible in the Swedish public sphere, no significant connection was made with the anti-apartheid movement. According to Håkan Thörn, this was partly due to a generational gap, partly to a different approach to traditional popular movement culture (*folkrörelse*) (Thörn, 2010, pp. 138–139).

11 I discuss this process of proliferation, translation and travel of the concept of hate crime and of the related legal definitions in more detail in Chapter 5.

12 In Sweden, apart from the already mentioned issues of Sweden's position during World War II, other troubling episodes of Swedish history were critically discussed, both among historians and in the broader public, such as scientific racism, sterilization laws, the state policy towards Sami people and Roma, as well as the country's colonial involvement (Rosenberg, 2002, p. 196).

13 One notorious example of such an attempt to overcome the problem of racism was the performance of the then minister of culture responsible for immigration issues, Birgit Friggebo, during a meeting with inhabitants of Rinkeby, a Stockholm suburb where mostly immigrants and their descendants live, in the aftermath of the shootings by the Laser Man. Confronted with expressions of fear and demands for action and justice, her response was to propose the gathered to rise and sing 'We shall overcome'.

14 The EU anti-discrimination directives are directly binding on Sweden and they have been, since the 2000s, the driving force for the introduction and reformulation of anti-discrimination legislation in the present form. The trend to address the questions of racism in the language of human rights and discrimination is related to a broader development of international human rights instruments. Moreover, national measures addressing racial discrimination originated in the United States, where they have been adopted since the 1960s to compensate for historical injustices towards certain groups. In this context, they have also been accompanied, not without controversy, by affirmative action (Fransson & Stüber, 2010, p. 33).

15 In reality, the Swedish protection of human rights, following international practice, is not universal but depends on citizenship. Non-citizens are treated differently by Swedish law and protected from discrimination to a varying degree

Making racism a crime 75

depending on the part of the world they come from. Citizens of the Nordic countries are in the most favourable position, followed by EU citizens, while citizens of Third World countries have their human rights least protected. This difference in legal protection, stemming from historically shaped political arrangements, reflects important ways in which the proximity and distance, similarity and difference have been defined in the construction of national community (Johnsson, 2005, pp. 176–178).

16 On the activity of the Swedish State Institute for Racial Biology, see Broberg (1995). On Swedish sterilization laws, see Tydén (2000). On eugenics in Scandinavia written in English, see Broberg and Roll-Hansen (2005).

17 The Swedish sterilization laws lasted for several decades, sanctioning the negative eugenics applied to tens of thousands of Swedish citizens, the overwhelming majority (93%) women (Tydén, 2000). One of the targets of the sterilization laws identified during a parliamentary debate in 1941 was the *tattare*. Considered antisocial and their travelling lifestyle unadjusted to modern society, they represented all that existed on the edges of the modern state. The reasons for their way of life were explained both socially and biologically, hence the belief in heredity of antisocial behaviour and need for sterilization. *Tattare* were believed to originate in the East and were often confused with Travellers and 'Gypsies', which meant that they were classified as racially different (Svensson, 1993). The *tattare* question gradually faded away and, in the mid-1950s, a state report asserted that they did not make up a separate people (*folkgrupp*), but were ethnically Swedish (Lindholm, 1995).

18 For the analysis of the retreat of scientific racism in the United States and the United Kingdom, see Barkan (2001) and Jackson and Weidman (2004).

19 This was the case of Black Nationalism as defined by Malcolm X or more generally the Black Power movement in the United States or of such movements as *Négritude* or Black Consciousness founded by black intellectuals and politicians from colonial countries.

20 In addition, religious affiliation was kept in the Swedish law, although the Convention did not cover religious discrimination (Egon, 1966). The decision taken by the UN to exclude religious discrimination from the Convention was a result of an intervention from some Arab countries, reflecting the Arab–Israeli conflict, backed up by Eastern European countries in which questions of religious discrimination were marginalized. The idea was that religious discrimination would be covered by a separate legal instrument, but until now, only two resolutions have been produced. This split between religious and racial discrimination present in international law has been questioned on several occasions. As a result, CERD explicitly recognized the intersection between racial and religious discrimination in 2009 (CERD, General Recommendation No 32, §7).

Bibliography

II kamm. prot. (1960). nr 2, p. 257.

Ahmed, S. (2006). 'The nonperformativity of antiracism.' *Meridians: Feminism, Race, Transnationalism*, 7(1), 104–126.

Ahmed, S. (2012). *On being included: Racism and diversity in institutional life*. Durham: Duke University Press.

Alexander, J. (2009). *Remembering the Holocaust: A Debate*. Oxford: Oxford University Press.

Andersson, L. & Tydén, M. (2007). *Sverige och Nazityskland: skuldfrågor och moraldebatt*. Stockholm: Dialogos.

76 Making racism a crime

Arbetsmarknadsdepartementet. (1981). *Om hets mot folkgrupp delbetänkande (SOU 1981:38)*. Stockholm: Allmänna Förlaget.

Arbetsmarknadsdepartementet. (1991). *Organiserad Rasism (SOU 1991:75)*. Stockholm: Almänna Förlaget.

Arendt, H. (2004). *The Origins of Totalitarianism*. New York, NY: Shocken Books.

Arendt, H. (2006). *Eichmann in Jerusalem: A Report on the Banality of Evil*. New York, NY: Penguin Books.

Barkan, E. (2001). 'The Retreat of Scientific Racism: Changing Concepts of Race in Britain and the United States between the World Wars.' In E. Cashmore & J. Jennings (Eds.), *Racism: Essential Readings*. London: Sage, pp. 326–335.

Bauman, Z. (2000). *Modernity and the Holocaust*. Ithaca, NY: Cornell University Press.

Berggren, L. (1999). *Nationell upplysning: drag i den svenska antisemitismens idéhistoria*. Stockholm: Carlsson.

Björkman, M. (2011). *Den anfrätta stammen: Nils von Hofsten, eugeniken och steriliseringarna 1909–1963*. Lund: Arkiv.

Borevi, K. (1998). 'Svensk invandrarpolitik under (om)fromulering.' *Politica, 30*(2), 168–183.

Borevi, K. (2012). 'Sweden: The Flagship of Multiculturalism.' In G. Brochmann & A. Hagelund (Eds.), *Immigration Policy and the Scandinavian Welfare State 1945–2010*. Basinstoke: Palgrave Macmillian, pp. 25–96.

Broberg, G. (1995). *Statlig rasforskning: en historik över Rasbiologiska institutet*. Lund: Avd. för idé- och lärdomshistoria, Universitet (Lund: Reprocentralen, Universitet).

Broberg, G. & Roll-Hansen, N. (Eds.). (2005). *Eugenics and the Welfare State: Sterilization Policy in Denmark, Sweden, Norway, and Finland*. East Lansing: Michigan State University Press.

Chakraborti, N. & Garland, J. (2015). *Hate Crime: Impact, Causes and Responses*. Los Angeles: Sage.

Diskrimineringskommittén. (2006). *En sammanhållen diskrimineringslagstiftning (SOU 2006:22)*. Stockholm: Fritzes.

Egon, S. (1966). 'The International Convention on the Elimination of All Forms of Racial Discrimination.' *The International and Comparative Law Quarterly, 15*(4), 996–1068.

Första lagutskottets utlåtande1948. nr 39.

Fransson, S. & Stüber, E. (2010). *Diskrimineringslagen: en kommentar*. Stockholm: Norstedts juridik.

Fraser, N. (2000). 'Rethinking Recognition.' *New Left Review, 3*, 107–120.

Goldberg, D. (2001). *The Racial State*. Malden, MA: Blackwell.

Goldberg, D. (2004). 'The End(s) of Race.' *Postcolonial Studies, 7*(2), 211–230.

Hammar, T. (1964). *Sverige åt svenskarna: invandringspolitik, utlänningskontroll och asylrätt 1900–1932*. Stockholm: Caslon Press.

Hammar, T. (1985). *European Immigration Policy*. Cambridge: Cambridge University Press.

Hammar, T. (1994). *Om IMER under 30 år: en översikt av svensk forskning om internationell migration och etniska relationer*. Stockholm: Socialvetenskapliga forskningsrådet.

Henry, J. (2009). 'Hate Crime Laws: A Critical Assessment.' In B. Perry (Ed.), *Hate Crimes*. Vol. 1. Westport: Praeger, pp. 183–204.

Making racism a crime 77

Jackson, J. & Weidman, N. (2004). *Race, Racism, and Science: Social Impact and Interaction.* Santa Barbara, CA: ABC-CLIO.

Jenness, V. & Grattet, R. (2001). *Making Hate a Crime: From Social Movement Concept to Law Enforcement Practice.* New York: Russell Sage.

Johnsson, C. (2005). *Svensk rätt i integrationspolitisk belysning: rapport från Integrationspolitiska maktutredningens forskningsprogram.* Stockholm: Fritzes offentliga publikationer.

Justitiedepartementet. (1968). *Lagstiftning mot rasdiskriminering betänkande (SOU 1968:68).* Retrieved from Stockholm: http://weburn.kb.se/metadata/478/SOU_8210478.htm

Justitiedepartementet. (2000). *Organiserad brottslighet, hets mot folkgrupp, hets mot homosexuella, m.m.—straffansvarets räckvidd (SOU 2000:88).* Stockholm: Fritzes.

Justitiedepartementet. (2001). *Ett effektivt diskrimineringsförbud: Om olaga diskriminering och begreppen ras och sexuell läggning (2001:39).* Stockholm: Fritzes.

Justitiedepartementet. (2005a). *Bortom Vi och Dom: Teoretiska reflektioner om makt, integration och strukturell diskriminering (SOU 2005:41).* Stockholm: Fritzes.

Justitiedepartementet. (2005b). *Demokrati på svenska? Om strukturell diskriminering och politiskt deltagande (SOU 2005:112).* Stockholm: Fritzes.

Justitiedepartementet. (2005c). *Sverige inifrån: Röster om etnisk diskriminering (SOU 2005:69).* Stockholm: Fritzes.

Justitiedepartementet. (2006a). *Arbetslivets (o)synliga murar (SOU 2006:59).* Stockholm: Fritzes.

Justitiedepartementet. (2006b). *Den segregerade integrationen (SOU 2006:73).* Stockholm: Fritzes.

Justitiedepartementet. (2006c). *Diskrimineringens retorik: En studie av svenska valrörelser 1988–2002 (SOU 2006:52).* Stockholm: Fritzes.

Justitiedepartementet. (2006d). *Hälsa, vård och strukturell diskriminering (SOU 2006:78).* Stockholm: Fritzes.

Justitiedepartementet. (2006e). *Integrationens svarta bok: Agenda för jämlikhet och social sammanhållning (SOU 2006:79).* Stockholm: Fritzes.

Justitiedepartementet. (2006f). *Mediernas vi och dom: Mediernas betydelse för den strukturella diskrimineringen (SOU 2006:21).* Stockholm: Fritzes.

Justitiedepartementet. (2006g). *Partierna nominerar: Exkluderingens mekanismer: etnicitet och representation (SOU 2006:53).* Stockholm: Fritzes.

Justitiedepartementet. (2006h). *Utbildningens dilemma: demokratiska ideal och andrafierande praxis (SOU 2006:40).* Stockholm: Fritzes.

Justitiedepartementet. (2006i). *Är rättvisan rättvis? Tio perspektiv på diskriminering av etniska och religiösa minoriteter inom rättsystemet (SOU 2006:30).* Stockholm: Fritzes.

Lag. (1999). 139 om etnisk diskriminering.

Lag. (2001). 1286 om likabehandling av studenter i högskolan.

Larsmo, O. (2007). '"Bollhusmötet" 1939. Konstruktionen av en rasistisk opinion.' In L. Andersson & M. Tydén (Eds.), *Sverige och Nazityskland: Skuldfrågor och moraldebatt.* Stockholm: Dialogos, pp. 193–228.

Levin, B. (2009). 'The Long Arc of Justice: Race, Violence, and the Emergence of Hate Crime Law.' In B. Perry (Ed.), *Hate Crimes* Vol. 1. Westport: Praeger, pp. 1–22.

Lindholm, G. (1995). *Vägarnas folk: de resande och deras livsvärld.* Göteborg: Etnologiska fören. i Västsverige.

78 Making racism a crime

Lööw, H. (2000). 'Incitement of Racial Hatred.' *Journal of Scandinavian Studies in Criminology & Crime Prevention*, *1*(2), 109–120.

Lööw, H. & Nilsson, L. (2001). *Hets mot folkgrupp.* Stockholm: Brottsförebyggande rådet.

Lundmark, L. (2008). *Stulet land: svensk makt på samisk mark.* Stockholm: Ordfront.

Motion. (1993/94:A35). *med anledning av prop. 1993/94:101 Åtgärder mot rasistisk brottslighet och etnisk diskriminering i arbetslivet.*

Motion. (1993/94:A36). *med anledning av prop. 1993/94:101 Åtgärder mot rasistisk brottslighet och etnisk diskriminering i arbetslivet.*

NJA. (1996). p. 577.

NJA. (1999). p. 702.

NJA. (2005). p. 805.

Palme, O. (1965). *Tal till Utlandssvenskar.* Retrieved from: www.olofpalme.org/wp-content/dokument/651225_vi_och_utlanningarna.pdf

Prop. (1948:80). *Kungl. Maj:ts proposition till riksdagen med förslag till lag om ändring i strafflagen m.m.* Stockholm: Stockholms slott.

Prop. (1970:87). *Kungl. Maj:ts proposition till riksdagen angående godkännande av konvention om avskaffande av rasdiskriminering, m.m.* Stockholm: Stockholms slott.

Prop. (1975:26). Stockholm: Regeringen. *Regeringens proposition om riktlinjer för invandrar- och minoritetspolitiken m. m.*

Prop. (1981/82:58). *Om ändring i tryckfrihetsförordningen och brottsbalken (hets mot folkgrupp m.m.).* Stockholm: Regeringen.

Prop. (1986/87:151). *Om ändringar i tryckfrihetsförordningen m.m.* Stockholm.

Prop. (1993/94:101). *Åtgärder mot rasistisk brottslighet och etnisk diskriminering i arbetslivet.* Stockholm: Kulturdepartamentet.

Prop. (1997/98:177). *Ny lag om åtgärder mot etnisk diskriminering i arbetslivet.* Stockholm: Inrikesdepartementet.

Prop. (1999/2000:143). *Ändringar i jämställdhetslagen m.m.* Stockholm: Näringsdepartementet.

Prop. (2001/02:59). *Hets mot folkgrupp, m.m.* Stockholm: Justitiedepartementet.

Rosenberg, G. (2002). 'The Crisis of Consensus in Postwar Sweden.' In L. Trägårdh & N. Witoszek (Eds.), *Culture and Crisis: The Case of Germany and Sweden.* New York, NY: Berghahn, pp. 170–201.

Said, E. (2003). *Orientalism.* London: Penguin.

SFS. (1962:700). *Brottsbalken.* Stockholm: Justitiedepartementet.

SFS. (2008: 567). *Brottsbalken.* Stockholm: Justitiedepartementet.

Straffrättskommittén. (1945). *Straffrättskommitténs betänkande med förslag till lagstiftning om brott mot staten och allmänheten (SOU 1944:69).* Stockholm: Kungl. Bokrtyckeriet. P.A. Norstedt & Söner.

Svanberg, I. & Tydén, M. (2005a). *Sverige och förintelsen: debatt och dokument om europas judar 1933–1945.* Stockholm: Dialogos.

Svanberg, I. & Tydén, M. (2005b). *Tusen år av invandring: en svensk kulturhistoria.* Stockholm: Dialogos.

Svensson, B. (1993). *Bortom all ära och redlighet: tattarnas spel med rättvisan.* Stockholm: Nordiska museet.

Sveriges Riksdag. (2018). *Beslutar om lagar.* Retrieved from: www.riksdagen.se/sv/sa-funkar-riksdagen/riksdagens-uppgifter/beslutar-om-lagar/

Making racism a crime 79

The Swedish Penal Code. (1999). Retrieved from: www.regeringen.se/rattsliga-dokument/departementsserien-och-promemorior/1999/01/ds-199936/

Thörn, H. (2006). *Anti-Apartheid and the Emergence of a Global Civil Society.* Basingstoke: Palgrave Macmillan.

Thörn, H. (2010). *Solidaritetens betydelse: kampen mot apartheid i Sydafrika och framväxten av det globala civilsamhället.* Stockholm: Atlas.

Tydén, M. (2000). *Från politik till praktik: de svenska steriliseringslagarna 1935–1975: rapport till 1997 års steriliseringsutredning.* Stockholm: Fritzes offentliga publikationer.

UN Committee on the Elimination of Racial Discrimination (CERD). 'General Recommendation No. 32, the Meaning and Scope of Special Measures in the International Convention on the Elimination of All Forms of Racial Discrimination.' 24 September 2009, CERD/C/GC/32. Retrieved from: www.refworld.org/docid/4adc30382.html

5 On the politics and poetics of hate-crime statistics

Two photographs are displayed on the cover of the report on hate crimes published in 2005 by Säpo, the Swedish Security Service. The upper photograph shows two outstretched arms with clenched fists. Black sleeves are rolled up. Behind the arms, knitted brows and shaved heads appear against the background of a Swedish flag. In the lower photograph, a crowd of masked people holds a banner. All are dressed in black and wear helmets leaving only their eyes visible. A banner in front of them, held like a shield, reads in black letters: 'Strike back against Nazism!' The report's title appears between the pictures: *Offences Related to National Internal Security 2004* (Säpo, 2005).

In 2010, Brå released its sixth report on hate crimes. The cover in black, green and white shows a sketch of four heads in different sizes, overlapping one another. All but one are just contours drawn in one line: a black outline of a large head turned somewhat back with short, thick hair; a white outline of a small head in profile, short hair again; and in the middle a white outline of a head in profile with a skullcap on. The fourth head is somewhat different: the contours are coloured black and the head is covered by a greenish veil. Below the sketch, the title of the report reads: *Hatecrimes 2009. Statistics of reports to the police where the motivation of the crime includes ethnic background, religious faith, sexual orientation or transgender identity or expression* (Molarin & Frenzel, 2010).

Statistics on hate crimes were first compiled in Sweden in 1993 by Säpo. In 2004, a new methodology for collecting data was elaborated. Certain words were automatically searched in the police reports on selected crimes, the appearance of which might indicate that the reported crime was motivated by xenophobia, anti-Semitism or homophobia. The police reports identified in this way were thereafter examined by the researchers responsible. In 2005, Brå took over the responsibility for compiling statistics and issuing annual reports on hate crimes. In 2008, Brå changed the definition of hate crime and expanded the data. The covers of the reports are expressive of some of the major shifts in the ways in which hate crimes in Sweden were identified, defined and the statistical data on them compiled during this time. In this chapter, by analysing Swedish reports on hate crimes, I will identify these shifts and explore the frameworks and contexts in which this type of violence is approached by the Swedish state.

There are two reasons why I found it important to analyse how the relevant national bodies identify, define and frame what they call hate crimes. The first reason is that the material presented in this book was accessed through one of these bodies, Brå. As discussed in Chapter 3, while my material is primarily composed of police files and court documents, the selection of the cases that I had a chance to get familiar with was made by Brå. It is thus central to present what this selection meant, what kind of acts I was able to see and what was left out. The second reason is that the analysis of hate-crime reports produced by national institutions is interesting for its own sake. By investigating the ways in which classifications are made, definitions are formulated, acts are counted and violence is described, it is possible to explicate official interpretations and understandings of this kind of violence. Moreover, looking into processes through which the knowledge, in the form of facts and figures, is produced, by whom and in what context, enables me to explore the politics of hate-crime statistics. As such, hate-crime statistics and the reports in which these are presented constitute an interesting repository of expert knowledge of the problem, which not only defines what a problem is but also collects evidence in accordance with this definition. By doing this, hate-crime reports create particular systems of visibility, materializing some things as a problem while leaving others opaque and diffuse (Prior, 2003, p. 73).

In this chapter, I will first propose a reading of Säpo's and Brå's reports,[1] where I will take into account contexts in which hate-crime statistics have been produced in Sweden, identify frameworks within which this knowledge has been situated and analyse the shifts these frameworks have undergone. This is my way of attending to the politics of hate-crime statistics. Second, I will investigate the role of the quantitative nature of the method adopted in the reports. What does it mean for the understanding of racist violence, or other types of biased violence, to approach it with a statistical lens? I have chosen to name this part 'the poetics of hate-crime statistics'. Third, I will track and examine the genealogy of the concept of hate crime in some international debates and developments, and explore its Swedish life. Finally, I will look at how the issue of anti-Muslim racism—or Islamophobia—is addressed in the hate-crime reports. In this way, I will situate the subject of this book in a broader discourse on hate crimes.

The changing politics of hate-crime statistics

The title of the Säpo report whose cover I described above reveals the initial location on which the hate-crime statistics were compiled. When in 1993 Säpo was entrusted with a task of mapping 'crimes with xenophobic, racist, anti-Semitic and homophobic background', this was done as a part of Säpo's work 'to prevent and expose offences against national internal

82 *On the politics and poetics of hate-crime statistics*

security'. Monitoring what a few years later would be called hate crimes was just a part of this larger work. The reports were produced by a branch of Säpo, which focused on 'political extremism' through the prevention of

> activities that, through use of violence, threat or undue force, aim at changing the constitution, influencing the political institutions or authorities to make decisions in a given direction, or preventing citizens from exercising their constitutional civil rights and freedoms.[2]
>
> (Säpo, 2005, p. 7)

Xenophobic, racist, anti-Semitic and homophobic violence is defined here as a threat to national internal security, understood partly as a threat to basic democratic values such as civil rights and freedoms, but also, and predominantly, as one kind of subversive activity of extreme groups defined as a threat to the stability of the Swedish political system. Thus, collecting hate-crime statistics is a by-product of the core work of Säpo, consisting in safeguarding the national security. One of the criteria for selecting offences to be included in this report is their link to organizations or movements that endorse 'anti-democratic views' (Säpo, 2005, p. 13). Racist violence appears next to crimes committed between individual members of what in the reports is presented as conflicting extremist groups or in mass confrontations between these groups, and next to saboteurs targeting the animal industry. What makes this violence a threat to the social order is not so much its racist nature as its undemocratic methods and destabilizing potential.

The militant salute performed with clenched fists, shaved heads and masked faces on the photographs of the Säpo report indicate the extreme nature of the offences described in the report. Violence is thought of as extreme in two different senses: it is extreme because it is extraordinary, exceeding and threatening the democratic order and thus the internal security of the country, as well as violating fundamental rules of conduct acceptable in a peaceful society; but it is also extreme because it is performed by extremists belonging to the margins of society. The organizations mapped and monitored in the report—those belonging to the 'white power movement', to the 'autonomous movements', including anarchist, syndicalist and anti-fascist groups, and to 'animal rights activism'—are depicted as equally dangerous and extreme.

Although the data gathered in the report reveal that only a fraction of offences with xenophobic, anti-Semitic and homophobic motives is linked to the White Power movement, this kind of violence is represented in the report as organized and ideologically motivated. This is at least the report's point of departure. The way that the categories of crimes are selected and formulated stems from a reading of the ideology of hatred within White Power extremism. For example, the following justification is given as to why offences with anti-Semitic motives are addressed in the report: 'special interest has been attached to this category because of the important role that

On the politics and poetics of hate-crime statistics 83

anti-Semitic representations have within the White Power movement' (Säpo, 2005, p. 24). Offences with homophobic motives are also included in the report because homosexuals have traditionally been treated as a 'moral enemy' within the White Power movement. Moreover, in most of the ideological programmes of the organizations within this milieu, there are texts expressing hatred towards and/or instigating violence against homosexuals (Säpo, 2005, p. 27).

Hence, Säpo's statistics are informed by research into White Power ideologies and also related to the surveillance of political extremism. This is one reason why the report includes an overview of White Power organizations and groups, of their ideas and activities. Situated in this context, hate crimes are understood as acts based on a coherent ideology: people are attacked on account of their colour, religion or sexual orientation, because they are perceived as 'enemies' according to a specific ideological view.

The photographs on the cover of the Säpo report reveal one more important feature of Säpo's approach to hate crimes: a focus on the perpetrators. Extremists are those who are the object of surveillance, hate crimes being just one part of their criminal activity that threatens the social order and the country's security. Moreover, the report presents no ordinary statistics when it comes to the methods of gathering information:

> In the selection and assessment process, the police reports are supplemented with information from other sources. Säpo's surveillance register may contain important information on suspects or victims and their connections to White Power or autonomous movements.
>
> (Säpo, 2005, p. 14)

Three profiles of a perpetrator are constructed in the report: one with a hate-crime motive and no White Power motive, one with connection to the White Power movement and one with connection to the autonomous movement. It is thereby noted that some hate crimes are not necessarily linked to White Power ideology on the level of the individuals involved.

Säpo's approach to hate crimes in the 2005 report is influenced by the climate of the 1990s, when Säpo began to collect the statistics. The focus on surveillance of extremisms, as both one of the research tools and one of the aims of the statistics, was a result of the attention given to the emergence of neo-Nazi and White Power organizations in Sweden. The feeling of urgency, created by attacks on refugee centres, cross-burnings, an expanding White Power music scene and other manifestations of right-wing extremism, triggered a reaction by the state in which the problem of racist violence—from now on called hate crime—was defined as a problem of security-threatening, ideologically based extremism.

Moreover, Säpo's statistics on hate crimes were inscribed in its larger surveillance activity, defined as aiming to protect Swedish society from anti-democratic movements. This definition must be understood, however, in the

84 *On the politics and poetics of hate-crime statistics*

context of Säpo's need to legitimize its own surveillance activity and to describe this in relation to the democratic order. Like similar security services in other countries, Säpo has been criticized and its practices and methods have been called into question as untransparent and undemocratic (Flyghed, 1997, p. 14).

The 2009 hate-crime report by Brå was the fifth one since the agency took over the responsibility for hate-crime statistics and, similar to the earlier Brå reports, the approach to hate crimes is already manifest on the report's cover. The focus shifts from extremism to ordinary crimes. Brå is explicit in that the statistics it presents challenge the dominant views on hate crimes:

> In the media, violent crimes are often portrayed as typical hate crimes, whereas the judiciary instead usually talks about agitation against a national or ethnic group and unlawful discrimination. In this report, the picture is different. The largest crime category is unlawful threat/molestation, which is nearly twice as large as the next category of violent crimes. The majority, 62 per cent, of hate crimes in 2006 thus belong to other crime categories than the ones portrayed as stereotypical.
>
> (Sporre, Klingspor & Wigerholt, 2007, p. 9)

Here Brå is reducing the emphasis on extremism, thereby shifting attention from extreme, extraordinary crimes to everyday, ordinary offences. This shift is only partly due to the evidence provided by the data gathered, since the level of what Brå called violent crimes has been relatively stable, both when Säpo collected the statistics and after Brå took over (cf. Sporre et al., 2007, p. 49). Rather, it marks a change in the context in which the statistics are produced and presented: no longer by Säpo, responsible for the surveillance of subversive activities of extreme groups, but by Brå, dealing with crimes in society at large. Hate crimes become situated *within* society instead of being pushed to its margins. At the same time, the acts denoted as hate crimes are now redefined from being treated as a threat to national security, to being treated as offences that, similar to other crimes, must be dealt with and prevented by the state. Which national body collects the statistics and for what purpose thus becomes significant regarding how hate crimes are represented.

The emphasis on the everyday nature of hate crimes runs through the Brå reports. It is visible in the language of the reports, with headers such as: 'Most Exposed in Everyday Life'. In addition, the design of the reports and the choice of what data should be included stem from this focus on the ordinary and everyday character of hate crimes. 'Ideologically motivated hate crimes' are still accounted for, but they constitute only a short section of the reports that is often introduced as a legacy of Säpo's method of collecting statistics (Sporre et al., 2007, p. 36). Beginning in 2006, new variables were created to describe hate crimes: the nature of the contact, the scene of the crime and the relationship between perpetrator and victim. This has

On the politics and poetics of hate-crime statistics   85

shifted the attention to the immediate context of the reported crimes, which has made it possible to reveal the ordinary settings in which these acts are performed. This information is presented to 'contribute to a more nuanced description of hate crimes' (Sporre et al., 2007, p. 12).

The focus on everyday or ordinary offences follows a development in much of the criminological research on hate crimes that has criticized the exaggerated focus on 'extreme, deviant, and isolated phenomena' (Wang, 2002, p. 1). The extensive attention given to statistically exceptional acts, such as murder, is claimed to have led to a neglect of the more ordinary experience of less extreme violence present in mainstream society, such as everyday discrimination, racial profiling or street harassment as well as other more mundane expressions of racist violence (Blee, 2005, p. 614). In part of the criminological literature, this criticism is often related to an attempt to move the problem of hate crimes from the margins to mainstream society. By doing so, these critical voices claim that hate crimes are rooted in existing and accepted forms of social inequality rather than a deviation from the norm[3] (cf. Perry, 2001; Young, 1988). While Brå's emphasis on the ordinary, everyday nature of hate crimes follows this trend, it does not endorse the critical component present in this literature. Rather, Brå's change in approach to hate crimes is part of a broader shift in criminological thought and practice in Sweden, towards everyday crime (Lidskog, 2006, p. 212).

This new focus is linked to the methodology of Brå's data collection that is designed in such a way that the most extreme cases of hate crimes— murder—most probably are not included in the statistics. This is recognized in the reports themselves as a problem: in cases of lethal violence, there is no account of the victim on which Brå could rely to discover possible motives for the crime, which is the usual way for Brå to identify hate crimes (Klingspor, Molarin, Sporre & Brottsförebyggande rådet, 2008, p. 31). Although it is possible to use other methods to spot the most extreme cases of hate crimes, this rarely seems to be done. It is impossible from the Brå reports to know the amount of lethal violence, since it is included in the larger category of 'violent crimes', together with assault and violence against a public servant. The acknowledgement of the seriousness of this kind of crime seems to be balanced against its statistical insignificance:

> The missing data concerning lethal violence do not, however, affect the overall level of hate crimes, as this type of crime is very rare. Nevertheless, it is important to map lethal violence, since it is the most serious crime in the penal code.
>
> (Klingspor et al., 2008, p. 31)

Thus, the framing of hate crimes as ordinary, everyday events, coupled with a characteristic statistical approach, has the peculiar effect of equalizing different types of crime and making the most extreme cases of violence invisible.

86 *On the politics and poetics of hate-crime statistics*

The cover of the Brå report reveals yet another shift in the representation of hate crimes: a focus on those exposed to hate crimes. The depiction of the perpetrators on the Säpo report is replaced by outlined profiles of victims. The question of who falls victim to hate crimes becomes central to the reports. Once again, this change is present on several levels. A new accounting unit, 'persons subjected to hate crimes', is included in the statistics. Additional data are drawn from another source, the Swedish Crime Survey, which examines the Swedish population's exposure to crime. Finally, emphasis is placed on the victim's perspective throughout the statistics. Thus, it is stated several times that, 'The hate criminality described in this report is based on the victim's feelings about the perpetrator's motive for his/her deeds' (Klingspor et al., 2008, p. 25).

This method of relying on the victim's account of the event, written down by a police officer, had already been adopted by Säpo. Nevertheless, it is only now stressed that this procedure is a victim-centred perspective. To be exact, the victim-centred perspective means here that the victim has reported the event as a crime to the police. Thus, the statistics consist of reported crimes, and not only the ones that have been identified as hate crimes by the judiciary or the police. Despite this approach, for an event to appear in the statistics, it must first fulfil Brå's criteria for classifying as a hate crime: the event must be reported to the police; the crime must be properly labelled; the police officer must register relevant information in the report that will include words found in Brå's word-search list; and, finally, the Brå coder must interpret the event as a hate crime (Klingspor et al., 2008, p. 39).

Also, by this focus on the victim, Brå's approach reflects a shift in criminological research in the 1980s and 1990s, where attention turned to the victims of crimes, their rights in the legal process, psychological effects of the crime, and the need for protection, compensation and support (Nilsson, 2003, pp. 25–30). However, while Brå's rhetoric is influenced by this new field of criminology—victimology—its epistemology is to a lesser degree affected by perspectives that seek to create knowledge from the standpoint of those affected by violence. This fracture is visible, for example, in how the difference in the number of hate crimes registered in the Swedish Crime Survey and the hate-crime statistics gathered by Brå is explained: 'it may be the case that the victim experiences the act as a hate crime, but that it is not defined this way according to hate crime statistics' (Klingspor et al., 2008, p. 24). It is Brå, through its definition of hate crime, that ultimately decides how many and what type of events will appear in the statistics.

The very definition of hate crime, too, has undergone major changes during the time Brå has been responsible for the collection of the statistics. Until 2008, the primary criterion for an event to be classified as a hate crime was that 'a majority person aggrieves a minority person' (Sporre et al., 2007, p. 15). This approach had been formulated by Säpo which, in turn, followed case law regarding penalty enhancement (Sporre et al., 2007, p. 15). 'Majority' and 'minority' were defined in different ways for different

On the politics and poetics of hate-crime statistics 87

motives: thus, for example, for anti-Semitic hate crimes, the victim must belong to a minority (either of Jewish origin or perceived as such by the perpetrator), while the perpetrator must belong to a majority (non-Jewish). As a consequence, an individual's status as a majority or minority member might shift depending on the category of crime that was described. The general idea was that individuals belonging to certain *groups* in Swedish society were targeted by hate crimes. Following this approach, one early Brå report included a section on victims of hate crimes, in which groups vulnerable to hate crimes were characterized: Sweden's population with foreign background affected by xenophobia, Muslims in Sweden by Islamophobia, Jews in Sweden by anti-Semitism and lesbian, gay, bisexual and transgender persons in Sweden by homophobia (Sporre et al., 2007, pp. 16–19). In addition to a description of groups, the section presents definitions of xenophobia, Islamophobia, anti-Semitism and homophobia. Some markers of this vulnerability are still represented on the cover of later reports: the Muslim veil and the Jewish skullcap.

In 2008, Brå redefined hate crime. The report is now no longer entitled *A summary of reports to the police of crimes motivated by xenophobia, Islamophobia, anti-Semitism and homophobia*, but *Reports to the police where the motivation for crime includes ethnic background, religious faith, sexual orientation, or transgender identity or expression*. The change in definition is thoroughly discussed and extensively justified. 'The new definition is more inclusive than before, and is only based on the motive for the crime', it is claimed. 'If the motive was to insult, there is no difference when it comes to group membership' (Klingspor, Molarin & Brottsförebyggande rådet, 2009, p. 16). In this way, the definition ceases to be related to particular groups that might be more exposed to certain crimes and instead focuses on individuals that are potentially targeted because of their identity. The inclusive way in which this identity is defined means that every individual in society might become a victim of a hate crime. This change is justified by a regard for the victim's perspective: 'Having a more inclusive and wider definition also gives a more comprehensive image of the exposure to hate crimes from the perspective of the victim' (Klingspor et al., 2009, p. 16).

This new definition has led to several changes. Different, more extensive, data are collected, now including offences against, for instance, ethnic Swedes or heterosexuals. The variables concerning motives are redefined and grouped in three sections: xenophobic/racist motives, including crimes against minorities, crimes among minorities and crimes against the majority; anti-religious motives, including Islamophobic, anti-Semite and other antireligious motives; and homophobic and heterophobic motives, where transphobic crimes are also included.

Against this inclusive tendency, two new additional categories are singled out within xenophobic/racist hate crimes: Afrophobic and anti-Roma hate crimes. Here, the justification is that the two groups are considered to be particularly exposed in Swedish society (Molarin & Frenzel, 2010, pp. 38–40).

88 *On the politics and poetics of hate-crime statistics*

Even in this case, however, the rhetoric is informed by the aim of being inclusive, as the following definition of the Afrophobic hate crime indicates: '*Anybody* can become exposed to an Afrophobic crime if the perpetrator is targeting people because of perceived identity' (Molarin & Frenzel, 2010, p. 38, my emphasis). In this way, hate crimes are transformed from crimes that affect some historically disadvantaged groups, because of phenomena such as anti-Semitism, racism, xenophobia, Islamophobia or homophobia, into crimes that can affect 'anybody'. Hate crimes are still seen as a result of a lack of respect for human rights and the equal value of people (Molarin & Frenzel, 2010, p. 16), a definition that runs through all the Brå reports. Now, however, the fight against hate crimes is detached from particular, historical struggles and placed within the framework of individual human rights. The former approach is deemed 'exclusionist' and 'unmodern' (Molarin & Frenzel, 2010, p. 10), while the latter is seen as truly inclusive.[4] This inclusive approach embodies a kind of liberalism that Sara Ahmed depicts as working 'to empty the place of the other, such that it can be filled by *anybody*' (2001, p. 359, original emphasis).

I argue that this kind of shift is symptomatic of a recent urge, present in Sweden and other countries in Europe, for social cohesion that stresses solidarity and equality between individuals in society. Brå's reports give us an atemporal, symbolic representation of hate crimes as targeting individuals detached from their social positions and disentangled from the histories of their communities. A shift thus takes place towards a liberal project of tolerance. One effect of this inclusive and individualistic approach to hate crimes is that the vulnerable position of some social groups is made invisible. So, the change in Brå's representation of hate crimes is embedded in a general discourse on crime in which vulnerable social *groups*, such as immigrants or women, are obscured (Lidskog, 2006, pp. 2014–2017) and instead the focus is placed on unsafe *individuals*. But it is also related to a more general backlash against multiculturalism that has been identified in several countries, despite the great variation in multicultural models in Europe (cf. Alexander, 2013; Lentin & Titley, 2012). The ways in which plural societies had attempted to recognize difference and to organize democratic life around this recognition have been called into question. One repeated criticism of multiculturalism has been that it divides rather than unites, thereby leading to resentment and fragmentation (for a discussion on the criticism of multiculturalism, see Meer & Modood, 2012, p. 187). In Sweden, multiculturalism has also been challenged in the political arena and media as well as in academia (cf. Bauhn & Demirbag-Sten, 2010; Carlbom, 2003). Multiculturalism has been blamed for, among other things, creating a segregated society, leading to the emergence of nationalism and for radicalizing minorities, in particular the Muslim minority (Carlbom, 2003). Its critics often describe it as a hegemonic ideology, whose 'values are forced onto all those actors who seek to say anything in public about cultural diversity' (Carlbom, 2003, p. 16). These voices feed into what Sara Ahmed argues is 'the hegemonic

On the politics and poetics of hate-crime statistics   89

position that liberal multiculturalism is the hegemony' (2008). The criticism of multiculturalism is intertwined with the idea that, in multicultural ideology, racism has become both the ideologically sanctioned explanation for issues of immigration and integration, and an accusation used to excommunicate those who oppose the hegemonic discourse (Carlbom, 2003, p. 52).

Although the demand for the inclusion of 'reverse racism' into the measures against hate crimes undertaken by the Swedish state has been mainly from the far-right in Sweden (cf. e.g. Motion, 1993/94:A35, for the position of New Democracy in the 1990s, and Motion, 2013/14:A353, for the position of Sweden Democrats in the 2000s), it would be wrong to understand Brå's changes in the definition of hate crime as yielding to the nationalists' discourse. My argument is that it is in the context of the general backlash against multiculturalism and a striving towards social cohesion that Brå's inclination towards inclusiveness and its transition from the focus on vulnerable groups to the emphasis on the universal vulnerability to hate crimes become intelligible.

The poetics of hate-crime statistics

While in the previous section I addressed the shifts in framings and definitions of hate crime and how they influenced the knowledge produced by the national bodies responsible for data collection, here I will address the impact that the adopted method and genre of the reports—what I call here 'the poetics of hate-crime statistics'—has on this knowledge. My argument is that the poetics of statistics shape, to a considerable degree, the understanding of hate crimes produced in the reports. Knowledge is produced in the form of figures that are divided into singled-out categories. The logics of the quantitative method impose a strict model of how facts are created, subordinating them to some fundamental criteria—such as reliability and comparability—as to what constitutes good scientific knowledge.

One of the central tools in statistical methods in general, and in the hate-crime statistics collected by Brå in particular, is categorization: the identified acts of violence are first of all categorized. Due to the nature of the statistical method, the categories are exclusive, which means that an act can only be categorized once. While Säpo's statistics included four categories of hate crimes—'crimes with xenophobic motive', 'crimes with anti-Semitic motive', 'crimes with homophobic motive' and 'crimes with white power–ideological motive' (Säpo, 2005)—Brå's way of building categories has undergone several changes. In 2006, the new category of Islamophobic crimes was created. A major reorganization of the categories took place in 2008, when the above-discussed new definition of hate crime was adopted. The new categories were as follows: 'xenophobic/racist hate crimes', including the subcategories 'Afrophobic hate crimes' and 'anti-Roma hate crimes'; 'anti-religious hate crimes', including the subcategories 'Islamophobic hate crimes', 'anti-Semitic hate crimes' and 'other anti-religious hate crimes'; 'homophobic,

90 *On the politics and poetics of hate-crime statistics*

biphobic and heterophobic hate crimes', with three subcategories: a new category 'transphobic hate crimes', previously included under homophobic hate crimes, and 'white power–ideological hate crimes'. In the methodological section of the reports, it is acknowledged that one crime might often have several possible motives. The procedure in such cases is to decide which of these is most 'prominent' and thereby to be chosen. When no prominent motive can be established, the category is decided on a random basis (Klingspor et al., 2008, p. 27). In this way, not only are the categories constructed as exclusive, a procedure indispensable to account for the actual number of hate crimes, but, also, different types of hate crimes are constructed as targeting one aspect of a person's identity, which thus becomes separable and independent from other aspects thereof. Accordingly, once it is decided that Islamophobia or anti-Semitism are about religion, other aspects of hate crimes that might, for example, target a person's colour, origin or ethnicity become invisible as the crimes' 'sub-motives' are not accounted for. The complexity and ambivalence of the examined violence are subordinated to statistical precision or the principle of randomization, which are assumed to guarantee a more reliable knowledge of hate crimes.

Apart from reliability, comparability is another driving force in the production of good statistical knowledge. Although, in the reports, several problems in comparing hate-crime statistics are identified and thoroughly described, the ideal is to enable comparisons within hate-crime statistics, both in time and between various categories of hate crimes, so that trends can be described and differences in the extent and nature of the categories of hate crimes can be identified. Such comparisons require a certain homogenization of the collected data. A uniform mould is created for all the categories and the same variables are accounted for in each of them. No specific data on types of hate crime are provided. The only trace that these might be different or similar and what these differences and similarities would encompass is left to the word-search lists used by Brå to select its cases. These lists are presented in an attachment to the reports. Otherwise, all the crimes are reduced so that they can be described with the help of the predefined variables. As a result, different types of violence—homophobic, anti-Semitic, racist or Islamophobic—are divorced from the historically specific contexts in which they have developed and forced into one uniform model of hate crimes. This uniformization or homogenization of different types of violence is particularly striking in the wording of the definitions of the various hate-crime motives. For example, the definition of xenophobic/racist hate crimes reads:

> [F]ear of, hostility towards or hatred of a person, group, their property or institution because of skin colour, nationality or ethnic background, and that activates a reaction against a person or persons that are, or are perceived to be, of foreign or Swedish origin, or representatives of persons of foreign or Swedish origin.
>
> (Molarin & Frenzel, 2010, p. 31)

In the definitions of other types of hate crime, the object of fear, hostility or hatred is different (Islam and Muslims in the case of Islamophobia, Judaism and the Jewish population in the case of anti-Semitism, etc.). But all types of violence are invariably defined as a reaction to some emotional state, described as fear, hostility or hatred. Apart from the above-discussed widening of the definition of those who can be targeted by hate crimes, the definitions have not changed during the time Brå has been responsible for the statistics.[5] In this sense, the homogenization of different categories of hate crime entails a uniform understanding of different types of violence, their reasons and mechanisms.

Also at a stylistic level, comparability leaves its imprint, repetition becoming the main trope in the reports. Different chapters are constructed following the same order, sections repeat the same sentences, and the same words and expressions are used in different parts of the text. The uniformalization and homogenization of the text and style make a search for statistical trends and deviations quick and easy, both in time and among the different types of hate crime. This gives an impression of a certain uniformity of the history of this type of violence in Sweden. Not much space is left to introduce different contexts and particular events that might have contributed to a more heterogeneous, complicated and dynamic image of the different types of violence at different points in time, opening up a more historical account of hate crimes. Not surprisingly, following this style, the cover of Brå's 2009 hate-crime report has also been replicated year after year since 2008. The only thing that changes is the colour of the background.

What is a hate crime? On the emotions of racist violence and travelling concepts

In the previous sections, I described how the politics and poetics of hate-crime statistics inform Brå's understanding of hate crimes. Here I will focus on the term itself—'hate crime'—chosen to denote the object of the statistics.

In the background section of the reports, the term 'hate crime' is presented as relatively new and ambiguous (cf. Klingspor et al., 2008, p. 16). It is said that the term entered the Swedish criminological vocabulary as late as 1999 through a study on crimes against homosexuals conducted by Eva Tiby (Tiby, 1999). It is stressed in the reports that the term is applied in different ways in different countries, but that there is a consensus that hate crimes are

> a result of a lack of respect for human rights and the equal value of people. A single hate crime has the power to injure twice, it creates insecurity and fear in the victim, as well as in the group to which the person belongs. For the individual, the crime may entail an attack against his or her identity and dignity.
>
> (Klingspor et al., 2008, p. 16)

92   On the politics and poetics of hate-crime statistics

Since 'hate crime' is not a legal term in Sweden, Brå's definition thereof and thus the hate-crime statistics cannot be directly drawn from law texts. However, Brå locates the origin of hate-crime statistics in legislation created in the 1990s, although the crimes defined by the older laws on agitation against a national or ethnic group and unlawful discrimination are also included in Brå's definition. This positioning strengthens the impression of the novelty of this kind of criminalization and situates Brå's activity in the larger, international trend of addressing racist violence as a special type of criminality: both the choice of the term and the timeframe are influenced by developments in other countries.

The Swedish word *hatbrott* is a literal translation of the English 'hate crime'. The term originated in the United States, where it was coined by a group of Democrats who in 1985 cosponsored a bill in the House of Representatives entitled the 'Hate Crime Statistics Act' (Jacobs & Potter, 1998, p. 4). The political idea of addressing particular kinds of violence in law goes back, however, to the 1970s and certain social movements, such as the Civil Rights movement, that opposed racist violence, and, somewhat later, the Gay movement struggling against the violence that homosexuals were exposed to. The efforts to legally address these types of violence coincided with the conservative crime-victim movement and groups that fought for more severe penalties, forming in this way a strange alliance between progressive radicals and conservatives (Jenness & Grattet, 2001, pp. 20–21). These social mobilization efforts established hate crimes as a problem to be dealt with by the legal system and resulted in the proliferation and diffusion of state laws addressing hate crimes, in different ways and diversely defined, in the 1980s and early 1990s (Jenness & Grattet, 2001, pp. 73–101). Thus, in the United States, 'hate crime' is an umbrella term mainly originating from the grass-root activities of different oppressed groups in their struggle for recognition and a legal remedy for the violence they had been experiencing. While this general concept offered a common language for the struggle of these different movements, it also opened the way for a broad application to other possible groups of victims, most importantly, women[6] and disabled people (Jenness & Grattet, 2001, p. 72). So, in the United States, the genealogy of the concept of hate crime embodies a history of a struggle above all against racial oppression rooted in slavery and the Jim Crow legislation, implicating a progressive and linear narrative of the transformation of the state's role from a perpetrator legitimizing racial violence to a protector of civil rights (Levin, 2009, p. 2). At the same time, the term 'hate crime' indicates a disconnection from this particular historical context, and a broadening of the idea of racist violence so that it could include other vulnerable groups.

A rapid diffusion of the concept of hate crime followed, resulting in its spreading into different national contexts in the 1990s. Sweden was one of the countries where the term took root, entering the vocabularies of criminology, policy and official statistics. Unlike in the United States and similar to, for example, in the United Kingdom,[7] the term was borrowed in

On the politics and poetics of hate-crime statistics   93

reaction to some developments and high-profile events involving racist violence. As discussed above, the term has since undergone a substantive transformation, not only opening the way for the inclusion of different grounds of bias, but also shifting the focus from vulnerable groups towards individuals, thereby creating an impression of universalism and ahistoricity of this kind of violence.

My understanding is that the concept of hate crime turned out to be suitable for this type of transformation, for three reasons: because of the term's vague, novel and strongly contested character (cf. Chakraborti, 2009; Mason, 2001; Ray & Smith, 2001; Stanko, 2001); because it highlights the emotional and thereby a more universal nature of this type of crime over other concepts; and because the very process of translation and transplantation from one context to another made it easier to divorce the term from the particular historical context in which it originally emerged. The case of the Swedish re-adaptation of this term is hence interesting, not because it reveals the possible meaning of the concept of hate crime, but because it discloses the work that this concept does.[8]

The element '*hat*' (hate) in the compound *hatbrott* has influenced Brå's definition of hate crime, in which hatred, along with fear and hostility, is singled out as a source of violence. Moreover, and most importantly, it effectively places an emphasis on the emotional state of the perpetrator towards the victim. Significantly, 'prejudice' or 'bias'—terms often used in the United States and the United Kingdom, both by scholars and in the context of law enforcement, interchangeably with 'hate' to denote this type of crime (Chakraborti, 2009, p. 17)—while sporadically used in the early reports to discuss hate crimes motivated by Islamophobia or anti-Semitism, disappear completely from later reports.

In combination with this trend towards the inclusiveness of the definition of vulnerability to hate crimes, the term 'hate crime' is separated from the historically rooted affects involved in the work of creating communities, and instead placed in free-floating individuals driven by emotions. In this sense, Brå's statistics reproduce an approach to hate crimes as an expression of a psychological disposition or a matter of individual psychology.[9] It is in this context of individualization that the specific way in which a crime is identified as a hate crime is significant. Following Swedish legislation, Brå identifies hate crimes based on motive. And just like in the case of the legislation, the challenge emerging from this definition is how to understand the concept of motive. Brå stresses that the statistics presented in its reports are independent from the categorizations and judgements made by law enforcement and the judiciary (Klingspor et al., 2008, p. 18); yet it still encounters similar problems related to the identification of motive. The general rule, stemming from Brå's victimological perspective, is the priority given to the narrative of the victim:

> If the victim considers or suspects that the motive for the crime is due to her or his being or being considered to be of foreign extraction, a

94 *On the politics and poetics of hate-crime statistics*

Muslim, of Jewish birth, homosexual or bisexual or a person of transgender, the event is usually considered to be a hate crime.

(Klingspor et al., 2008, p. 26)

In this sense, Brå's interpretation of the motive follows the victims' interpretation thereof. This is, however, not the only way to identify hate crimes in the reports. Other ways to select possible hate crimes include the perpetrator's use of certain words or symbols and interpretations produced by other actors, such as the police, the media or witnesses. Still, not necessarily all crimes experienced as hate crimes by the victims or interpreted as such by others are included in the statistics. It is actually the coder who determines, based on Brå's definitions, whether a reported crime should be included.

Thus, Brå's general definition decides what a 'hate-crime motive' is. This definition is, as I have discussed, both vague and ambivalent, directing us to psychological states of individual perpetrators that are difficult to see through. After all, how are we to decide whether a person is driven by fear or hate in his or her acts? On the other hand, Brå's definition of hate-crime motive is based on assumptions that might seem technical, but that in fact are quite revealing. One such assumption follows the common idea, present in criminological literature (Tiby, 1999, p. 223), that the crime would not have happened if the victim and the perpetrator had the same (ethnic, religious, sexual) identity. Accordingly, Brå assumes a position that a crime is a hate crime if it is clear that it is caused by a 'hate-crime motive' and not by another motive, such as economic gain (Molarin & Frenzel, 2010, p. 20).[10] Another assumption is visible in the choice that possible hate crimes are searched for only in selected categories of crimes. When in 2008 the Swedish police introduced a special hate-crime box in the computer system that police officers fill in when registering a crime, which must be ticked if they suspect a hate crime, it turned out that some potential hate crimes were not included in Brå statistics because they did not belong to the crime categories that Brå searches for hate crimes. The largest individual crime category of this sort was professional misconduct (*tjänstefel*), which is a crime by civil servants in the exercise of their public authority. By excluding this crime category from the statistics, Brå indirectly defines hate crime as occurring predominantly among citizens, understood as private persons detached from the institutional contexts in which they act. Such an approach parallels the exclusion of the anti-discrimination legislation from the penal law[11] and, thereby, cases of discrimination from the hate-crime statistics.

The search-word lists elaborated by Brå for each motive included in the reports play a central role in identifying potential hate crimes. It is here that the operationalization of different motives actually takes place. The lists are updated every year according to previously identified hate crimes and to include time-specific wordings linked to particular events that occurred in a given year and that might have triggered violence. These lists include, among other things, words denoting certain identities. What is significant here is that the operationalization of the definition is not based on individuals'

On the politics and poetics of hate-crime statistics 95

motivations. Instead, by searching certain words, it draws on attributes assigned to some groups in acts of violence and on specific, historically situated vocabularies and imaginaries of racism, anti-Semitism, Islamophobia and homophobia. This suggests that, despite an overall emphasis that a hate crime is defined through a motive and despite a representation of hate crimes as motivated by some states of mind, the practical work of identifying hate crimes encounters obvious obstacles in relying on motives alone or even in determining the motive in the first place.

I have argued here that the development that hate crime has come to be defined as the domain of individual and private persons, disentangled from historical contexts and detached from institutional settings, was facilitated by the character given to the term 'hate crime'. I have also suggested that the different ways in which the term travelled contributed to gradually detaching it from its historical roots of collective struggle. The first travel was initiated in the United States: from social movements to law and policymaking and to the academic field of criminology. The second travel was from the political reality of liberalism in the United States to the Swedish context in a time marked by the eruption of violent racism and the above-mentioned backlash against multiculturalism. Here again, the context changes and the term travels back from academia and criminological research to the domain of policymaking.[12]

Islamophobia as a hate crime

In this last section, I turn to the subject of this book to explore the definitions of anti-Muslim racism in official statistics on hate crimes. The issue of accounting for 'Islamophobic hate crimes' as a separate category in hate-crime statistics was raised for the first time in the early 2000s in the aftermath of 9/11. Several times, questions about measures against Islamophobia have been raised in the Swedish Parliament (cf. e.g. Motion, 2004/05:K460; Motion, 2004/05:Ju254; Skriftlig fråga, 2002/03:855; Skriftlig fråga, 2002/03:96). As a result, since 2006, when Brå took over the hate-crime statistics, it also began to collect statistics on crimes motivated by Islamophobia.

A definition of Islamophobia was adopted that has not changed since and was based on the general template of Brå's definition of hate crime. It reads:

> Fear of, hostility towards or hatred of Islam or Muslims and that activates an anti-Islamic reaction against Islam, Muslim property, its institutions, or a person or persons that are, or are perceived as, Muslims or representatives of Muslims.
>
> (Sporre et al., 2007, p. 25)

What has changed throughout the years is the location of Islamophobic hate crimes in relation to other types of hate crime. This location, I argue, is significant because, lacking differentiation in treatment of distinct types of hate crime by Brå and in the context of the uniform language used to

96 On the politics and poetics of hate-crime statistics

describe different hate-crime motives, it shows that the understanding of Islamophobic hate crimes has nevertheless undergone a transformation. In the first report accounting for Islamophobia, Brå writes:

> Islamophobia is a relatively new concept that scientifically has been debated and used to a limited extent. Formerly the term was often incorporated in xenophobia. To some degree this is still the case.
>
> (Sporre et al., 2007, p. 17)

Also, when discussing how the creation of the new category influences the comparability of the data, Brå notices that Islamophobic hate crime had before most probably been included in the numbers on xenophobic hate crime (Sporre et al., 2007, p. 8). At this early stage, Islamophobia was thus defined as a type of xenophobia directed against Muslims, although it was also noticed that the concept of Islamophobia had been criticized because

> prejudice affects primarily Arabs and not all Muslims. This is because the Arabs' appearance better meets the stereotypical idea of who is a Muslim than, for example, Muslims from the Balkans.
>
> (Sporre et al., 2007, p. 17)

The early approach to Islamophobic hate crime recognized the relation between this type of prejudice and the prejudices directed against people because of their ethnicity, nationality or because they are immigrants. It was also underlined on this occasion that Islamophobia must be linked to behaviour and acts rather than to ideology and opinions (Sporre et al., 2007, p. 17). This is the only type of hate crime in regard to which such a remark is made. It can be explained by a common approach that Islamophobia should be differentiated from legitimate forms of criticism. This seems to be a response to how debates about Muslim minorities in Europe are framed.[13] What is also interesting as to how the definition of Islamophobic hate crime has evolved since is that in the first definition it is underscored that

> the difference between secular and practicing Muslims is less important when it comes to exposure to hate crimes, as the crime affects both people perceived as Muslims and practicing Muslims.
>
> (Sporre et al., 2007, p. 18)

In this way, by both noting that Islamophobic acts are often targeting particular groups of immigrants on the basis of their ethnicity rather than religion, and by underscoring the exposure regardless of the actual relation to religion of the victims, Islamophobia is still located in the realm of xenophobia rather than violence based on religious intolerance.

In 2008, together with the major change in Brå's definition of hate crime, the location of Islamophobic hate crime in relation to other hate crimes

On the politics and poetics of hate-crime statistics 97

changed as well. In the report from that year and in a couple of years that followed, they have been accounted for under the general heading of anti-religious hate crimes. Brå gave less attention to this type of hate crime: they were not singled out in a separate section of the report, nor does the word 'Islamophobia' appear in the title of the report or in the table of contents. In the 2009 report, the numbers regarding Islamophobic hate crimes are accounted for separately in a few tables only. So, while data about Islamophobic hate crimes were clearly prioritized in Brå's statistics in the mid-2000s, this seemed to have changed in the late 2000s. In the later reports, the category of Islamophobic hate crimes was included in a larger category of anti-religious hate crimes and thus made less visible.[14]

This move from an understanding of Islamophobia as close to xenophobia to an understanding of it as anti-religious hate crime shows a deeper change in how violence targeting Muslims is perceived. One of the consequences of calling violence against Muslims an anti-religious hate crime is that it stresses the importance of the Muslims' religion and thereby might suggest that the violence they are exposed to could be situated in the realm of alleged tensions between the secular and the religious. Framed in this way, Islamophobic hate crimes are implicated in the broader discourses on religion and secularism and their relation to modern democracy (for a discussion of these in relation to Islam, see Asad, 2003). As a consequence, Muslims become perceived primarily as a *religious* minority.

Conclusions

In this chapter, I have explored the ways in which statistical knowledge of hate crimes is produced in Sweden. I have identified the main shifts in the definition and understanding of this particular type of violence: from a focus on extreme violence perpetrated from the margins of society to everyday and ordinary crimes; from a focus on the perpetrators pictured as political extremists committed to undemocratic ideologies to a focus on the victims; from the context of protection of some historically marginalized groups to the context of protection of all individuals whose universal rights are threatened. All of these shifts are embedded in the larger processes and changes in the discourses that I have identified in the criminological literature and in the work on crime prevention. I have argued that the ways in which hate crimes have been defined and understood have had to do with both the politics and the poetics of the statistics.

Notes

1 I focus in particular on Säpo's last report on hate crimes published in 2005 and on Brå's reports from 2006, 2007, 2008, 2009 and 2010. Each report addresses hate crimes that had been committed in the previous year.

98 *On the politics and poetics of hate-crime statistics*

2 When the reports were translated into English, I used this translation. In the remaining cases, the translation is mine. In the case of Säpo's 2005 report, no English version is available, but large parts of the report are the same as the 2001 report that was translated into English.

3 For a comprehensive overview of the sociological explanations of hate crime, see Barbara Perry (2009). One of the mainstream interpretations of hate crimes in criminology that Perry identifies draws on Robert Merton's strain theory. Hate crimes are here explained as a deviant response to the pressures of capitalism by some individuals who treat minorities as scapegoats (Walters, 2011).

4 This reinterpretation follows some recent developments in the field of criminology concerned with hate crimes, with a turn away from an understanding of hate crimes as a mechanism of power and oppression targeting some traditionally marginalized groups (Perry, 2001) and a move towards a more inclusive understanding that departs from the victim's vulnerability and difference (Chakraborti & Garland, 2012). An argument often used in this debate is that hate crime legislation leads to social fragmentation and undermines social solidarity (Jacobs & Potter, 1998, p. 131).

5 Säpo had different definitions for different types of hate crime: xenophobia was about 'a negative attitude, disrespect or hatred directed against a person or a group on the grounds of colour, ethnic or cultural background'; it included racism, which consisted in 'negative treatment of some individuals based on the conception that there are several human races'. Anti-Semitism was defined as 'hostility towards Jews, Judaism and Jewish property', with both religious and ideological causes. Homophobia consisted in 'dislike and fear of homosexuality and homosexuals' (Säpo, 2005, pp. 12–13).

6 According to Jenness and Grattet, while the Feminist movement was important in that it shed light on the forms of violence that women are exposed to in ways similar to the Civil Rights movement's struggles against racist violence, it has not been involved specifically in the mobilization around hate-crime legislation in the United States. Gender as a basis for protection was included in some state hate crime statutes in the 1990s, more as a result of the diffusion of these acts than as lobbying activities of some particular feminist groups (2001).

7 The concept of hate crime made its entry into the United Kingdom in the aftermath of the murder of Stephen Lawrence and the subsequent publication of the Macpherson Report that brought the issue of institutional racism within the police to the fore (Lawrence, 2002).

8 I am here influenced by Meke Bal's work on concepts (2002).

9 Here I have been inspired by the work of David Theo Goldberg (1997), Sara Ahmed (2001, 2004) and Kathleen Blee (2003), who, in different ways, discuss and criticize the psychologization and individualization of hate crimes.

10 The legal interpretation of the penalty enhancement provision is different, hate motive being just one, and not necessarily the primary, motive for the crime.

11 One effect of this development is that discrimination is actually not included in hate-crime statistics. The act on unlawful discrimination (*olaga diskriminering*), as discussed in Chapter 4, has been applied to a very limited degree; instead, the anti-discrimination legislation formulated in the Civil Code has been used. In 2009, Brå started to account in footnotes for the cases conducted by the Equality Ombudsman (DO). Still, these numbers are not included in Brå's statistics.

12 This last travel turned out to be somewhat troublesome. As mentioned above, since 2008, police officers have been asked to tick a special box on the form they fill out when registering a crime report if there is an indication that a crime is a hate crime. Brå did an evaluation of this procedure and found that the majority of the crime reports marked as hate crime by the police did not have a hate

crime motive in Brå's understanding. This divergence seemed to be a result of misunderstanding of the term 'hate crime'. One of the common mistakes made by the police was, for example, to mark as a hate crime those crimes in the course of which the perpetrator expressed hatred against the victim. This does not, however, mean that the police lack the language for describing the particular character of this type of violence when such is noticed and recognized. My analysis of the police reports concerning Islamophobic hate crimes reveals that the word 'racism' or 'racist' appears in the free text of the police reports three times as often as the word 'hate crime'.

13 In no other type of hate crime is an explicit distinction made between legitimate ideology and opinion and the criminal act. However, in a somewhat similar way, albeit with a distinct justification, Brå argues that crimes 'that are related to the State of Israel and its policy are not coded as hate crimes, on the grounds that the crime is not in this case specifically targeted against the Jewish population or Judaism' (Klingspor, Molarin & Sporre, 2008, p. 29).

14 This decrease in attention given to the Islamophobic hate crimes was temporary. In the reports from the 2010s, the Islamophobic hate crimes are again reported in a separate section and their visibility re-established.

Bibliography

Ahmed, S. (2001). 'The Organisation of Hate.' *Law and Critique, 12*(3), 345–365.

Ahmed, S. (2004). *The Cultural Politics of Emotion.* Edinburgh: Edinburgh University Press.

Ahmed, S. (2008). '"Liberal Multiculturalism is the Hegemony—Its an Empirical Fact"—A response to Slavoj Žižek.' *dark matter.*

Alexander, J. (2013). 'Struggling Over the Mode of Incorporation: Backlash against Multiculturalism in Europe.' *Ethnic and Racial Studies, 36*(4), 531–556.

Asad, T. (2003). *Formations of the Secular: Christianity, Islam, Modernity.* Stanford, CA: Stanford University Press.

Bal, M. (2002). *Travelling Concepts in the Humanities: A Rough Guide.* Toronto: University of Toronto Press.

Bauhn, P. & Demirbag-Sten, D. (2010). *Till frihetens försvar: en kritik av den normativa multikulturalismen.* Stockholm: Norstedt.

Blee, K. (2003). 'Positioning Hate.' *Journal of Hate Studies, 3*(1), 95–105.

Blee, K. (2005). 'Racial Violence in the United States.' *Ethnic and Racial Studies, 28*(4), 599–619.

Carlbom, A. (2003). *The Imagined versus the Real Other: Multiculturalism and the Representation of Muslims in Sweden.* Lund: Dept. of Sociology, Lunds Universitet.

Chakraborti, N. (2009). 'Crimes against the "Other": Conceptual, Operational, and Empirical Challenges for Hate Studies.' *Journal of Hate Studies, 8*(1), 9–28.

Chakraborti, N. & Garland, J. (2012). 'Reconceptualizing Hate Crime Victimization through the Lens of Vulnerability and "Difference".' *Theoretical Criminology, 16*(4), 499–514.

Flyghed, J. (1997). *Säkerhetspolisen och det demokratiska samhället.* Stockholm: Kriminologiska institutionen, Stockholms Universitet.

Goldberg, D. (1997). *Racial Subjects: Writing on Race in America.* New York: Routledge.

Jacobs, J. & Potter, K. (1998). *Hate Crimes: Criminal Law & Identity Politics.* New York: Oxford University Press.

100 On the politics and poetics of hate-crime statistics

Jenness, V. & Grattet, R. (2001). *Making Hate a Crime: From Social Movement Concept to Law Enforcement Practice.* New York: Russell Sage.

Klingspor, K., Molarin, A. & Brottsförebyggande rådet. (2009). *Hatbrott 2008: polisanmälningar där det i motivbilden ingår etnisk bakgrund, religiös tro, sexuell läggning eller könsöverskridande identitet eller uttryck.* Stockholm: Brottsförebyggande rådet (BRÅ): Fritze.

Klingspor, K., Molarin, A., Sporre, T. & Brottsförebyggande rådet. (2008). *Hatbrott 2007: en sammanställning av anmälningar med främlingsfientliga, islamofobiska, antisemitiska och homofobiska motiv.* Stockholm: Brottsförebyggande rådet (BRÅ): Fritze.

Lawrence, F. (2002). 'Racial Violence on a "Small Island": Bias Crime in a Multicultural Society.' In P. Iganski (Ed.), *The Hate Debate.* London: Profile, pp. 36–54.

Lentin, A. & Titley, G. (2012). 'The Crisis of "Multiculturalism" in Europe: Mediated Minarets, Intolerable Subjects.' *European Journal of Cultural Studies, 15*(2), 124–138.

Levin, B. (2009). 'The Long Arc of Justice: Race, Violence, and the Emergence of Hate Crime Law.' In B. Perry (Ed.), *Hate Crimes.* Vol. 1. Westport: Praeger, pp. 1–22.

Lidskog, R. (2006). *Staden, våldet och tryggheten: om social ordning i ett mångkulturellt samhälle.* Stockholm: Daidalos.

Marshall, G. & Scott, J. (2005). *A Dictionary of Sociology* (3rd edn.). Oxford: Oxford University Press.

Mason, G. (2001). 'Not Our Kind of Hate Crime.' *Law and Critique, 12*(3), 253–278.

Meer, N. & Modood, T. (2012). 'How Does Interculturalism Contrast with Multiculturalism?' *Journal of Intercultural Studies, 33*(2), 175–196.

Molarin, A. & Frenzel, A. (2010). *Hatbrott 2009: statistik över polisanmälningar där det i motivbilden ingår etnisk bakgrund, religiös tro, sexuell läggning eller könsöverskridande identitet eller uttryck.* Stockholm: Brottsförebyggande rådet.

Motion (1993/94:A35).

Motion (2004/05:K460).

Motion (2004/05:Ju254).

Motion (2013/14:A353).

Nilsson, B. (2003). *Brottsoffer: offerskapets innebörder och villkor i (o)säkerhetens kultur.* Umeå: Boréa.

Nussbaum, M. (2012). *The New Religious Intolerance: Overcoming the Politics of Fear in an Anxious Age.* Cambridge, MA: Belknap Press of Harvard University Press.

Perry, B. (2001). *In the Name of Hate.* London: Routledge.

Perry, B. (2009). 'The Sociology of Hate: Theoretical Approaches.' In B. Perry (Ed.), *Hate Crimes.* Vol. 1. Westport: Praeger, pp. 55–76.

Prior, L. (2003). *Using Documents in Social Research.* London: Sage.

Ray, L. & Smith, D. (2001). 'Racist Offenders and the Politics of "Hate Crime".' *Law and Critique, 12*(3), 203–221.

Säpo. (2005). *Brottslighet kopplad till rikets inre säkerhet.* Stockholm: Säkerhetspolisen.

Skriftligfråga (2002/03:855).

Skriftligfråga (2002/03:96).

Sporre, T., Klingspor, K. & Wigerholt, J. (2007). *Hatbrott 2006: en sammanställning av polisanmälningar med främlingsfientliga, islamofobiska, antisemitiska och homofobiska motiv.* Stockholm: Brottsförebyggande rådet.

Stanko, E. (2001). 'Re-Conceptualising the Policing of Hatred: Confessions and Worrying Dilemmas of a Consultant.' *Law and Critique, 12*(3), 309–329.

Tiby, E. (1999). *Hatbrott?: homosexuella kvinnors och mäns berättelser om utsatthet för brott*. Stockholm: Kriminologiska institutionen, Stockholms Universitet.

Walters, M. (2011). 'A General *Theories* of Hate Crime? Strain, Doing Difference and Self Control.' *Critical Criminology*, 19(4), 313–330.

Wang, L.-I. (2002). 'Hate Crime and Everyday Discrimination: Influences of and on the Social Context.' *Rutgers Race & the Law Review*, 4, 1–32.

Young, I. (1988). 'Five Faces of Oppression.' *Philosophical Forum*, 19(4), 270–290.

6   In search of a racist subject

The worship room is located in a large block of flats ...

The room is spartanly furnished with just a simple bookcase at one of the room's narrow ends. The floor is covered with rugs. Under the rugs there are sleeping-mats and flattened cardboard boxes to make the floor softer ...

The picture shows the seat of the fire below the window. Above the window there is a curtain rail. ... Parts of the rail are still white and thereby unaffected by smoke and soot, indicating that one or several curtains had been hanging in front of the window.

The soot deposits on the wall below the window indicate there may have been at least two seats of the fire ...

The investigation could not establish any break-in damage to windows, doors or locks of the room. According to gathered information the worship room had been open and unlocked.

The cause of the fire is unknown. No natural cause for fire can be ascertained. There was no electrical wiring at or close to the seat of the fire that could have been the source of ignition ...

That the fire was premeditated cannot be excluded. The soot deposits on the walls below the window indicate that one or several curtains had been set on fire by means yet unknown. Burning chunks of fabric may have fallen to the floor under the window and set the carpet on fire.

(Crime scene report, Case 8)

On a June night, on his way to morning prayer, Mustafa Al-Basri discovered that the local mosque situated in a flat in a residential block in Manby—a small village in Sweden—was burning. He called the fire brigade. The fire-fighters soon arrived and put out the fire. The room's curtains were burnt, as well as the rugs that stretched across the floor. The walls were covered with soot and the flat was filled with smoke, which had started to spread into the communal stairwell. Mustafa Al-Basri also found a Koran thrown on the ground outside the mosque. Over the following days, the police would receive several religious books that belonged to the Muslim community and had been kept in the mosque, but were now found all around the village.

In the course of the investigation, it became clear that the fire had been started by somebody, and a local young man, Sven Persson, confessed that he had entered the mosque twice that night. On the first occasion, he took some books from a bookshelf and afterwards threw them away in different places around the village while wandering the streets with a group of friends. On the second occasion, he dropped a match in the mosque. Persson was charged with theft and arson and, some months later, his trial took place.

When a police officer filed the crime report on the morning after the fire, in his description of the crime he wrote:

> An unknown perpetrator has set fire to a mosque located in a place where there is an extensive risk of property damage, and is guilty of ATTEMPTED ARSON. *The crime may also be suspected of having a character similar to a hate crime.*
>
> (Police report, Case 8, my emphasis)

Throughout the entire investigation, the idea that Sven Persson's acts could constitute a hate crime was evident. Sometimes it was manifested explicitly in the police notes. For example, in the records from the interrogation of the suspect, in the box asking for 'reason for interrogation', it was stated that:

> The crime should be considered a hate crime, since the acts were directed and perpetrated against a space and scriptures used by Muslims to exercise their religious faith. The scriptures were later found thrown away in various places in the village of Manby. And by intentionally setting fire to the curtain, [the suspect] has caused damage to the Muslim prayer room/mosque.
>
> (Interrogation records, Case 8)

This thread of the police investigation disappeared from the indictment, however. Nowhere in the judgement was there any indication that this aspect of the act had been taken into consideration by the court. Nor did the prosecutor demand the statutory penalty enhancement.

In this chapter, I will analyse the ways in which justice was dispensed in the Manby case. The penalty enhancement provision that is included in the Swedish Penal Code and that I discussed in Chapter 4 suggests that recognition of a particular nature of a racist act is an indispensable part of the process of doing justice. But what makes a crime a racist one? How does the judiciary proceed to identify racism? In other words, what is necessary for an act to be judged as racist in a Swedish court?

The analysis of the Manby case will be carried out in two stages. In the first part of the chapter, I will trace different narratives presented in court: those by the witnesses from the local Muslim community on the one hand,

104 *In search of a racist subject*

and those by the defendant and his friends, who witnessed the acts, on the other. These narratives are embedded in the very specific context of a trial. I will read this context as a *scene of address* that, by imposing an agonistic structure on the dispute, deeply shapes the narratives of those involved according to the roles of the defendant, the injured party and the witnesses. Following Judith Butler (1997, 2005), I claim that the working of such a scene of address is constitutive: the law's and the court's impact on what can be said and how it can be framed goes much deeper than just to inform the ways in which justice is claimed or innocence pled, strongly shaping the *accounts* of those involved in the trial. I will claim that the narrative strategies adopted by those involved disclose what kind of responsibility is claimed, denied or questioned and how the injury is defined. Most importantly, they help to create a particular *account of the self* and thus a particular subject that can be held responsible or absolved of blame. Butler insists that an account of the self is always dependent on the terms in which it is possible to talk about oneself and on the accessible modes of attending to one's own actions and motivations (2005, pp. 15–21). Thus, the trial will be read here as a frame providing the language and terms for claiming injuries, defining motives and constructing accounts of the self *in relation to* the legal definitions of injury, motive and subject as well as in relation to the court's understanding of racism. The deconstruction of the narratives in this case will help me answer the following questions: What language is available to describe the performed violence? What did the acts mean to those involved? How is the injury conceived? In what terms are the motives defined?

As discussed in Chapter 3, the material that I use to reconstruct the case and the trial are police files and court documents produced during the investigation and as a result of the trial. This means that I rely on the police's and court's voice in order to recover the narratives in which I am interested. They come to me mediated in the third person by police officers and judges. I receive them in the form of concise, impersonal summaries of the testimonies of the witnesses, captured in the laconic style of official language. One aim of the analysis will be to recreate the polyphony of voices present in court, which will enable me, I hope, to reach a complex and deeper understanding of the dynamics of justice and recognition or the lack thereof.

In the second part of the chapter, I will turn to a discourse of the judiciary represented by different actors of the system who have the power to define the case—most importantly, the prosecutor, the district court and the court of appeal—in order to deconstruct their definitions of the crime and the process of dispensing justice. By analysing the rationale behind the judgement, my aim will be to understand the ways in which the act is defined by the court and to examine what kind of definition of racism is adopted. Also, I will explore how justice is comprehended and dispensed and how responsibility is defined. I will end by contrasting the Manby case with another case of a mosque fire that had taken place in the town of Holmstad several years earlier and that had been judged in a very different way. This comparison will be aimed at clarifying some aspects of the judiciary's ways of approaching racism.

The value of a mosque

The police and court documents contain the testimonies of those who discovered the fire in the mosque. From these we learn how members of the Muslim community noticed the fire and tried to extinguish it, how they called the emergency services and what they saw at the crime scene. The documents also include a description of what kind of space it was and what role it played for the Muslim community in Manby. Moreover, they provide some details concerning the religious books that had been taken from the mosque and later on found in different places in the village.

It seems that these testimonies were most prevalently and most directly structured by questions asked during the police interviews and the trial. The questions were tailored to the judiciary's need to reconstruct the course of events, to gather reliable evidence and evaluate the damage done to the property. The material dimension of the acts and of the injury sustained seemed to be of central importance here. And so, for instance, during a police interview, one of the witnesses and a member of the Muslim community was asked to estimate the value of the books. His response is summed up as follows:

> Mustafa states that he cannot give the value/price of the books (the sacred scriptures handed over to the police) that were found in various locations in the village and outside the window. Mustafa states that all Muslims living in Manby have bought these together. Mustafa further states that people of the Muslim faith experience the treatment of the religious scriptures as very painful, the fact that they were thrown onto various locations in the village and that the Koran was on the ground.
>
> (Police interview, Case 8)

Mustafa Al-Basri seemed to have been unwilling to define the loss in the formal language in which harm is measured in economic terms. Instead, he tried to expand the meaning of the term 'value' and thereby the material frames in which the judiciary tried to contain and measure the injury, and according to which the compensation might have been weighted. In a similar way, a description of the character and functions of the place made in the testimonies comprised more than just a physical and material valuation of the space. In the judgement, the following summary of the account by Mustafa Al-Basri can be read:

> The space was used as a prayer room. It feels like a mosque to him. Prayers take place there five times a day, and, in addition, the space is

106 *In search of a racist subject*

used for Friday prayers. Attempts have been made to turn it into a mosque, but the authorities have not approved this.

(Mustafa Al-Basri's testimony, Judgement, district court, Case 8)

The mosque was presented here, despite the ordinariness of the physical space in which it is located—a simple flat in a block—as fulfilling a special function and having emotional significance to members of the local Muslim community. A similar account can be found in a letter signed by members of the Muslim community and included in the crime report filed, which conveys more than just a description of a crime scene:

> Mustafa came back and picked up the Koran that was lying outside, because the Koran, according to religious teachings, must not be placed in an unclean place or on the ground. ... It was particularly painful and insulting that the Koran, sacred to all Muslims, was thrown on the street. The arson in the mosque and this offence against the sacred scriptures are clear evidence that the incident is a case of vandalism and an open attack on the religion and feelings of Muslims. We still fear for our safety.
>
> (Crime report, Case 8)

These accounts reflect the accessible modes of defining the suffered injury. According to the testimonies of the Muslim witnesses, the material loss central to the legal logics of investigation and trial, here understood as vandalism, is just one of the aspects of the injury. In their accounts, they seem to express a particular affect that reflects the significance of the Koran as a sacred book and of the mosque as a place of worship, of the community's collective life, and a particular sign of the community's presence (Metcalf, 1996, p. 6). This suggests that to understand the interpretation of the meaning of the transgression and the kind of injury that the acts of throwing the Koran on the ground and putting the mosque on fire entailed for at least some members of the Muslim community, it is necessary to take into account the nature of this attachment and consider the possibility that the destroyed flat is an affective space (Verkaaik, 2012, pp. 162–163). In part, the Muslim witnesses' accounts are thus an attempt to go beyond not only the material but also the secular frames of the investigation and the trial.

In her essay on the Mohammed cartoons controversy, Saba Mahmood turns away from the understandings of the conflict as between the secular and the religious. Trying to understand the personal loss expressed by many Muslims, Mahmood proposes an understanding of moral injury as different from the Western definitions of blasphemy that were put forward during the controversy. She writes that 'for many Muslims, the offence the cartoons committed was not against a moral interdiction ..., but against a structure of affect, a habitus, that feels wounded' (Mahmood, 2009, p. 78). She continues by claiming that the judicial language and structural constraints of secular law in Western liberal nation-states limit the possibilities in which injury can be defined and rendered intelligible. I would like to argue that the Muslim witnesses in the Manby case encountered this type of constraint of the legal vocabulary offered by secular law, in which they had to define the harm they experienced. A particular concept of property, value, personal injury and reparation shaped the ways in which their loss was understood and treated by the police and the court.[1]

Mustafa Al-Basri's testimony in court reveals yet another story: that of the failed attempts to transform the space from a prayer room into a mosque. This attempt was rather nominal and did not involve any actual change as is the case when purpose-built mosques are constructed. The local authorities' resistance to support this symbolic act, whatever the reason, can be read as an act of unrecognition of the Muslim community in Manby. With this history, the prayer room represents a double invisibility. There is a physical invisibility through the prayer room's location in a semi-private space, a solution predominant in Sweden as well as in many other European countries, where most mosques are placed in basements, industrial buildings, warehouses, former shops or simply flats (Allievi, 2009, p. 18). There is also a symbolic invisibility through the resistance to transform the prayer room into a mosque. The story mediated by Mustafa Al-Basri is one of incapacity to gain visibility and, at least partially, to transfer Islam from semi-private to public space (Cesari, 2005, p. 1018).

During the police investigation and the trial, Mustafa Al-Basri and other mosque regulars emphasized that the mosque had been open that night, as it usually was: 'The doors of the mosque are kept unlocked so that anyone can come in at any time' (Mustafa Al-Basri's testimony, Judgement, district court). This emphasis had again to do with the description of the circumstances of the fire—the lack of traces of burglary—but it can also be understood as a statement about openness. Recent research into mosque architecture in Europe underscores the burden of representation that mosques are loaded with (Verkaaik, 2012, p. 163). These places are constantly confronted with voices that define them in terms of a particular Muslim identity. Cases of mosques being designed as literally transparent have been explained as a response to the discourse that frames Muslim religious spaces as a site of shady political practices and in particular as a breeding ground for terrorists (Verkaaik, 2012, p. 168). This kind of discourse was present in Europe in its most extreme form in the campaigns before the Swiss referendum on the ban of minarets, in which minarets were depicted on posters as missiles. But it could also be heard when conflicts emerged over the construction of mosques in Sweden (cf. Karlsson Minganti & Svanberg, 1995). In this context, the statement about the openness of the Manby mosque can be interpreted as a similar declaration of transparency.

One aspect present in these testimonies is that the arson is understood in a broader context. It becomes one event in a series of other events. The above-mentioned denial of granting the status of mosque to the worship

108 *In search of a racist subject*

room is one example. Other examples come expressed as past grievances enumerated by members of the Muslim community in their letter sent to the police:

> Before this happened, youngsters in Manby had openly offended our religion. They would throw bottles at our little children, scare them and make fun of them. When we went to the mosque, they would shout 'Allahu Akbar!' after us. Some young men had threatened our comrade—Ibrahim Hassani's—life by making a gesture of moving the hand across the throat. On the weekends, after 9pm and until the morning, drunk youngsters would make a mess with loud partying in Manby so that neither we nor our children could fall asleep.
>
> We perceive the arson of our mosque as an expression of racism, religious intolerance and incitement to ethnic hatred.
>
> We still live in fear for our safety.
>
> (Crime report, Case 8)

Narrated in this way, the mosque fire and the debasement of the sacred books are seen as another attack in a series of daily violence, harassment and threat. From this point of view, the prolonged effect of the event cannot be reduced only to the immediate damage, but is understood as a process of accumulation of often less serious events. This process of accumulation can only be fully apprehended from a longer time perspective. What happens, however, is that this kind of perspective is irrelevant according to the legal logics of the trial, that is of necessity concerned with concrete events that are being judged and, most importantly, with a concrete defendant who is being charged.[2] These logics entail a type of 'legal temporality [that] cannot admit, cannot include, cannot acknowledge timelessness' (Felman, 2002, p. 153). Shoshana Felman claims that the trial will always strive to delimit, close and totalise the event that is being judged, excluding from the picture all that is considered as not having any connection to this event.[3]

To sum up, in their accounts in court, members of the Muslim community attempted to convey an interpretation of the events of that night and to define the injury those produced. These accounts were framed by the language and the logics accessible in a judicial process. First of all, the testimonies were structured according to the ways in which injury can be claimed and proven in court. Here, one of the most important things was the legal understanding of value, property and damage, in which the material dimension of harm is the predominant one. In an attempt to expand this strict definition, members of the Muslim community brought attention to other dimensions of the injury caused by the arson. In their narratives, they conveyed a complex significance of the mosque not only as an affective space for prayer and for community life, but also as a symbol of the presence of the Muslim community in the village, defined through its invisibility in the public space and its openness. These accounts were to a large extent shaped by a resistance and in opposition to a particular imaginary of the mosque existing in Swedish, and more broadly Western, debates and disputes. This was evident both in the descriptions of the mosque as an open space and in the accounts of its marginalization and vulnerability.

Even when challenging these legal understandings of value and harm, the testimonies given by members of the Muslim community had to use a language that could be intelligible for the judiciary—only in this way could their claims be attended to. They could be read in the context of 'the political emergence of the question of the victim at the forefront of criminal jurisprudential debates' (Felman, 2002, p. 226) that have been translated into a growing significance of the role of victims in criminal processes globally and in Sweden (Asp, 2016, pp. 154–158). This development opened up for claims of vulnerability, but it also contributed to a kind of victimization narratives that needed to live up to and reproduce a specific idea of victim and injury.

But rather than reducing the accounts of witnesses from the Manby Muslim community during the investigation and the trial to the testimonies of suffering and victimization, one could read them as what Shoshana Felman calls an act of 'reclaiming legal subjecthood' (2002, p. 226).[4] Considering that the history of vulnerability and marginalization of the Muslim community in Manby was partly at least a result of the lack of recognition on the part of local authorities, an act of filing a complaint and of witnessing in court might be understood as resistance to marginalization and exclusion. In a way, the very form of one of the documents in which their testimony is given—the letter written to the police—enhances this aspect of their account. In contrast to most of the accounts in this case, the letter is archived among the police documents in its original form and not related in indirect speech. Rather than reading minutes produced by a police officer and summarizing the accounts of witnesses, we are dealing with a piece unique in the sense that it is formulated in the first person plural—*we*. The document could be read, following Felman's analysis, as an alternative indictment in which the crime is being defined from the vantage point of the Muslim community. What is, moreover, important is that the 'we' in the document constitutes a collective act, underscoring the impact of the event not on particular Muslims in Manby as individuals, but on the Muslim community there as a whole.

The innocence of a joke

As the introduction to the judgement informs, Sven Persson confessed to theft. He also admitted that he had caused the fire, but he pleaded that he had had no intent to commit arson or aggravated arson. In court, he said that he had been drinking with his friends and thus was intoxicated during the occurrence. He also added that 'he and his friends were walking about, not talking about anything in particular. The conversation had not at all

110   *In search of a racist subject*

been related to immigrants and he has nothing against them' (Sven Persson's testimony, Judgement, district court, Case 8). At the same time, Sven Persson admitted that he knew the flat was used by immigrants and he said that he went in there because he got curious. He wanted to look around. He took the books with him and then threw them away while wandering the village with his friends. 'They looked a bit in the books/booklets but did not talk so much about it' (Sven Persson's testimony, Judgement, district court, Case 8). Then he returned to the prayer room and lit a match. According to his explanation, he did so in order to get the attention of his friends who were standing outside. The friends did not react and he did not notice when the match fell; 'he never thought it could be dangerous' (Sven Persson's testimony, Judgement, district court, Case 8). It was only when he was back with his friends outside that he noticed the flames. This threw him into panic:

> He panicked and told his friends that he had started the fire. They all ran. He has no particular opinion about immigrants, but may find large numbers of people and high unemployment tiring. His mother ran a foster home and Muslims had lived with them. He has no negative thoughts about Muslims.
>
> (Sven Persson's testimony, Judgement, district court, Case 8)

In Sven Persson's account, the whole event unfolded as almost accidental: a result of a mixture of drunkenness, curiosity and an accident. There had been no plan and no explicit intent. Moreover, Sven Persson claimed that he had been unaware of the risk that the fire could cause. The acts were a banal incident that happened as if in the background of these youngsters' ordinary night of common drinking, idle chatter and aimless wandering. A dropped match utterly changed that innocent climate; a sudden panic and chaotic escape disrupted the ordinariness of the night. It was in this moment of panic that Sven Persson confessed that 'he had started the fire'. The confession was the key moment in the testimonies of Sven Persson's friends who were with him that night. One of Sven Persson's friends recalled the discovery of the fire in the following way:

> He saw that there was a fire in the room. He asked Persson what he had done, but got no reply. They panicked and they got scared and ran away. They stopped by a balcony and he and Edberg wondered why Persson had done it. The next morning, he asked Persson if he was stupid, and Persson replied 'I don't know'.
>
> (Judgement, district court, Case 8)

The testimonies suggest that the immediate realization of the seriousness of Sven Persson's act transformed the atmosphere of that night from carefree to weighty. That seemed to be the breaking point. However, already earlier that night, there had been some signs that they understood the significance of what was going on. Erik Andersson, another friend, recounted the night in the following way:

> Persson had gone off and came back with the books. ... They also talked about the books. He told Persson that it could be a problem for him if anyone saw that he had these books since they belonged to the Muslims.
>
> (Judgement, district court, Case 8)

The testimonies reveal that those who witnessed the events that night were aware that an acceptable and legal boundary had been transgressed. They also seemed to realize that the act of stealing books belonging to the Muslims could be understood as problematic because of the nature of these books and to whom they belonged. At the same time, however, both Sven Persson and his friends seemed to dismiss in court any serious motives behind Sven Persson's acts. Time after time they repeated:

> There were no racist jokes between them. Persson is not like that. He cannot remember, but it is possible that one of them made a Taliban *joke*. He thinks Persson took the books *for fun*. Persson is not a racist or anti-immigrant.
>
> (Testimonies, Judgement, district court, Case 8, my emphasis)

The main argument as to why the acts performed by Sven Persson that night were not racist was the assertion that Sven Persson was not 'like that', he was not racist. Tough, blatantly racist opinions were here denied and the only thing left was a petty 'Taliban joke'.

The framing of possible utterances about Muslims as jokes and of Sven Persson's acts in terms of a funny prank builds on a dichotomy between racism as a serious matter and the banality of humour. In his analysis of racist jokes, Michael Billig refers to a conventional justification used by those who joke when accused of being racists—'it's just a joke'—and he elaborates that a just-a-joke defence assumes a binary opposition between the seriousness of racism and the triviality of humour (2001, p. 269; cf. also Weaver, 2011, p. 8). In such a justification, humour is contemplated from a celebratory and positive stance, praising the human capacity for laughter and enjoyment, while racism is constructed as a serious and humourless matter underlying organized and ideologically motivated violence. Conceived in this way, racist humour is treated as innocent and placed in opposition to *real* expressions of racism. Moreover, humour is often seen as a matter of rebellion against the established order, the joke as a weapon against power (Billig, 2005, p. 210). Billig draws on Freud's theories of aggressive humour, according to which the pleasure of the joking person, who expresses prohibited contents in socially acceptable ways, is denied

112   *In search of a racist subject*

(Billig, 2001, p. 286). The just-a-joke defence is thus used to give meaning to acts of violence, by framing them as trivial and harmless. In this sense, the claim of the humorous character of Sven Persson's acts can fulfil exculpatory functions, as it is supposed to refute the charge of racism and thus to prove the banality of the incident. By defining an act as a joke, a fun thing to do, the inherent violence of the act is exonerated (Weaver, 2011, p. 2). Moreover, the source of the offence can, in this way, be relocated from the inherent rhetoric of humour to those at whom the joke is directed. Thereby the offence is perceived as stemming from an inclination to get offended and a lack of humour. Such 'offendability', as Sara Ahmed calls it, has been attached to some people more than to others. She suggests that it has been defined as a hallmark of Muslims, in particular in the aftermath of the Mohammed cartoons controversy and similar events (2011, p. 126), in which the humour was located within the scope of freedom of speech. Ahmed examines 'how "being hurt or offended" by racism becomes seen as the "problem" of Muslims who don't integrate, such that Islam becomes what offends "our freedom", what challenges our freedom' (2011, p. 126).

In Sven Persson's and his friends' testimonies, the just-a-joke defence seems, however, paradoxical and out of place considering that he actually confessed to having set fire to the mosque. Sven Persson did not just use jokes to imagine a transgression and to break perceived taboos; he actually performed violence. While the just-a-joke defence is usually used to construct a dichotomy between the polysemy and ambiguity of a joke on the one hand, and the blatancy and clear-cut nature of a serious racist act on the other, here this boundary is blurred. The act of violence was itself presented as a joke and its seriousness thereby obliterated.

Sven Persson's account seemed to be guided by the questions he was asked and by the investigation, in which from the beginning an assumption had been made that the arson was a hate crime. In this sense, his account of the events of that night, and perhaps even more deeply his account of himself, was shaped by the ways in which racist violence is imagined as a serious affair, stemming from certain explicit and articulated opinions and thoughts, preceded by a devised plan and executed with premeditation. I suggest that Persson's account of his state of mind, intent and motives might be seen as a counter-narrative to the dominant view of what a hate crime is. The focus in this account shifted from the acts themselves to the motives that underlay these acts and to the person who performed them. The strong emphasis was on demonstrating Persson's lack of negative opinions or thoughts about immigrants. Similarly, the reference to his mother having kept a foster home and to his experience of having lived with Muslims seems to reflect an idea that knowing Muslims, particularly through some kind of personal relationship, could be treated as evidence of closeness and sufficient proof of openness and tolerance.[5] Finally, according to his account, the events of that night emerged as trivial and almost accidental acts performed as a part of some youngsters' tomfoolery and meant to

In search of a racist subject   113

amuse friends. It was in this context that the meaning of the acts of stealing the Koran and other books, of throwing them around in the village and of setting the mosque on fire was constructed as an innocent joke.

Dispensing justice

The district court's main concern in the Manby case was to establish whether the fire had been started intentionally or was a result of negligence. Once the version presented by Sven Persson—who claimed that, by lighting a match, he tried to communicate with his friends—had been rejected as incompatible with the crime scene report, the district court proceeded to decide whether Sven Persson had had the intent not only to start the fire, but also whether he had intended 'the fire ... to pose a threat to another's life or health or of extensive damage of another's property, which is a necessary condition for an act to be classified as arson' (Judgement, district court, Case 8).

The district court did not find that such intent existed in Sven Persson's act, and the justification for this conclusion was as follows:

> Sven Persson *for some reason* decided to set fire to one of the curtains hanging there. ... However, *nothing has emerged in the case that would suggest that Sven Persson had the intent* to cause such a danger or that he realized there was a risk of such a danger and that he would have been indifferent to this risk. *The mere fact that Sven Persson and his friends may, at some point, have expressed that there were many immigrants in Manby or joked about the Taliban does not mean that Sven Persson aimed at causing such a danger.* Thus it is not shown that Persson had the intent to put another's life or health at risk, nor to extensively damage another's property, which is why the act shall not be classified as intentional arson.
>
> (Judgement, district court, Case 8, my emphasis)

On the basis of this argument, the district court downgraded the crime's classification from aggravated arson, which the prosecutor was charging Sven Persson with, to aggravated damage to property.

The procedure of assessing the evidence of the existence of intent is the one usually applied in Swedish courts. In cases that have to do with arson, this translates into the following definition of liability: 'To be responsible [for arson] the defendant must ... have had the intent to start the fire. Furthermore, the intent must also include that the fire creates a risk of extensive damage to another's property' (cf. NJA, 2009, p. 149). The district court in the Manby case did not discuss the issue of the intent in depth, and limited itself to stating that nothing in the trial suggested that Sven Persson had had the intent to cause a risk to somebody's life or health.[6] In this context, the remarks about immigrants and the Taliban jokes exchanged between the

114   *In search of a racist subject*

friends were mentioned, but no connection was made between these and Sven Persson's act of setting the mosque on fire.

In addition to establishing that Sven Persson lacked intent to cause a risk to somebody's life or health, the district court assessed that the probability of harm was low. The potential risk of harm caused by the act was analysed based on testimonies given by fire experts. The district court's conclusion was that the risk of harm caused by fire or smoke was small, 'as long as the doors of the flats were not opened' (Judgement, district court, Case 8). The act was thereby defined as harmless and its gravity was played down.

In contrast to this, the prosecutor claimed that the crime should be treated as particularly serious and thereby fall under the provision on aggravated arson, since the space was of special cultural value. In response to this, the district court argued:

> It can be noted here that the space has been used as a prayer room and that it has had special significance to the Muslim community in Manby. *It has not, however, been established that the space has any special significance in the sense that it is of cultural interest outside the Muslim community,* which is why this circumstance does not affect the crime classification.
>
> (Judgement, district court, Case 8, my emphasis)

The ways in which the district court reconstructed the events, defined the crime and established the degree of responsibility of the defendant arguably contributed to the interpretation of the acts as trivial. This was done by downgrading the crime from arson to property damage, by estimating as low the possible risk to the life or health of those who were in the building, and by denying the cultural value of the Manby mosque. But the court did even more: by recognizing the significance of the mosque for the Muslim minority but not outside of it, and by not applying the provision of aggravated arson, the court's decision actually reinforced the marginalization and exclusion of the Manby Muslim community. Thereby not only was their access to justice restricted, but also their status as a part of Swedish society put into question.

The district court sentenced Sven Persson to probation and community service. The prosecutor lodged an appeal against the sentence. The court of appeal changed the sentence, by reclassifying the crime as arson and sentencing Sven Persson to prison. Another reading of the testimonies given by the fire experts was made and the conclusion drawn was that the prayer room would have burnt out completely had it not been for the intervention of the fire brigade. Already the smoke that had spread in the stairwell had put others' life and health in concrete danger, the court of appeal affirmed. Moreover, the court of appeal took up the issue of Sven Persson's intent to cause the risk of endangering others' lives. It established that in this case direct intent was not required. It was instead sufficient that the defendant knew that such a risk existed when he started the fire. The court of appeal referred to an earlier decision of the Supreme Court, which established that in cases of arson, in which people's lives are at risk, there is no possibility to judge the crime as minor. Thus, following the case law, Sven Persson had to be sentenced to prison.

The decision of the court of appeal offered a new interpretation of the act, returning to it its gravity and meting out justice accordingly. The penalty was imposed according to this interpretation of the act. However, the district court's evaluation of the lack of cultural value of the place exposed to the fire was not changed—it remained unrecognized. In this regard, the courts in both instances performed, albeit to different degrees, a kind of exclusionary practice against the Manby Muslim community in their decisions.

When racism becomes invisible

While both court instances were concerned with the issue of intent, neither touched upon the possible motives of the crime in the judgement, nor did the prosecutor ask for the application of the penalty enhancement provision. Nevertheless, the issue surfaced in the case. As mentioned, when deciding whether it was proven that Sven Persson had the intent to put the life or health of those who lived in the building at risk, the district court discussed the remarks on the arrival of more immigrants to the village and the Taliban joke made by the youngster earlier that night. These were, however, dismissed as possible proof of intent. Similarly, the ambivalence expressed in Sven Persson's statement that he 'finds large numbers of people and high unemployment tiring' (Judgement, district court, Case 8), linking immigrants with overpopulation and unemployment in one utterance, was not commented on in judgement.[7] The court did not even consider whether a racist motive was plausible, despite the fact that this was the interpretation of the Muslim community in Manby and the interpretation in relation to which the defendant and his friends narrated their accounts of that night. Why did the prosecutor not refer to the penalty enhancement provision? Why did the court not take it into consideration when deciding on the penalty? Why was the possible racist nature of the crime not addressed in the judgement? And, more generally, what would be required for an act to be considered racist by a Swedish court?

Since these questions are not openly addressed in either of the two instances, the answers must be found in the ways that the courts built their rationale when establishing responsibility for the acts and when constructing a subject that bears this responsibility. The first point that can be made is that the courts' main focus in the entire investigation was on Sven Persson's state of mind when performing the act. It was his intent that mattered as well as his understanding of what he was doing and what his act might have resulted in. In this sense, the courts approached the defendant as a rational subject in control of his actions and cognizant of the significance thereof. If

116   *In search of a racist subject*

the crimes in dispute were to be considered a manifestation of racism or religious intolerance, as the Muslim community in Manby claimed, this, according to the penalty enhancement provision, would have to be identified in a particular *motive* that guided Sven Persson. As a consequence, the courts, rather than investigating the racist *nature* of the acts, were compelled to identify motives and intent of a racist *subject*.

Judith Butler, drawing on Nietzsche and his investigation into the genealogy of morals, writes that certain forms of morality require that a subject be installed to which the responsibility for the injury may be assigned. The subject thereby emerges as 'the prior and causal origin of a painful effect that is recast as an injury' since such a moral framework 'seeks to isolate the "cause" of [painful] effects in a singular and intentional agent' (1997, pp. 45–46). In the Manby case, this kind of morality seems to be at work. Thus, in order for the court to recognize the harm done to the Muslim community that would be defined not merely as financial loss and the exposure to a risk, but also as an injury provoked by racism, a particular kind of accountable racist subject had to be identified.

To examine what kind of subject can be attributed responsibility for a racist act in a Swedish court, I will look at a case of another mosque arson that happened in Holmstad several years earlier. In that case, the defendants openly admitted that they had performed the act in order for 'politicians to understand that there are too many immigrants in Sweden' (Judgement, Case 9). One of them was a member of an openly racist organization and another confessed that he sympathized with this organization. Moreover, during the trial, they offered an interpretation of their action that could hardly be ignored by the court. On the night of the fire, they 'were talking about there being too many immigrants in Sweden and that one should do as in Germany, where one had burned down refugee centres' (Judgement, Case 9). They planned what to do and chose their target. They decided that 'it would be a shame to burn down a refugee centre where there could be people' (Judgement, Case 9). They considered a cultural centre, but finally chose a mosque 'because it would attract more attention' (Judgement, Case 9). According to their testimonies, the event of that night was carefully planned and rationally weighed: they wanted to get their political message out, at the same time as they did not wish to cause harm to people. They were strategic and open in their plan and the performed act was not only explicitly premeditated and thought through, it was also designed as a political message.

This political act, performed by ideologically articulated subjects, was treated by the court as 'a crime with xenophobic overtones' (Judgement, Case 9). The recognition by the court of the racist nature of the crime influenced the severity of the penalty. The court saw in it 'strong reasons to react forcefully' (Judgement, Case 9). One additional circumstance that bore influence on how the case was adjudicated was that it 'caused indignation in Sweden and abroad' (Judgement, Case 9). Thus, public pressure and shame

In search of a racist subject 117

about racism seem to have been an additional driving force for the judiciary in the process of dispensing justice. The court was clear about its interpretation of the act and weighing of the different dimensions of the harm done:

> The act has meant an attack on a place where Muslims exercise their religion and where they also gather for different activities. This also means it is an attack on the freedom of religion established in the Swedish Constitution. It has also caused great cultural and economic damage. The act has thus affected property of particular importance. The arson shall therefore be classified as aggravated arson.
>
> (Judgement, Case 9)

The court's unequivocal recognition of the harm, its interpretation of the act as bearing xenophobic signs and targeting the fundamental right to freedom of religion, and the severe sentence backed-up rhetorically, all contributed to the impression that it was the *racist nature* of the act as such that was recognized, judged and condemned in the trial. It is this focus on the meaning of the act as racist that makes this case different from the Manby case. While the court in the Holmstad case highlighted the racism in the act, the court in the Manby case made this possible dimension of the act invisible and opaque. The court seemed to have no problem in reading acts as racist in the Halmstad case, where those performing them were explicit about their motives and cognizant of the meanings of their actions. These were self-reflecting and ideologically declared subjects. In the Manby case, on the other hand, the defendant spoke equivocally about his motives. He claimed that he was unaware of the risks involved in his acts. Sven Persson emerged from the judgement as a young man acting in a state of drunkenness, in search of fun and trying to impress his friends. He clearly denied any negative opinions about Muslims or immigrants, thereby presenting himself as a non-racist. Nor were any other objective circumstances, such as membership of an extreme-right party or organization, brought to court to prove that racist motives might have pushed him to set fire to the mosque. If the court was looking for an ideologically declared supporter of hatred against people of different religion or ethnicity, they certainly did not find it in the case of Sven Persson.

It might be significant that these two cases are more than a decade apart. In the early 1990s, the time that in Chapter 4 I have referred to as a period of crisis, racism was more often flagrant. This did not necessarily manifest itself in the degree of violence of the events, but instead in the way these events were talked about and understood. This was apparent in the Holmstad case, in which the language was used of an openly hostile ideology expressed with an almost naïve sincerity. The events in the Holmstad case were treated as a serious political message, both by those who performed them and by the judiciary. In the late 2000s, similar acts were performed with ambiguity and almost light-heartedness and narrated in a subtle and

118 *In search of a racist subject*

coded language of jokes and trifling remarks that are only decipherable if certain anti-immigrant and anti-Muslim discourse is taken into consideration.

Conclusions: unintelligible acts and unrecognized harm

In this chapter, I have analysed a case of a mosque fire in order to explore the Swedish judiciary's ways of dealing with racism. I have argued that the court's interpretation of the acts in dispute, in which the possibility of the racist motive is not taken into consideration, has to do with the ways in which the court conceives of racism. When I contrasted the Manby case with the similar case of the Holmstad mosque fire, it became evident that courts, in order to be able to approach an act as bearing the hallmarks of racism, look not so much for a specific kind of event as for a particular kind of motive and a subject from which such a motive originates. Such a racist subject, constructed as rational, independent and ideologically self-conscious, becomes the primary site of a racist act.[8]

By locating the source of a racist nature of an act in a racist subject performing it, courts seem to rely on an idea of identity as fixed, one-dimensional and stable. In his *Short Introduction to Racism*, Ali Rattansi suggests that in adjudicating the racist nature of statements and behaviours, emphasis is often placed on a particular racist identity. Racist identity is presented as sharply opposed to non-racist identity and both are essentialized and fixed to individuals. Influenced by the postmodern debates on identity, Rattansi proposes that we should instead think about racist identities as ambivalent and contradictory (2007, pp. 119–123). In a similar tone, but in another context, Sara Ahmed shows how the focus on the figure of 'the racist' makes it difficult to address racism. She writes:

> The very appearance of this figure is what allows a reduction of racism to an individual person who suffers from a false set of beliefs. The figure can do a great deal of work: it is relatively easy for someone to respond to a critique of racism by insisting or even showing they are not that figure.
>
> (2012, p. 150)

My argument is that this is what happened in the Manby case. Responsibility for a racist act was denied by the refutation of the presence of the figure of a racist, and the court did not consider the racist nature of the act because of its inability to imagine a racist act as originating from an inconsistent and ambivalent subject.

When the court relied on and thereby legitimated one interpretation of the event in dispute—locating the source of the meaning in the intent and in the motives of the person performing the act—this was done at the expense of other readings of the same event. As a result, other interpretations, most importantly those put forward by the Muslims testifying in

In search of a racist subject   119

court, were ignored. The court's reading was, however, also done through abstracting the act from the discourses that inform the ways in which the act becomes meaningful. In this way, the act was neither interpreted in its communicative context nor as a meaningful practice in a given social formation and historical moment. The communicative aspects of racism were thereby ignored, making the act unintelligible.[9] Thus, the act was never examined as an aggression against the property and place of piety of a particular minority. It was never considered whether this act had drawn on or re-established a particular imaginary of the Muslim minority and how it became entangled in a chain of practices and discourses that construe mosques as attackable.

Notes

1 As discussed in Chapter 4, in Sweden, the laws against racism include religion as one of the grounds for special protection. In this way, and unlike the system in the US and in the international legal instruments against racial discrimination, some consideration is given to religion in this type of legislation. Still, Saba Mahmood's argument applies to the general framework in which the value, injury and reparation are defined and measured in law in Sweden.
2 A tension between a perspective of criminal law that focuses on singular events and a perspective from which these events are understood and experienced as a part of a larger context has been one of the questions discussed in the debates on hate crime in the US and the UK (see, for instance, Bowling, 1993). The main issue here was how racist violence should be defined and measured and where the source of a specific kind of harm entailed by these kinds of crimes should be located. These debates have proposed an understanding of what they call racist victimization originating from a process of a continuous exposition to violence, harassment and threat rather than from one concrete event (Chakraborti & Garland, 2015, p. 5).
3 See Andersson (2016) as to how in Sweden this kind of focus of the criminal law has been challenged in legislation concerning domestic violence and what kind of obstacles this meets.
4 In her analysis of the Eichmann trial, Shoshana Felman argues for an understanding of this trial as a historical and a unique one with respect to victims and as having revolutionized the role of victim in a criminal proceeding. For Felman—in contrast with the later victims' rights movement—the Eichmann trial was not so much about victims' rights as it was about the victims' authority. In this regard, Felman writes:

> In my view, the victims/witnesses are not simply expressing their suffering: they are *reclaiming legal subjecthood* and autobiographical personhood. They *change within the trial* from being merely victims to something else. *They are carrying out a prosecution* (a "J'accuse" articulated through a legal process). Through this recovery of speech and this recovery of history, they reinvent an innovative logos that is *no longer simply victims' logos* but constitutes a new kind of legal language.
> (2002, pp. 226–227, original emphasis)

5 This resonates with an understanding of racism defined as xenophobia—a fear of the unknown, different and distant—something that is possible to remedy by enlightenment, education and community life. According to this approach, reduced segregation and increased interaction between groups contribute to the reduction of

120 *In search of a racist subject*

prejudice and discrimination (Allport, 1954). The definition is implicit in several surveys and studies done in Sweden of Islamophobia and other forms of racism in which the respondents' intolerance was correlated with lack of knowledge of Islam and contacts with Muslims (cf. Hvitfelt, 1991; Integrationsverket, 2006a, 2006b; Ring & Morgentau, 2004). It has been also influential in qualitative studies (Andersson, Natland & Berg, 2001) that suggested that a kind of 'lived tolerance'—tolerance that is a product of a common everyday life—created a concept of a mediated Orientalism resulting from lived renegotiation of the Orientalist representations of Muslims.

6 The question of intent is crucial in criminal cases in Sweden, as with other legal systems. Intentionality (*mens rea*) is a necessary condition for acts to be considered crimes. There is a scale of criminal intent that begins with direct intent, malice, in cases where it can be proven that a person's aim was to commit a given crime. Such intent is easiest to prove in premeditated crimes. However, Swedish case law also recognizes other types of intent. The case law regarding more indirect types of intent has changed recently. Some terms have been abandoned, such as indirect intent (*indirekt uppsåt*) or possible intent (*eventuellt uppsåt*), while others have been introduced, such as insight intent (*insikts uppsåt*), which refers to situations in which a person is aware of the risks his or her actions entail. Most importantly, the term 'intent of indifference' (*likgiltighets uppsåt*) has been introduced to describe acts in which the perpetrator not only is aware of or realizes that there is a risk of an effect of his or her action, but also remains indifferent to this risk (NJA, 2004, p. 176). Having to do with the state of mind of the person performing the given act, the issue of intent is often difficult to prove in court (cf. Asp, 2004/05; Rung, 2006/07).

7 This statement can be read in the context of the representation of immigrants that has spread from the extreme-right into mainstream discourse in Sweden, and more generally in Europe, which blames immigrants for taking an undeserved place in the nation or welfare state and, by taking the jobs that belong to natives, contributing to unemployment (cf. Gardell, 2011; Malm, 2009).

8 This insight is also inspired by such important contributions as Hannah Arendt's analysis of the Eichmann trial in which she identified the clash between the modern legal system's fundamental assumption—that intent to do wrong is a necessary condition for a crime to be committed—and the huge difficulties in establishing and proving particular motives in the case against Eichmann. Her concept—*the banality of evil*—is aimed at capturing this unresolved tension:

> When I speak of the banality of evil, I do so only on the strictly factual level, pointing to a phenomenon which stared one in the face at the trial. Eichmann was not Iago and not Macbeth, and nothing would have been further from his mind than to determine with Richard III 'to prove a villain.' Except for an extraordinary diligence in looking out for his personal advancement, he had no motives at all. And this in itself was in no way criminal. ... He *merely*, to put the matter colloquially, *never realized what he was doing*. It was precisely this lack of imagination which enabled him to sit for months on end facing a German Jew who was conducting the police interrogation, pouring out his heart to the man and explaining again and again how it was that he reached only the rank of lieutenant colonel in the S.S. and that it had not been his fault that he was not promoted. ... And if this is 'banal' or even funny, if with the best will in the world one cannot extract any diabolical or demonic profundity from Eichmann, that is still far from calling it commonplace.
>
> (2006, pp. 287–288, original emphasis)

9 I am here inspired by Kathleen Blee's discussion of theoretical and legal approaches to racial violence in the United States (2005). Blee describes racist

In search of a racist subject 121

violence in terms of communicative events that send a message both to the targeted community and to other audiences, a message that may communicate vulnerability or empowerment (Blee, 2005, p. 106). She and others stress that the ways in which such messages are interpreted are not completely fixed and thus they are not always effective as tools of spreading fear (Ahmed, 2004, p. 60; Blee, 2007, p. 264). Drawing on her work on women involved in the Ku Klux Klan and white supremacist skinheads, Blee proposes a reconceptualization of racist violence from what she identifies in the literature as an overemphasis on perpetrators' intentions and motives, towards an understanding of racial violence as an interactional and communicative act addressing certain audiences (2005). Blee discusses how her interviewees, the women active in the Klan, could become involved in events such as cross-burnings in the Southern United States in the 1920s for several different reasons not necessarily directly related to some explicit racist ideology. She shows how many treated these events as a 'carnival of conviviality, a chance to enjoy the company of the community' (2005, p. 609). In other words, the interviewed women's motivations to join the Klan and to participate in violent events could be complex and diverse. Yet, Blee claims that to deny—based only on this difficulty in capturing racist motives—the racist nature of cross-burnings would be to miss the message of racial empowerment and racial vulnerability that these events were communicating and thereby to be unable to understand their racist impact on the victims and audiences (2005, p. 610). Blee claims that the reliance on the notion of intent and motive and the focus on a particular figure of the perpetrator, both of which are derived from criminal law where motivation is the main explanatory narrative, entail some analytical problems that make it difficult to understand how racial violence works (2005, p. 601).

Bibliography

Ahmed, S. (2004). *The Cultural Politics of Emotion*. Edinburgh: Edinburgh University Press.

Ahmed, S. (2011). 'Problematic Proximities. Or Why Critiques of Gay Imperialism Matter.' *Feminist Legal Studies, 19*(2), 119–132.

Ahmed, S. (2012). *On Being Included: Racism and Diversity in Institutional Life*. Durham, NC: Duke University Press.

Allievi, S. (2009). *Conflicts over Mosques in Europe. Policy Issues and Trends*. London: Network of European Foundations' Initiative on Religion and Democracy in Europe and Alliance Publishing Trust.

Allport, G. (1954). *The Nature of Prejudice*. Cambridge, MA: Addison-Wesley.

Andersson, Å., Natland, S. & Berg, M. (2001). *Där hemma, här borta: möten med Orienten i Sverige och Norge*. Stockholm: Carlsson.

Andersson, M. (2016). *Grov fridskränkning och grov kvinnofridskränkning: fridskränkningsbrotten som rättslig konstruktion*. Uppsala: Iustus.

Arendt, H. (2006). *Eichmann in Jerusalem: A Report on the Banality of Evil*. New York: Penguin Books.

Asp, P. (2004/05). 'Uppsåtets nedre gräns—en efterlängtad sequel.' *Juridisk tidskrift, 2*, 385–396.

Asp, P. (2016). 'Straffrätten—igår, i dag ochimorgon.' *Svensk Juristtidning*, pp. 138–161.

Billig, M. (2001). 'Humour and Hatred: The Racist Jokes of the Ku Klux Klan.' *Discourse and Society, 12*(3), 267–289.

122   *In search of a racist subject*

Billig, M. (2005). *Laughter and Ridicule: Towards a Social Critique of Humour.* London: Sage.

Blee, K. (2005). 'Racial Violence in the United States.' *Ethnic and Racial Studies, 28* (4), 599–619.

Blee, K. M. (2007). 'The Microdynamics of Hate Violence: Interpretive Analysis and Implications for Responses.' *American Behavioral Scientist, 51*(2), 258–270.

Bowling, B. (1993). 'Racial Harassment and the Process of Victimization—Conceptual and Methodological Implications for the Local Crime Survey.' *British Journal of Criminology, 33*(2), 231–250.

Butler, J. (1997). *Excitable Speech: A Politics of the Performative.* New York; London: Routledge.

Butler, J. (2005). *Giving an Account of Oneself.* New York: Fordham University Press.

Cesari, J. (2005). 'Mosque Conflicts in European Cities: Introduction.' *Journal of Ethnic and Migration Studies, 31*(6), 1015–1024.

Chakraborti, N. & Garland, J. (2015). *Hate Crime: Impact, Causes & Responses.* Los Angeles, CA: Sage.

Felman, S. (2002). *The Juridical Unconscious: Trials and Traumas in the Twentieth Century.* Cambridge, MA: Harvard University Press.

Gardell, M. (2011). *Islamofobi.* Stockholm: Leopard.

Hvitfelt, H. (1991). 'Svenska attityder till Islam.' In S. Holmberg & L. Weibull (Eds.), *Politiska opinioner: SOM-undersökningen 1990.* Göteborg: Statsvetenskapliga institutionen, Göteborgs Universitet: Institutionen för journalistik och masskommunikation.

Integrationsverket. (2006a). *Integrationsbarometer 2005: en rapport om allmänhetens attityder, erfarenheter och kunskaper inom områdena integration, mångfald och diskriminering.* Norrköping: Integrationsverket.

Integrationsverket. (2006b). *Rasism och främlingsfientlighet i Sverige: antisemitism och islamofobi 2005.* Norrköping: Integrationsverket.

Karlsson Minganti, P. & Svanberg, I. (1995). *Moskéer i Sverige: en religionsetnologisk studie av intolerans och administrativ vanmakt.* Uppsala: Svenska Kyrkans Forskningsråd.

Mahmood, S. (2009). 'Religious Reason and Secular Affect: An Incommensurable Divide?' In T. Asad (Ed.), *Is Critique Secular?—Blasphemy, Injury & Free Speech.* Berkeley, CA: University of California Press, pp. 64–100.

Malm, A. (2009). *Hatet mot muslimer.* Stockholm: Atlas.

Metcalf, B. (1996). *Making Muslim Space in North America and Europe.* Berkeley, CA: University of California Press.

NJA. (2004). p. 176.

NJA. (2009). p. 149.

Rattansi, A. (2007). *Racism: A Very Short Introduction.* Oxford; New York: Oxford University Press.

Ring, J. & Morgentau, S. (2004). *Intolerans: antisemitiska, homofobiska, islamofobiska och invandrarfientliga tendenser bland unga.* Stockholm: Brottsförebyggande rådet.

Rung, A. (2006/07). 'Likgiltighetsuppsåt—En ny form av uppsåtets nedre gräns?' *Juridisk Tidskrift, 1,* 254–274.

Verkaaik, O. (2012). 'Designing the "Anti-Mosque": Identity, Religion and Affect in Contemporary European Mosque Design.' *Social Anthropology, 20*(2), 161–176.

Weaver, S. (2011). *The Rhetoric of Racist Humour: US, UK and Global Race Joking.* Farnham: Ashgate.

7 Hate speech, linguistic injury and language in court

The telephone rang. Abdul Hassan, who worked in the shop, answered and heard: 'Fucking Arab! Muslim idiot! Wife-beater who imported your wife!' Abdul Hassan recognized the voice of Axel Berg, the ex-husband of one of his employees, who had been calling the shop several times a day for some weeks now. He asked Axel Berg not to offend his family and warned that he would call the police. Axel Berg hung up. A few minutes later Abdul Hassan received a text message on his mobile phone saying: 'An extremely stupid move to threaten me you little Arab fag'.

Insulting language features frequently in cases collected in Brå's hate-crime reports. Often it is the very language, its nature and possible meanings, which is the subject of dispute in court. In the above case, Axel Berg was charged with unlawful threat, molestation and insult towards his ex-wife and several other persons. The insults directed towards Abdul Hassan constituted one of the points of the indictment. The district court adjudicating the case decided that:

> Although there were accusations from both sides and although there was only short mention of Abdul Hassan's race and religion, the acts must be regarded as molestation and insultand the crimes shall have increased penal value.
>
> (Judgement, district court, Case 10)

The decision was appealed and the court of appeal changed the sentence, arguing that:

> considering that nothing has shown that Axel Berg's motive with the acts was to offend Abdul Hassan because of race, or the like, there is no reason to apply the aforementioned penalty enhancement provision.
>
> (Judgement, court of appeal, Case 10)

The court based its decision partly on the fact that the penalty enhancement provision requires that one of the motives for the crime is to aggrieve a person by reason of race, religion or the like. However, Axel Berg stated

124 *Hate speech, linguistic injury and language in court*

during the trial that he did not hold any xenophobic views nor did he sympathize with xenophobic groups. The decision of the court of appeal was not unanimous. One of the judges in the court of appeal expressed a dissenting opinion in which he stated:

> Axel Berg insulted Abdul Hassan with several offensive names. Some of these names—such as Muslim bastard, fucking Arab and Arab fag—must, in my opinion, have been chosen to offend Abdul Hassan because of his ethnic origin or religion. In any case, *the choice of these names shows that the motive for the crime was to offend* Abdul Hassan in the manner mentioned.
>
> (Judgement, court of appeal, dissenting opinion, Case 10, my emphasis)

The divergence, not only between different instances but also within the court of appeal, suggests that the case was difficult to decide. While the main argument in this case was about how to define a particular motive, the presence of the insulting language played a central role for some judges, those in the district court and the dissenting judge in the court of appeal, in pinpointing the site of racism in the discussed act.

In this chapter, I will analyse the role of language in cases involving anti-Muslim violence, focusing on assaults that produce what Judith Butler calls 'linguistic injury' (1997, p. 4). Hate speech and racist slander have become especially susceptible to being addressed by recourse to the law (for the debate in the United States, see Butler, 1997; MacKinnon, 1994; Matsuda, Lawrence III, Delgado & Williams Crenshaw, 1993; for the development of the European Court of Human Rights case law concerning hate speech, see Weber, 2009) and thus are often treated in court as *the* site of racism. Moreover, slander often helps to identify the racist nature of the physical violence or other types of acts that it accompanies. Part of this development has been that communicative practices not necessarily involving words have often been treated by courts as speech. This has happened in cases involving bearing certain symbols or other behaviours that have a symbolic significance (Lööw, 2000, p. 117).[1]

This development has not been unique to Sweden. Similarly, in the United States, practices such as cross-burnings have been approached in court as potentially exceeding the freedom of speech. Injurious utterances have been used in court as a model for defining injurious behaviour, leading to a certain conflation of speech and conduct (Butler, 1997, p. 40). In the Swedish legal system, this focus on acts involving a scene of utterance has been present from the very inception of the first law against racism—the act on agitation against a national or ethnic group—which I described in Chapter 4. The act on agitation against a national or ethnic group has been interpreted as a restriction of freedom of speech, indispensable for certain norms and values to be respected in a democratic society. Moreover, the law on insult has recently been interpreted to cover racist slander (cf. NJA, 1989,

Hate speech, linguistic injury and language in court 125

p. 374). In this chapter, I will analyse a case in which offensive language was adjudicated.

One December morning, a local politician from a mainstream party, Fatima Ameen, checked her work mailbox and discovered several emails sent from the same email address. The first email, entitled 'The terrorist visit', read:

> Hi!
>
> What are you, your party's 'billboard import' and friend of a terrorist organization, doing now, are you still trying to bring your friends from Hamas here?
> What a nice disservice you are doing to your party, I hope they remember your terrorist contacts in the elections this autumn.
>
> Lars (Police file, Case 11)

The second email had no title and just stated: 'Damn, you're ugly!' The third email was entitled: 'On Muslim niggers' and repeated: 'Damn, you're ugly!!!!! Shouldn't you be motioning about banana cultivations and not about Hamas! Lars'. The fourth email, this time with the title 'Jungle!', read: 'Take away your awful jungle picture from the municipality's website!!!! Lars'. Fatima Ameen opened the fifth email, in which, in a large font, was written: 'Go home to Africa, fast as hell, billboard n_gg_r!' The last email read: 'Crazy darky bastard, terrorist lover!' Fatima Ameen contacted the police the same day and filed a report. She attached the received emails and gave the address from which the emails had been sent. The address served the police to identify the suspect, a retired teacher, Lars Nilsson, and made it possible for the prosecutor to issue an indictment. The case was adjudicated by a district court and later by a court of appeal. The final decision was furthermore appealed by the defendant to the Supreme Court. No review permit was granted by the Supreme Court, however.

This chapter will explore the court's philosophy of language in general and in particular its ways of defining and understanding injurious, racist language. I will analyse the court's judgements in the case against Lars Nilsson, in an endeavour to answer the following questions: How is the scene of utterance delimitated and treated during the trial? How are the meanings of the utterance in dispute defined, interpreted and fixed by the court? Where is the source of injurious speech located? What kind of language doctrine does the court apply in this case? And how does it itself use the language in the judgement? The aim of the chapter will thus be to examine the court's understanding of the use of abusive language, and in particular of linguistic injury. However, the reading of the court's approach to language will not be limited to an analysis of the content of the case, but will also include an examination of the court's use of language. I will analyse the judgements of the courts of the two instances as speech acts, in which a particular rhetorical work is done. Here, my point of departure is an idea that the court

126 *Hate speech, linguistic injury and language in court*

documents present yet another opportunity and, at the same time, a challenge: the judgements often seem to be saying things in different ways and on different levels. There is the message of the judgement, expressed in the verdict and measured off in the penalty. This is the act of justice being performed *through* the words in judgement. The justice is performed by means of the categorical words of the verdict: guilty or not guilty. But judgements also communicate something through the rhetoric, through the selection of words, through the tone of the document. In this respect, the language of the court documents reveals the logics and the workings of justice, thereby becoming an important focal point for my analysis. I will deconstruct how the documents are structured and composed and will explore how their structure, composition and rhetoric are related to the ways in which justice is performed. In this sense, in order to understand how justice is being done, I will need to look at how meanings were created at the intersection between the judgements' form and content. Thus, my analysis will, on the one hand, address the explicit language doctrine endorsed in the judgements and its consequences for the possibility to remedy the linguistic injury embedded in racist speech. On the other hand, I will examine the rhetorical status and work of the decisions, in order to attend to the courts' use of language as a performative tool when dispensing justice.[2]

Staging the conflict

The trial in the district court, as related in the judgement, opened with the claims presented by the parties involved in the case. The public prosecutor charged Lars Nilsson with insult and in addition invoked the penalty enhancement provision, claiming that one of the motives for the crime had been to aggrieve the injured party by reason of her race, colour, national or ethnic origin and religious belief. The six emails were presented as evidence. Lars Nilsson, with whose name the emails had been signed and from whose address they had been sent, admitted that the emails had been sent from his computer and he owned up to writing the first one. He denied, however, authorship of the remaining emails and claimed that the one he had composed did not contain any offensive invective or accusations. Fatima Ameen, on the other hand, supported the prosecutor, but demanded that the act be classified as aggravated insult and requested that Lars Nilsson be obliged to pay her damages (Judgement, district court).

The district court, after having presented the positions of the parties, turned its attention to establishing, first of all, whether the acts in dispute had been committed by Lars Nilsson, and second, if they constituted the crime as the prosecutor maintained. In his testimony, Lars Nilsson claimed that, when the emails had been sent from his mailbox, he had had several guests at his home. They had been drinking and talking. He also suggested that one of his guests had written and sent the remaining emails from his computer, which was on in another room the entire time. He did not,

Hate speech, linguistic injury and language in court 127

however, give any names of his guests on that day, nor was he willing to offer any details as to how a guest could have managed to send emails to the same addressee as Lars Nilsson had earlier; moreover, he did not give details about the other circumstances surrounding the sending of the emails when the court requested him to do so. Due to this lack of concrete information, the court found his account diffuse and unclear and decided to approve the version presented by the prosecutor, namely, that Lars Nilsson authored all six emails (Judgement, district court, Case 11). Once the question of authorship had been decided, the court began to approach the second question, of whether the emails contained expressions that fulfilled the necessary conditions to be classified as punishable insult. This question was the core of the deliberations as presented in the judgement.

The first thing that the court established was that Fatima Ameen was a representative of the local authority. It was also affirmed that both her photograph and email address appeared on the municipal website, which, according to the court, should be seen as an invitation for the public to contact her. The court continued:

> The fact that the representatives of the municipality are presented in this way cannot be perceived in any other way than that they want—or at least must be prepared for—contact with the public, both from sympathizers and opponents. In a democratic society, every citizen must have the right to freely contact a representative of the municipality to give both positive and negative criticism of his or her party's positions in individual questions or propose measures.
>
> (Judgement, district court, Case 11, my emphasis)

Through this introduction, the court framed the case in a particular way. The dispute was defined as a conflict between, on the one hand, a representative of authority—not a private individual hurt by the offensive utterances, but as a person of power, representing the state—and, on the other hand, a representative of the public—a citizen, whose democratic rights and freedoms were at stake. In this way, the court indirectly positioned itself in relation to the claim made by the prosecutor. The reference to the penalty enhancement provision by the prosecutor was an attempt to frame the case as racist speech. By putting the claim at the centre that the insult involved this particular kind of harm, the prosecutor presented the case as one in which a member of a minority was offended not by accidental or casual slander, but by an insult that, by referring to her skin colour, ethnic origin and religion, threatened not only one particular individual but also the norms and values of equality and freedom from racial discrimination rooted in the Swedish constitution and protected by Swedish law. The court, however, instead repositioned the power relations in the case, as a result of which the defendant emerged as the weak party whose rights and freedoms might have been curtailed by the power of the state. In this move, the issue

128 *Hate speech, linguistic injury and language in court*

in dispute was also redefined. The focus shifted from the question of protection from racism to the question of freedom of speech. Also, rather than understanding the dispute as a tension between two rights, both recognized in a democratic society, the court staged the conflict as being about the citizen's right to criticize a representative of the state. Simultaneously, the court placed itself, and its own authority, as external to the conflict, thus establishing itself as an objective and autonomous guard of freedom of expression. In this way, the court presented itself as detached from the oppressive functions of the state apparatus, obliterating the mechanisms of power and symbolic violence of the trial.

Thereafter, the district court mentioned the scarcity of case law involving insult in Sweden. It defined this type of crime as minor and its prosecution as depending on the injured party's readiness to seek legal redress:

> The fact that only a few cases concerning insult have been judged by the Supreme Court is much because insult is basically a crime where few are prosecuted by the injured party alone. If an individual feels offended by what someone else has said to him or her and decides to privately prosecute, it easily leads to the legal action being designed in such a way that the case, if it reaches the Supreme Court, is considered to have *little value as a precedent* and as a consequence review permit is refused. *Other people who feel offended by what has been said to them usually avoid going to court.*
>
> (Judgement, district court, Case 11, my emphasis)

The act was framed as balancing on the limit of legality. At the same time, Fatima Ameen was presented as one of few who sought redress for this type of injury in court and thereby suggested to be relatively sensitive. This, combined with the fact that she was approached as a person with power, where public exposure is part of her function, weakened her claim to justice. In Chapter 6, I discussed how the injury of the insult inherent in a particular type of humour is displaced from the rhetoric of the joke onto the sensitivity of those at whom the joke is targeted. I also referred to Sara Ahmed's claim that Muslims have recently been defined in Europe as particularly offendable. They have been represented as embodying oversensitivity that is at odds with what is required by the freedom of speech defined as one of the pillars of a democratic society. Such an image of Muslims has become particularly widespread in Europe in the aftermath of the Mohammed cartoons controversy, in which a categorical dichotomy between secular critique and religious censorship was established. Thereby, blasphemy was construed as a sign of Western civilization. At the same time, Muslims were imagined as lacking democratic traditions and unable to grasp the significance of secular freedom, which includes offending. The source of the alleged oversensitivity was located in their religiosity (Asad, 2009, pp. 21–23). Analysed in this context, the way in which the district court attached the source of the injury to the

Hate speech, linguistic injury and language in court   129

sensitivity of Fatima Ameen introduced this imaginary to the court, framing the conflict in a particular way.

The rightness of slander or the limits of legitimate criticism

Once the conflict in dispute had been framed as one between the democratic right of a citizen to criticize authorities and the right of a person representing the authorities to be protected from insult, the court went on to decide whether Lars Nilsson had abused his right. This part of the judgement starts with the repetition of the defendant's statement that the reason why he sent the email was that Fatima Ameen had contact with representatives of a certain political organization. The issue of the contact with Hamas was also the first one referred to in the summary of the injured party's testimony: 'Fatima Ameen has among other things stated: it is true that she has had contact with representatives of the Hamas movement' (Fatima Ameen's testimony, Judgement, district court, Case 11). Contact with Hamas was thereby brought in as a reason for the utterance to occur in the first place. The court in this context stated: 'Lars Nilsson was free as a citizen to criticize Fatima Ameen directly' (Judgement, district court, Case 11) and continued in a similar vein:

> Nilsson was also free to suggest that Fatima Ameen should propose to support a certain kind of fruit plantation instead of the Hamas movement, see the text of the email in appendix 3 to the judgement.
> (Judgement, district court, Case 11)

The court introduced its deliberations as consisting in deciding what a legitimate criticism of a person in power may be. At the same time as the court found it legitimate to criticize contact with Hamas, it also established that the suggestion of support for 'a certain kind of fruit plantation' lays within the sphere of rightful communication between a citizen and a municipal representative. I will return to the fruit plantation suggestion later on. But first I will try to identify where the limits of legitimate criticism were drawn by the court. The court referred to the fact that a necessary condition for an utterance to be considered an insult under Swedish law is that it vilifies another person by an insulting epithet or accusation or by other infamous conduct. In order to decide whether this condition was fulfilled in this case, the court proceeded:

> The emails, however, contain some noteworthy choices of words. The question in the case is whether Nilsson, by using these, is guilty of an insult.
> (Judgement, district court, Case 11, my emphasis)

By pointing to 'noteworthy choices of words', the court suggested that the limits of the freedom of speech and citizens' democratic right to criticize their government lie in the form—the strong words—used to utter their criticism. A

130 *Hate speech, linguistic injury and language in court*

certain choice of words through which the message is presented and communicated can transform a legitimate message into an illegal insult. The task that the court took upon itself was to decide whether the *form* of Lars Nilsson's utterance was acceptable or not.

The court proceeded in the following way: first, it enumerated the expressions that aroused its suspicion that the limits of acceptable speech had been overstepped. These were: 'billboard import', 'Damn, you're ugly!', 'Muslim niggers', 'Jungle!', 'Take away your awful jungle picture from the municipality's website!!!!', 'Go home to Africa, fast as hell, billboard n_gg_r!', 'Crazy darky bastard, terrorist lover!' These expressions were then carefully examined and their use adjudicated by the court.

The court referred thereafter to one of the few cases in which the Supreme Court had decided that certain utterances were an insult (NJA, 1989, p. 374). It was established that the expression 'fucking wog' (*svartskalle*), when directed towards a person of foreign origin, was to be considered an insult.[3] Following this precedent, the court decided that 'billboard n_gg_r!', 'crazy darky bastard' and 'Muslim niggers' were punishable insults. All three expressions build on classic racist slander: two of them included the word '*neger*' (nigger) and the third one used the word '*svarting*' (darky), alluding to the blackness of the person at which it is directed (*svart* means black in Swedish). But also, the three were drawn from a classic repertoire of slander referring to biological racism in which physicality, in particular skin colour, was used to classify people. The court thus had no difficulty in identifying overt racist slander and—following case law—in establishing that it constituted an insult punishable under Swedish law.

The court also classified the expression 'jungle picture' as an insult. This was done, however, in a rhetorically less categorical way: 'Also the use of the *somewhat vague expression* "jungle picture" should be considered to be within the scope of criminal insult' (Judgement, district court, Case 11, my emphasis). The court took that decision almost as if instinctively feeling that the expression had to do with some kind of racist offence. No explanation followed and the vagueness of the expression suggested that the court itself had difficulty in identifying what exactly was disturbing in this utterance. In this context, the district court's decision not to consider that the already mentioned suggestion directed at Fatima Ameen 'to support a certain kind of fruit plantation' could be offensive gains new significance. As I introduced earlier, the email in question actually read: 'Damn, you're ugly!!!!! Shouldn't you be motioning about banana cultivations and not about Hamas! Lars'. By replacing the word 'banana' with the generic 'fruit', the court obscured the link between the utterance and a particular imaginary in which black people, by being associated with such attributes as bananas and jungle, are portrayed as close to apes.

This kind of imaginary has its roots in Western scientific doctrines that created classifications that portrayed the idea of racial progress. Such a progress was imagined to be from ape to human, from black to white, from

Hate speech, linguistic injury and language in court   131

nature to culture, from the archaic to modern and from the barbaric to the civilized (McClintock, 1995, p. 38). Placed in the vicinity of apes, blacks were represented as atavistic and located on the boundary between nature and culture. The link between the European *mission civilisatrice* or the 'white man's burden' and the image of the other as biologically inferior was popularized through the use of images of the monkey in popular culture and commercials during the colonial era (McClintock, 1995, p. 214). Monkeys themselves stayed in an ambiguous position for Western people, occupying a territory between nature and culture and representing what it means to be almost human (Haraway, 1989, pp. 1–2). This imaginary, in which race-marked bodies are construed through the icon of the ape, has persisted until today and manifests itself, for instance, at football games, when bananas are thrown at black players.

By removing the reference to bananas, the court extracted Lars Nilsson's utterance from this imaginary and obscured the meaning of the message. The racist dimension of the suggestion to support banana plantations became thereby unintelligible, which made it possible to treat the utterance literally as a proposition for a concrete political measure. This made the historical correlation invisible between representing a person as an ape and the project of domination and oppression in the name of progress, supported by the above-mentioned scientific idea of biological hierarchy.

The rigid adherence to the Supreme Court's interpretation of the law on insult in a case of racist slur made it possible for the district court to identify a certain injury resulting from the most overt and blatant expressions of the racist sort. Yet such an interpretation of the Supreme Court's decision was insufficient to detect even slightly coded racist utterances. These were read as senseless or unclear. Moreover, the district court recognized racism in those expressions that were shaped by classic racism in which the colour of the skin was the primary marker of difference and hierarchy, but missed those that, building on the same scientific doctrines, imagined blacks as inferior but without directly mentioning skin colour. In this way, the so-called 'colour-blind racism' (cf. Bonilla-Silva, 2006), manifesting itself in coded language devoid of blatant or classic racist epithets and references, went unrecognized. This narrow interpretation exposed the court's difficulties in identifying the changing forms of racist vocabularies. So, when—in response to the taboo of overtly racist epithets—new ways of naming, representing and offending have emerged, these seemed to be difficult for the court to understand as racism.

The impoliteness of racist speech or racism as a class problem

There was yet another dimension of the district court's procedure to distinguish between punishable and unpunishable utterances. By distinguishing between legitimate criticism and an inappropriate *form* that obscures the actual *message* of the criticism, the district court located the problem of

132 *Hate speech, linguistic injury and language in court*

insult in the form of the utterance, thereby defining insult as inherent to a
certain feature of language. Referring to the above epithets, which the court
considered insults, the district court stated:

> None of these statements were in any way appropriate to express the
> criticism that Nilsson had the right to express against Fatima Ameen;
> rather the effect of their use was that the form hid the actual message.
>
> (Judgement, district court, Case 11, my emphasis)

The inappropriateness of the utterance was thereby identified in its vulgarity.
Established in this way, the legality of the offence was limited by the rules of a
certain type of civility and politeness inscribed in an ideal of civil conduct and
in established norms for appropriate communication. The coarse and vulgar
vocabulary was considered to violate these norms and thereby to overstep the
limits of what is legal. Thereby the court reinforced the ideal of civility and
deemed a certain type of speech illegal.

The racist slur was reduced to the question of bad manners and lack of
civility and its site identified in a vulgar language. This way of defining slander as impolite had already appeared in the police interrogation when the
suspect himself, being confronted with the emails sent from his mailbox,
reacted quite strongly:

> He comments on the content of the emails with: 'Oh, holy shit. Oh, did
> I write and send this?' He says that it is racist and mean. When asked if
> he recognizes it, he answers that he recognizes the choice of words but
> did not realize it was so, in his opinion, mean.
>
> (Police interrogation, Case 11)

In a similar way, the court's identification of offence as an unacceptable form
of expression reduced it to an issue of what kind of exchange of ideas is per-
missible in a society guided by a certain ideal of civility. Lars Nilsson was able
to recognize and approve of this ideal and showed shame when confronted
with the evidence of his bad manners.

Locating the offence in what was considered to be vulgarity also had an
effect of linking offensive speech with class: in the end, the vulgarity of language—its commonness and ordinariness—has often been socially constructed as a feature of a certain social position, and at the same time
served to delimit the lower classes.

In his analysis of blasphemy trials in nineteenth-century England, Joss
Marsh reached the conclusion that blasphemy was almost exclusively treated as 'class crimes of language', with vulgar working-class utterances being
brought to court, but not polite middle- or upper-class speech (1998, p. 8).
Drawing on Marsh's research, Talal Asad claimed that 'the identification of
blasphemy helped to constitute class difference in which asymmetrical
power was repeatedly inscribed' and suggested that blasphemy in these

Hate speech, linguistic injury and language in court 133

cases should be seen 'as an indicator of the shape that free speech takes at different times and in different places, reflecting, as it does so, different structures of power and subjectivity' (2009, p. 35). There are some similarities between the blasphemy trials in England in the nineteenth century and the cases against hate speech today.[4] Overt racism manifested in vulgar racist utterances is identifiable as an attribute of some classes, as rooted in the *masses'* tendencies towards irrational sentiments and in *populist* political jargon. Hence, racism emerges as a *popular* phenomenon (Balibar, 1991, p. 204). This makes it possible to externalize the problem of racism and to leave the classes assumed to be 'cultivated' above suspicion. At the same time, the historical genealogy of the idea of race as primarily used to denote class or estate in the European aristocracy's discourse about itself and slave-owners' discourse about their slaves (Balibar, 1991, p. 207) is hidden.

This understanding of racism as located in the masses is particularly visible in the ways the growth of right-wing extremism has been defined as a problem of populism, both in Sweden and elsewhere in Europe. For instance, in their review of the literature on right-wing parties, Diana Mulinari and Anders Neergaard identify and criticize the literature that places the origin of the popularity of these kinds of parties in the underprivileged groups' response—read 'the working class's response'—to the economic crisis. Such an approach, they claim, not only naturalizes the response as a logical consequence of a state that is external to the liberal nation-state, but also presents it as marginal and caused by irrational emotions of people in a particular social position. This makes it impossible to see 'racisms as ideologies with the ability to appeal to different classes and different societal groups for different projects and tactics' (Mulinari & Neergaard, 2010, p. 71, my translation).

Forbidden speech and the judicial doctrine of language

The distinction established by the district court between the legitimate message and the illegal form in which the message is conveyed draws on a particular understanding of language. It echoes the Saussurean distinction between the signifier and the signified, but puts it in such a rigid manner that the message becomes separable from the form and the insult is located only in the materiality of the sign. Saba Mahmood claims that this firm distinction between the form and the message constitutes a crucial aspect of a Western semiotic ideology, embedded in secular ideas of what it means to be modern. This ideology has shaped a widespread understanding of how words and images work (2009, p. 72). According to this understanding, linguistic practices are mostly denoting reality and the primary task of signs is the communication of referential meaning.

The district court's concern with the form as a possible punishable site of insult and its separation from the message that is protected by law can also be understood as a way of promoting freedom of speech conceived as the free circulation of ideas in a democratic society, and, in this case in

134 *Hate speech, linguistic injury and language in court*

particular, protecting the right of every citizen to express criticism of their government. In this sense, the theory of language underlying the judgement in the case of the insulting emails is similar to that present in the decisions in cases regarding fighting words in courts in the United States.[5] In her analysis of the decision of the Supreme Court of the United States in *R.A.V. v. St. Paul*,[6] Judith Butler identifies a similar mechanism:

> In his effort to protect all contents of communication from proscription, [Justice] Scalia establishes a distinction between the content and the vehicle of that expression; it is the latter which is proscribable, and the former which is not. He continues, 'fighting words are thus analogous to a noisy sound track.' What is injurious, then, is the sound, but not the message, indeed, 'the government may not regulate use based on hostility—or favoritism—towards the underlying message expressed'.
>
> (1997, p. 56)

The ideology of language that distinguishes between the noise and the message proper is deeply rooted in a specific genealogy of freedom of speech and shaped by the ideal of 'the free marketplace of ideas'. It has some significant consequences for how racist slander is defined and treated by the judiciary and, moreover, for an understanding of what constitutes a racist offence. By being treated as noise devoid of meaning itself, racist slander becomes detached from the historical context that actually makes of racist utterances *meaningful* acts of exclusion and oppression. The separation of the content from the form and the detachment of both these from the historical context of racist speech make it impossible to attend to the racist message of an utterance. Racist speech acts are thereby treated in court only in the immediate scene of utterance, isolated from the historical connotations that are activated in particular slander through racist imaginary.

In her analysis of racist speech, Judith Butler claims that the speaking subject, although clearly responsible for a particular speech, is rarely its *originator*. Rather, racist speech works through the invocation of a convention (Butler, 1997, p. 34), through citation of previous uses recalling the memory of a particular historical experience of racist oppression encoded in language:

> Clearly, injurious names have a history, one that is invoked and reconsolidated at the moment of utterance, but not explicitly told. This is not simply a history of how they have been used, in what contexts, and for what purposes; it is the very way such histories are installed and arrested in and by the name. The name has, thus, a historicity, what might be understood as the history which has become internal to a name, has come to constitute the contemporary meaning of a name: the sedimentation of its usages as they have become part of the very name, a sedimentation, a repetition that congeals, that gives the name its force.
>
> (Butler, 1997, p. 36)

Sara Ahmed created the concept of 'sticky signs' in order to name this process of sedimentation of meanings in injurious names. She writes in relation to the use of the word 'Paki' in the United Kingdom:

> We could argue that signs become sticky through repetition; if a word is used in a certain way, again and again, then that 'use' becomes intrinsic; it becomes a form of signing. ... The resistance to the word acquiring new meaning is not about the referent; rather the resistance is an effect of these histories of repetition ... The sign is a 'sticky sign' as an effect of a history of articulation, which allows the sign to accumulate value. The stickiness of the sign is also about the relation or contact between signs. ... To use a sticky sign is to evoke other words, which have become intrinsic to the sign through past forms of association. The word 'Paki' might then stick to other words that are not spoken: immigrant, outsider, dirty, and so on. The association between words that generates meanings is concealed: *it is this concealment of such associations that allows such signs to accumulate value.* I am describing this accumulation of affective value as a form of stickiness, or as 'sticky signs'.
>
> (2004, pp. 91–92)

From this perspective, the meaning conveyed by racist slander is located in its 'stickiness', that is, its citational character, and consists in recalling a certain history of exclusion. The court, however, by separating the form from content, seemed unable to attend to this violent dimension of the message carried by the form of the racist slander—its sound or shape—and limited itself to whether or not to punish the vulgarity of certain expressions.

Guilt, punishment and epilogue

The court concluded the judgement by taking a stance on Fatima Ameen's demand to classify the insult as aggravated because of the reference to her race and on her mentioning that the threats and insults had forced her to resign from her position. The court stated that '[Nilsson] can naturally not be convicted of another deed than the one he is guilty of' (Judgement, district court, Case 11) and thus the court rejected Fatima Ameen's demand and kept the prosecutor's crime classification.

This dissonance between the injured party's sense of harm and the impossibility of this type of sense to be addressed in a criminal case, that necessarily requires a defendant and a clear demarcation of his or her responsibility for certain defined actions, is not a mere reflection of Fatima Ameen's ingenuousness. Rather it seemed to be an attempt on her part to define the injury she had suffered as embedded in a larger context and impossible to limit to a single scene of utterance.

Fatima Ameen's attempt to express this type of injury can be understood in two ways. First, she tried to put the utterances in the broader context of

136   *Hate speech, linguistic injury and language in court*

intimidations and threats that made an important impact on her life, finally leading her to resign from the political post she was holding. In this sense, every insult contained in every single expression so scrupulously analysed by the court was adding to the harassment already suffered. The way in which the court analytically treated the utterances, separating one from another, isolating them from their context and examining them in their singularity, was fragmenting and diffusing the nature of the harm of this type of racism that consisted in the accumulation and repetition. In her analysis of systematic, recurrent, familiar practices involving socialized attitudes and behaviours that add up to what she named 'everyday racism', Philomena Essed writes:

> [T]he experience of everyday racism is a cumulative process. New experiences are interpreted and evaluated against the background of earlier personal experiences, vicarious experiences, and general knowledge of racism in society.
>
> (1991, p. 8)

The meaning of everyday incidents is shaped and interpreted in the light of previous experiences. The court's procedure in establishing the possible injury resulting from the insults occluded the possibility to recognize harm of this particular nature, thereby making it difficult to address the actual source of the injury.

There is yet another dimension to this cumulative nature of racist slander, inherent not so much in the repetitive character of the experience of everyday racism as in the way language in general, and in particular the language of oppression, works through accumulation and recollection of a history that is carried and reinstalled in the injurious words as well as through interpellation. Drawing on Althusser's idea of a subject as constructed through the interpellation of a particular ideology, and thus of a subject that is brought into linguistic existence through a speech act, Judith Butler examines excitable speech as illocutionary, producing a subject in a position of subordination. The use of injurious language or name-calling repeats and re-establishes a history of injury—it recalls a particular legacy (1997, pp. 24–28). Butler is careful, on the one hand, to recognize the possibility of a subversive use of language and, on the other, to stress the speaker's responsibility for the language they use. She writes:

> I would argue that the citationality of discourse can work to enhance and intensify our sense of responsibility for it. The one who utters hate speech is responsible for the manner in which such speech is repeated, for reinvigorating such speech, for re-establishing contexts of hate and injury. The responsibility of the speaker does not consist of remaking language ex nihilo, but rather of negotiating the legacies of usage that constrain and enable that speaker's speech.
>
> (1997, p. 27)

Hate speech, linguistic injury and language in court 137

This suggests that the repetition and accumulation of injurious speech have these two dimensions: they are cumulative because of the nature of the process in which they are experienced in everyday life. In the case of Fatima Ameen, the numerous emails sent by Lars Nilsson added to already experienced threats and intimidation, having a significant impact on her life. But they are also cumulative through the workings of an insulting word that gathers and carries the past meanings and the history of a particular subjugation. Thus, the words addressed to Fatima Ameen brought with them the racist imaginary of biological inferiority, political threat, suspicion and not belonging, which activated distinct but at the same time converging histories of European domination.

The court seemed unable to attend to these dimensions of the language that was being judged and to understand and address the harm that Fatima Ameen tried to describe in her testimony. Moreover, by holding on to a very strict reading of what a punishable insult is and by lacking the flexibility to follow and capture the ever-changing and disguised racist speech, the district court did not identify the less vulgar, coded racist language.

In the end, the way in which law is practised in court—by fixing meanings to acts and words, by omitting what is ambiguous, subtle and indefinite in clear-cut interpretations, and by drawing sharp distinctions between what is legal and what is not—made it impossible for the court to address the essence of racist language that is ever-moving and fluctuating, always adjusting itself to new contexts, trying to conceal its nature.

Most importantly, however, the court partly obscured the racist dimension of the utterance. This was done by rhetorically redefining the scene of utterance, from consisting in an offence of a member of a racial and religious minority, to consisting in a criticism formulated by a citizen towards a representative of the state. This resulted in the imposition of a relatively light penalty in terms of the amount of the fine and of low damages to be paid to the injured party and led to an appeal lodged by both the prosecutor and the injured party. While the prosecutor demanded higher fines for Lars Nilsson, Fatima Ameen insisted that the act be classified as aggravated insult and requested higher damages. The defendant dismissed these changes. All the parties agreed that the court of appeal should take as a starting point the district court's judgement regarding the guilt. The analysis of the scene of utterance and of the range of its illegality was thus not put into question.

The court of appeal first considered the injured party's claim. It argued that in order for an act to be classified as an aggravated insult, the offence must be very serious and occur in certain circumstances that transform the insult into harassment or other suppressive behaviour. The court of appeal stated:

> Lars Nilsson has without doubt abused Fatima Ameen in a serious way. It shall thereby be especially considered that one motive for the crime

138　*Hate speech, linguistic injury and language in court*

clearly has been to aggrieve a person because of skin colour, ethnic origin and creed. This situation, according to Chapter 29 section 2 (7) of the Penal Code, constitutes an aggravating circumstance when deciding on the penalty.

Based on this, the court of appeal considers this crime to have a much higher penalty than established by the district court.

(Judgement, court of appeal, Case 11)

Still, the court of appeal did not find any reason to classify the case as aggravated insult: 'a number of email messages that were sent on the same day to a representative of local authorities at her official address cannot be considered aggravating to the extent that the deed should be regarded as an aggravated offence' (Judgement, court of appeal, Case 11). It doubled the fines imposed and the damages awarded by the district court. In doing the latter, the court of appeal invoked the preparatory works and stated:

Apart from what is stated in the provision, it has been particularly underscored in the preparatory works that when determining the damages for insult it must be considered if the attack is in conflict with fundamental societal values, e.g. the equal value of all human beings (Prop. 2000/2001:68 p. 51; see also NJA, 1989 p. 374). This is definitely the case with the present crime.

(Judgement, court of appeal, Case 11)

The court of appeal, even though it dismissed the injured party's demand to reclassify the crime, rhetorically reframed the case as one about a racist offence. Both when deciding the fines and the damages, the court referred to the particular character of the crime: that offending a person because of her skin colour and religion violated some of the values fundamental to Swedish society.

The decision of the court of appeal was appealed by the defendant, who was unsatisfied with the higher fines. When requesting a review permit at the Supreme Court, his attorney argued that:

The cause of the demand for changing the sentence of the court of appeal is that the penalty given in the district court is balanced and the damages are appropriate. On the whole, the judgement is well elaborated and clearly justified.

In the district court, my client was declared guilty of, during the same day, sending a number of email messages to a representative of local authorities at her official address. The messages were offensive. They had been caused by my client feeling insulted by the injured party, in her office, promoting that Sweden should initiate talks with the terrorist-labelled organization Hamas. The question of liability has not been tried in the court of appeal.

(Application for review permit, Case 11)

Hate speech, linguistic injury and language in court 139

The application concluded with a quote from the judgement of the district court, in which the court referred to the democratic right of every citizen to criticize people in power. Thus, the reason for this attempt to bring the case to the Supreme Court was not the issue of responsibility for the crime, nor the court's interpretation of some words as punishable insults— an interpretation that was neither appealed nor reviewed by the higher court—but the framing of the conflict. Of course, the fine and damages were also an issue. Still, considering that these are generally comparatively low in Sweden, it was rather the way in which the case was formulated and interpreted—the more symbolic dimension of justice—that was of crucial importance. In this sense, the conflict in court was over what the district court itself would call the form, and not the message, of the judgement. The meaning, the significant part of the court's decision, and its symbolic power (cf. Bourdieu, 1991), was identified in the rhetoric used by the court. This suggests that the court's use of language in the trial, by communicating meanings through the rhetoric of the judgement, stood in contradiction to the court's linguistic philosophy, which strictly separated the message from the form of the utterance.

Conclusions: racist language on trial

In this chapter, I have analysed a case in which a specific language—racist slander—was in question. My objective has been to understand the *court's philosophy of language* and to identify the sites in which the insult is located. I have argued that the court decided on the illegality of a speech by looking at the form: the court considered vulgar, blatantly racist language as harmful, while it experienced difficulty in identifying an insult uttered in more 'polite' speech. This approach resembles the procedure of identifying a racist subject: in both cases, it is the overt racism that is noticed and defined as illegal, while ambiguous, disguised manifestations thereof are difficult for the courts to spot. I have claimed here that this identification of racist language with vulgarity contributes to projecting the problem of racism as an attribute of some social classes.

I have furthermore argued that the court's distinction between form and message, and the location of racist speech in an inappropriate choice of words, made it difficult for the court to see the form of racist speech as already carrying a particular message. Following Judith Butler and Sara Ahmed, I have claimed that the nature of the linguistic injury of this type of speech lies in a certain stickiness of racist insults, because such words carrying with them an accumulated history of oppression. This makes it difficult to neatly separate the abusive form from the message. This was the reason why the court's procedure in the case of insults directed against Fatima Ameen was insufficient to recognize the linguistic injury caused by racist speech.

Finally, this chapter has served as an illustration of the *use* of language in judicial speech acts—judgements. This has helped me to demonstrate how

140 *Hate speech, linguistic injury and language in court*

justice is dispensed at several levels: not only in the sentence and decision on damages, but also in the rhetoric of the judgement, the ways in which the case is framed and how what is at stake is defined by the court through these rhetorics. It is here, I have claimed, that the court frames the conflict, defines the roles of the parties and establishes the truth about the events. It is here that some claims are legitimized and others disregarded. It is also in the rhetoric of the judgement pronounced in this case that I locate the court's unrecognition of the racist injury.

Notes

1 The Swedish Supreme Court found, for instance, that bearing symbols associated with National Socialism and white-supremacy movements constituted agitation against a national or ethnic group (NJA, 1996, p. 577). In the 1990s, many cases of agitation against a national or ethnic group involved making the so-called Hitler salute. Similarly, the law on insult does not only forbid offensive slander, but also other types of behaviour, such as obscene gestures, although it is difficult to find cases where this rule is applied (Jareborg & Friberg, 2010, p. 82).
2 I am here inspired by Judith Butler's reading of the decision of the Supreme Court of the United States in the case R.A.V. v. St. Paul (1997, pp. 52–60).
3 The case from the Supreme Court concerned an assault and insult. The injured party, a refugee, after having missed her bus, walked along the road, when a car started to follow her and a young man inside screamed 'fucking wog' (*svartskalle*) at her and tried to grab her through an open window. He threw a bottle at her and thereafter jumped out of the car, knocked her over and took a stranglehold on her. The district court found the defendant guilty of assault, but acquitted him of insult; both the court of appeal and the Supreme Court changed the first sentence and found him guilty of insult. Moreover, the Supreme Court awarded damages to the injured party, recognizing a particular harm of the insult that, in referring to her ethnic origin, not only hurt the injured party but also violated fundamental values of Swedish society.
4 This similarity can already be found in the definition of blasphemy that Marsh formulates. He calls it 'genuinely indefinable', sliding into obscenity, and into slander and libel. Marsh himself mentions hate speech and fighting words as descendants of blasphemy (1998, p. 7). In the context of offence directed at the Muslim minority in Europe, the comparison has yet another dimension, as we have seen in the case in Chapter 6, when religious spaces are targeted, thereby hurting a particular kind of affect and resulting in an injury difficult to redress through a secular legal system.
5 I want to be cautious in making this comparison, being aware of the substantive differences between the definitions of freedom of speech in the two legal systems, the US and the Swedish one. While the First Amendment doctrine carries much weight in the United States, shaping the more libertarian conception of free speech, the European experience of the Holocaust and World War II pushed most European countries to place some restrictions on speech that might incite racial hatred (Mahmood, 2009, p. 84). As I have discussed in Chapter 4, this is the case of the Swedish act on agitation against a national or ethnic group. This difference is also reflected in the way the European Court of Human Rights allows the restriction of freedom of speech if this is required by the functioning of democratic societies (Weber, 2009, p. 2). However, it is important to stress that freedom of speech in both the United States and Europe is mostly balanced, not

Hate speech, linguistic injury and language in court   141

so much by a particular kind of responsibility imposed on individuals and states, as by an idea of the free human as a self-owning individual. Material property becomes the key to defining individuals in this type of liberal system: 'the right to choose how to dispose of what one owns is integral to the liberal subject—and the subject's body, affection, and speech are regulated as *personal property* because they constitute the person' (Asad, 2009, p. 30).

6 The case was concerned with establishing the constitutionality of an ordinance that prohibited public placement of symbols and the like that might arouse resentment on the basis of race, colour, religion, etc. A white teenager was charged under this ordinance for having burned a cross in front of the house of a black family. The Supreme Court declared that the cross-burning was not an instance of fighting words forbidden under the ordinance, but an act of expressing an opinion protected under the First Amendment.

Bibliography

Ahmed, S. (2004). *The Cultural Politics of Emotion*. Edinburgh: Edinburgh University Press.

Asad, T. (2009). 'Free Speech, Blasphemy, and Secular Criticism.' In T. Asad (Ed.), *Is Critique Secular?—Blasphemy, Injury & Free Speech*. Berkeley, CA: University of California Press, pp. 20–63.

Balibar, É. (1991). 'Class Racism.' In É. Balibar & I. Wallerstein (Eds.), *Race, Nation, Class: Ambiguous Identities*. London: Verso, pp. 204–216.

Bonilla-Silva, E. (2006). *Racism without Racists: Color-Blind Racism and the Persistence of Racial Inequality in the United States*. Lanham: Rowman & Littlefield Publishers.

Bourdieu, P. (1991). *Language and Symbolic Power*. Cambridge, MA: Harvard University Press.

Butler, J. (1997). *Excitable Speech: A Politics of the Performative*. New York; London: Routledge.

Essed, P. (1991). *Understanding Everyday Racism: An Interdisciplinary Theory*. Newbury Park: Sage.

Haraway, D. (1989). *Primate Visions: Gender, Race, and Nature in the World of Modern Science*. New York; London: Routledge.

Jareborg, N. & Friberg, S. (2010). *Brotten mot person och förmögenhetsbrotten*. Uppsala: Iustus.

Lööw, H. (2000). 'Incitement of Racial Hatred.' *Journal of Scandinavian Studies in Criminology and Crime Prevention*, *1*(2), 109–120.

MacKinnon, C. (1994). *Only Words*. London: HarperCollins.

Mahmood, S. (2009). 'Religious Reason and Secular Affect: An Incommensurable Divide?' In T. Asad (Ed.), *Is Critique Secular?—Blasphemy, Injury & Free Speech*. Berkeley: University of California Press, pp. 146–154.

Marsh, J. (1998). *Word Crimes: Blasphemy, Culture, and Literature in Nineteenth-Century England*. Chicago, IL: University of Chicago Press.

Matsuda, M., Lawrence, III, C., Delgado, R. & Williams Crenshaw, K. (1993). *Words that Wound: Critical Race Theory, Assaultive Speech and the First Amendment*. Boulder, CO: Westview Press.

McClintock, A. (1995). *Imperial Leather: Race, Gender and Sexuality in the Colonial Contest*. London: Routledge.

142 Hate speech, linguistic injury and language in court

Mulinari, D. & Neergaard, A. (2010). 'Sverigedemokraterna och det teoretiska fältet.' In M. Deland, F. Hertzberg & T. Hvitfeldt (Eds.), *Det vita fältet: samtida forskning om högerextremism*. Uppsala: Swedish Science Press, pp. 45–73.

NJA. (1989). p. 374.

NJA. (1996). p. 577.

Prop. (2000/2001:68). *Regeringens Proposition 2000/01:68. Ersättning för ideell skada*. Stockholm: Justitiedepartementet.

Weber, A. (2009). *Manual on Hate Speech*. Strasbourg: Council of Europe Publishing.

8   On judging and responsibility

> The injured party, Nizar, recounts that he got a taxi fare from a restaurant at Stortorget to Visbygatan. He picked up a male and drove him to Visbygatan. The man did not speak during the ride.
>
> When they arrived at Visbygatan, Nizar stopped the taxi and printed the receipt for 105:- [Swedish kronor]. The man said he did not have any cash and handed over a bank card to Nizar, who explained that the man could not pay with that card. The man became irritated and took his card back, saying to Nizar that he would go and get cash. Nizar also got out of the taxi and told the man he had to leave some form of security until he returned with the cash.
>
> The man then headbutts Nizar's nose, causing pain and bleeding. The man also called Nizar a 'Taliban' and a 'terrorist'. The man then enters a stairwell on Visbygatan 7. A male with a dog approaches Nizar and helps him call the emergency [services].
>
> (Police report, Case 12)

The above fragment comes from a police report filed by Nizar Jamal in 2008. A couple of months after the event, the defendant, Ola Johansson, was tried and sentenced. The court found Ola Johansson guilty of insult and violence against a public servant and sentenced him to 50 hours of community service. The focus of the judgement was the racist nature of the offence. Not only was the penalty enhancement provision applied, but the court also awarded Nizar Jamal higher damages due to the racist nature of the injury he suffered.

One year later, another report was filed against Ola Johansson. This time the crime description provided by the injured party, Babak Rostami, and introduced into the police files stated:

> The injured party recounts that he was driving a man from Stortorget to Visbygatan. The ride cost 103 kronor, but the man had no money to pay with. The man asked the taxi driver to follow him to his flat, where he would get the money. The injured party followed him up to the fifth floor and in to the hall to his flat. It read O. Johansson on the door. The man looked around, but had no money. He then started

144   *On judging and responsibility*

to become unpleasant and said some racist things about the taxi driver, such as that he was a Muslim and had come to Sweden to work. He also gave the injured party the finger. The injured party did not see any point in standing there, instead he left saying he would report it to the police.

The man then followed the injured party out, and when they reached the entrance, the injured party turned around and the perpetrator then swung a kick that the injured party blocked with his left arm, in such a way that the kick hit the left forearm. The injured party then left and called the police.

(Police report, Case 13)

This case too ended up in court. The court declared Ola Johansson guilty and sentenced him to probation combined with community service and drug treatment. The sentence took note of the previous cases against Ola Johansson. Nothing in the judgement indicates, however, that the court considered the possible aggravated nature of the crime or whether to apply the penalty enhancement provision.

Despite certain clear similarities between the events that were tried in the two cases against Ola Johansson—the acts of physical violence combined with verbal assault performed against two taxi drivers by the same customer unwilling to pay for his trip—the two cases unfolded during the police investigation and the trial in very different ways. They also resulted in two different judgements, not so much in terms of the sentence, for in both cases the defendant was found guilty, but with respect to how the crime was understood by the courts. While the judgement in the 2008 case paid attention to the injured party and the prosecutor's claim about the racist nature of the crime, and the justice included a rhetorical recognition of racism, the judgement in the 2009 case took no notice of this possible aspect of the crime, nor did it seem to have been part of the indictment.

In this chapter, I will analyse the development of the two cases throughout the judicial process, from the first police interrogations, through the activities of the prosecutor, the indictments and trials as presented in the court documents, to the judgements. My objective will be to identify the differences in the cases and to understand in what these differences consisted, that is, to explore when racism was made visible and how it did, or did not, become part of the process of dispensing justice. The core of the chapter will be a reading of the two judgements in the cases against Ola Johansson, a reading in which I will be mainly interested in how justice was done on the rhetorical level, that is, through the ways in which the acts on trial were named, defined, explained and judged by the judges. My point of departure will be that the two cases, by concerning similar acts performed by the same person and yet leading to different judgements, offer an opportunity to identify the reasons for the different approaches to racism in court.

The two cases

After Nizar Jamal's report, the police succeeded in tracking his customer and Nizar Jamal was able to identify him. Thereafter, the police interrogated the suspect, who claimed he did not remember a thing from that night, since he had a blackout caused by a combination of a medical remedy he had taken and the alcohol he had drunk that night. He knew, however, from the diary he kept that he had been out that night and that he felt bad the day after. He maintained that nothing like that had ever happened to him before. A couple of days after the interrogation, a note was made in the police files saying:

> The suspect states that he wants it on record that he did not call the injured party the things that the injured party had stated during the police interview. Johansson may, at the utmost, have said 'fucking Arab', or the like.
>
> (Police report, Case 12)

Thus, from the beginning, the attitude of the suspect, and later the defendant, was ambivalent or even contradictory. He denied having any memory of the evening and, at the same time, he was sure he had not uttered the slander of which the injured party was accusing him. He had moreover admitted that he might have been insulting towards Nizar Jamal in another way. Yet, paradoxically, the slander he admitted he could have uttered was, in legal terms, not less offensive as it referred directly to an ethnicity.

The insults played an important part also in the testimony given by the injured party. During the police interview, Nizar Jamal elaborated upon this in the following way:

> While doing this [performing violence] the man shouts 'fucking Taliban' and 'terrorist' at Nizar. The man also said other racist things, such as, that Nizar was a foreigner that had come to Sweden to live for free. Nizar found this to be very offensive.
>
> (Police interview, Case 12)

When formulating the indictment, the prosecutor took this part of the act into consideration and charged Ola Johansson with both violence against a public servant and insult, which he described in the following way:

> On the same occasion, Johansson had abused Nizar Jamal by calling him 'fucking Taliban', 'terrorist', and other *racist* invectives.
>
> (Indictment, Case 12, my emphasis)

By directly referring to the racist nature of the slander, the prosecutor brought this to the fore and attempted in court to present the case as a hate

146   *On judging and responsibility*

crime. Thus, in the 2008 case, the prosecutor sustained the injured party's version of the events and followed his claim that the acts of violence performed by the defendant had a racist nature.

The inconsistency in Ola Johansson's testimony became even more visible in court, when he changed his version, claiming that he remembered the evening and that he had indeed hit the injured party, but that this was accidental. He also admitted that he had called him names, but disputed what the actual insults were. He stated, as described in the judgement:

> He [Ola Johansson] has, furthermore, acknowledged that he said 'Arab bastard' and 'fucking Arab' or similar expressions to Nizar Jamal. He has left it to the court to decide whether this act is punishable.
>
> (Judgement, Case 12)

The inconsistency of Ola Johansson's testimony was taken up by the prosecutor in court as a way to discredit his version of the events. It became also the basis for the court to found its decision on the version presented by the injured party. Thus, the court decided on the issue of responsibility by establishing that Ola Johansson had both intentionally hit Nizar Jamal and insulted him in the way stated by the latter.

The 2009 case differed from the 2008 case in several regards. During the police interrogation Ola Johansson confessed directly to the crime. The police files from the interrogation read:

> When questioned about it, Ola said he did not remember that evening, but that he had no reason to believe that the taxi driver had not told the truth.
>
> ... When asked about it, Ola stated that he does not get violent when drinking. However, it happens that he talks back. Ola stated that he can become 'cheeky' when drinking.
>
> ... Ola was remorseful during the interrogation and ashamed of what had been communicated to him. He stated that he had to stop drinking alcohol in this way.
>
> ... Ola stated that he wanted to contact the driver and pay for the taxi ride.
>
> (Interrogation with Ola Johansson, Police report, Case 13)

No remark was made during this interview about the insults. They were mentioned, however, during the interview with the injured party—Babak Rostami—as reported by the police:

> the guy had started to say things to Babak. He had said nasty things about Babak coming to Sweden to work and that Babak was a Muslim, and the guy had called Babak a wog.
>
> (Police interview with Babak Rostami, Police report, Case 13)

On judging and responsibility   147

Already during the first police interview, when asked whether he had claims for damages, Babak Rostami stated that he thought the defendant should pay his debt for the trip; he had no further claims. A couple of days later, Babak Rostami called the police and informed them that Ola Johansson had contacted him, paid his debt and apologized.

In the course of the investigation, the prosecutor contacted Babak Rostami once again. The police files suggest that the prosecutor, the same person who had pressed charges against Ola Johansson in 2008, reacted to information provided in an early interview with Babak Rostami, where Babak claimed that Ola Johansson had made racist remarks against him. In the police records, it is stated that 'the injured party Babak did not want to elucidate exactly what Ola Johansson had said, but instead dismissed it saying that he had found Ola Johansson drunk and stupid' (Police interview with Babak Rostami, Police report, Case 13). Suspecting that the report made by Babak Rostami potentially included one more offence—insult—the prosecutor contacted him to get more details about the offences and to ask if he wanted to report this crime for legal action. Pressing charges for insult could have brought the racist dimension of the crime into the trial. What happened, however, was that Babak Rostami did not wish to press charges for insult. He seemed reluctant to talk about this aspect of the act of violence directed against him. On several occasions, he maintained that he did not harbour a grudge against Ola Johansson for what had happened.

The lack of initiative from Babak Rostami's side to claim redress for insult limited possible legal action in this regard.[1] The prosecutor's attempt turned out to be futile and, in the indictment, no reference was made to the racist insults that had been uttered in the course of events. As a result, Ola Johansson was charged with one crime only: violence against a public servant.

These two cases suggest that the course of a trial and its outcome are not only influenced by legal procedures and the law itself. The cases illustrate that there is always some scope for different persons involved in the case to act and that their agency bears an impact on how the cases will unfold. The scope for agency of different actors will depend, to different degrees, on their roles in the judicial process, but will not be completely predetermined by it. Thus, in the 2008 case, the injured party was explicit in his claim for justice, not only when it came to physical violence, but also to verbal abuse. He was also stressing the racist nature of the attack he had suffered. In the 2009 case, on the other hand, the injured party was reluctant to talk about the racist aspects of the event and did not wish to press charges for insult. He had no particular claims for extra damages; he just wanted to be paid for his work. Still, even in this case, the injured party referred to the insults, both during the police interview and the trial, and called them 'racist'. The defendant in the 2008 case gave contradictory testimonies, denying responsibility for any crime. His account when it came to the racist nature of the attack was even more ambivalent. He denied the injured party's accusation and, at the same time, admitted that he had cast insults at him, but

148 *On judging and responsibility*

suggested that his insults could be considered not criminal. In the 2009 case, the same defendant was repentant and apologized. He also openly admitted to having a drinking problem that he identified as a source of his offensive behaviour. The difference in how the cases ended up being defined in the indictments was thus a result of a combination of the legal framework applied, of the actions and attitudes of the parties in the cases, and, last but not least, of the agency of the prosecutor, who in the 2008 case succeeded in framing the case as having racist aspects, while in the 2009 case failed to do so. In what follows, I will begin by exploring what this scope for agency of the injured party means in the context of a trial and how the identification of the racist nature of a crime may depend on their claiming a particular type of injury. In the later part of the chapter, I will turn to an analysis of the acts of deciding a case and writing a judgement.

Racism and victimology

The two cases are interesting in several respects. One is that they instantiate the work of a prosecutor who attempts to bring the racist nature of the acts of violence to the fore, and thereby show what is required by the legal system to do so. In Chapter 6, I discussed how the judiciary needs a certain kind of racist subject in order to identify and recognize racism in the acts on trial. In addition, the cases against Ola Johansson suggest that the ways in which the injury is claimed may be decisive for the possibility of recognizing racism in court. In Chapter 6, I analysed how members of the Muslim community in Manby, who filed the complaint and witnessed in court, drew on the accessible frames of narrating a type of injury that could be intelligible to the judiciary. I also described how the emergence of these kinds of frames was related to certain shifts in the legal approach to victims and their place in the judicial process. Here, I will show what happens when accounts of an injured party cannot be contained in such frames.

Babak Rostami was reluctant to talk about the racist insults he had heard from the defendant and he decided not to report them for prosecution. This made it difficult to include insult into the indictment and, already at this stage, made the racist nature of the acts less visible in the judicial process. This indicates how the possibility of the judiciary to identify racism in this type of act of violence is dependent on an individual victim's claiming a particular type of injury, and thus racist violence is understood exclusively in terms of the immediate effects on the victim. Such an exclusively individualist approach obscures the broader social consequences of racist insults, or racist violence more generally, that, if understood through their communicative and contextual effects, can be seen as having lasting consequences for larger communities. As Kathleen Blee puts it:

> The damage of hate crimes is not merely to the immediate victim, but can convey long-enduring messages of vulnerability or empowerment to

those quite far removed from the crime. They can seal borders of racial identity. And they can obscure deeply entrenched, institutional forms of racial violence. These, rather than the issue of consequences to the immediate victim, may be more politically effective examples of harm to use in the effort to retain hate crime legislation.

(2005, p. 615)

With this approach to racist violence, it is not really relevant whether a speech act works or fails to work at the personal level, Sara Ahmed claims (2004, p. 60). It is rather the social dimension thereof that makes it a racist insult. As such, a speech act operates by bringing about particular stories of harm towards *communities*. Ahmed maintains that the risk of focusing on the personal dimension of a racist speech act is that its public or systematic dimension becomes concealed (Ahmed, 2004, p. 198). With her concept of 'sticky signs', she addresses this property of abusive hate speech, which, even when it fails to work in the case of an individual, can still operate by attaching itself to the body of a community.

Seen in this way, racist insults always bear a potential of injury and they act by imposing a certain racialized identity onto those to whom they are addressed, *regardless* of the insults' actual effectiveness in offending. In this sense, they operate *both* on the individual level, by involving 'forms of power that are visceral and bodily' (Ahmed, 2004, p. 56), and at a social level, by drawing on investments in social norms and reopening particular histories of subjugation.

Law's self-containment and the discretion of judges

The above discussion shows the importance of the agency of those involved in trials. This also applies to different representatives of the judiciary. Such a reading of the cases requires some reconsideration of the understanding of the workings of law and the judiciary. According to legal formalism, law is a self-determining system of rules and principles. The jurisdiction—that is, the way the law is exercised by courts—shall happen independently of extra-legal considerations, such as moral or political values (Veitch, Christo-doulidis & Farmer, 2012, p. 117). In this way, an image of the law is created as insusceptible to different interpretations, clear and stable in its message, and an image of the judiciary as objective and predictable. It is through this reliance on its internal coherence and self-containment that the legal system establishes itself as independent of other types of power, most importantly of executive power. The validity of a court decision is not evaluated in terms of its justness or fairness, but in terms of its conformity with the established law (Lacey, 1998, pp. 7–11).

This self-image of law as a coherent and self-contained *system* of rules and principles, predictable and expressing the objective and neutral voice of the law, has penetrated into my analysis of the courts' ways of dealing with

150 *On judging and responsibility*

cases involving racism. In the previous two chapters, I dedicated myself to spotting problematic sites within this system that made it difficult, if not impossible, to address racism in court. This I did by deconstructing the definition of racism applied by the courts. I found that the racist nature of an act was attributed to an individual actor and based on particular motives, understood as recognized and explicit reasons provided by the defendant to explain their conduct. I further argued that, by focusing on motives, the court was looking for a particular type of racist subject, one ideologically open and self-aware. In a similar manner, the injurious language could be classified as racist almost exclusively when it used blatant slander related to classic, biological racist imaginary. In my analysis, I addressed legal definitions and concepts such as intent, motive, injury, legal subject and, more indirectly, the ways in which racism is conceived in the law and by the judiciary. To do this, I accepted the vision that there is one established definition and understanding of each of these concepts and that the courts, in the cases I have analysed, had only one possible way of reasoning if they wanted to pronounce a valid decision.

This focus on what in the workings of the legal system made it difficult to fight racism with the help of law was reflected in the vocabulary of my accounts in Chapters 6 and 7, where the active subject was 'the court' and not 'the judges'. This was intentional and reflected my analysis where emphasis was placed on the *structural* and *institutional* frames that limited the ways in which legislation against racism could be applied, by creating obstacles for a certain type of justice. I therefore suggested that the failure of the judiciary to address the problem of racism in general, and anti-Muslim racism in particular, stems from the ways racism is defined and understood by the judicial knowledge regime.

My lack of attention to those involved in the judiciary, and most importantly to the figure of the judge, was consistent with the legal positivist tradition in which law makes itself audible during the trial through a speech act performed by the judge when passing a sentence. The voice of the judge is, from this point of view, equal to the voice of the law. In order to comply with the ideals of objectivity, impartiality and neutrality, judges must proceed in a formal way to determine how to apply legal rules in order to decide a particular case. Ideally, judges should be well trained in their craft and able to apply law almost mechanically.

This is also the dominant ideal of judges in Sweden. Already the university training of lawyers and the subsequent specialized training of judges are focused mainly on technical aspects of the law. The judge should know how to find the right solution to a case in accordance with law and use proper legal methods as defined by the legal doctrine (Ställvik, 2009, pp. 196–197; Stefan Strömberg in SvJT2004, p. 312, quoted in, Ställvik 2009, p. 194).

Yet, if we look at it historically, we can see that several different traditions have influenced today's Swedish judiciary. Often these traditions represent different ideals of a judge. They all, in one way or another, have left a

On judging and responsibility 151

trace on how the role of the judge is understood in Sweden today. After having been influenced for centuries by German legal thought, a break occurred at the beginning of the twentieth century and a national legal culture developed in Sweden (Wennström, 2005, p. 15). The legal positivist tradition and the legal realist tradition, developed through Scandinavian Legal Realism (*Uppsalaskolan*), combined to produce an ideal of the judge as neutral and impartial in skilfully applying legal regulations, without any interference of his or her own moral or political judgement. With the establishment of the People's Home (*Folkhemmet*, the Swedish version of the welfare state developed in the 1930s), an ideal of the judge as a public official, closely linked to and loyal to the state, flourished. The boundaries between the judicial, legislative and executive powers became blurred, and judges started to be thought of as social engineers (Modéer, 1994, p. 61). There has also been a long tradition in Sweden of lay judges that has survived up to the present day. These lay judges have represented different values in different periods, from the consciousness of the community to a modern symbol of democratic representation in court (Modéer, 1994, pp. 41, 63). Today, the main justification for the presence of lay judges in court is that through a kind of public inspection they 'help to maintain public confidence in the judicial system and lend court decisions legitimacy' (Justitiedepaterementet, 2013, p. 27), which is particularly important considering that the deliberation during which the sentence is decided upon is held behind closed doors, as opposed to the trial, which is open to the public. The lay judges, unlike their role historically, are not supposed to provide a popular vision of justice (Modéer, 1994, p. 41), but rather to constitute a kind of democratic control of the system (Justitiedepartementet, 2013, pp. 120–122).

Despite this rich tradition with different, often contesting ways of describing the role of judges, the prevalent ideal of the judge in Sweden, as implemented in education and training and as defined in the doctrine, imagines judges as public servants loyal to the legal system, dutiful and independent of moral, political or religious values (Ställvik, 2009, p. 196). Their task is to apply the rules and principles in an almost mechanical way and to be expert in the technicalities of the law, which enables them to find the right solution to a case. This ideal presupposes that there is one proper solution to every case. It also builds on a vision of the law in which the meaning of every rule is decided once and for all.

Nevertheless, as in the cases that I described in the two previous chapters, the image of a judge as merely expressing the discourse and the will of the law has been clouded several times. The fact that the district courts and the courts of appeal made different decisions, both in the case of the Manby mosque fire and in the case of insults against Fatima Ameen, is testament to a first such instance. A second instance, and one that is perhaps more telling, was the dissenting opinion to which I shortly referred in the opening of Chapter 7 that concerned the insults uttered over the telephone to Abdul Hassan. While the court of appeal in this case overturned the decision of

152 *On judging and responsibility*

the district court, by arguing that it was not shown during the trial that the defendant had the motive to aggrieve Abdul Hassan because of his ethnicity or religion, one judge presented a different interpretation of the law. In this dissenting opinion, the judge's role as an interpreter of the law was revealed, showing that the court actually *practises* law through a constant interpretation of rules. Thereby the idea of the meaning of legal regulations as firmly established, clear and unambiguous was undermined. The dissenting opinion is usually articulated in the judgement in the first person, which enables the court to stress the subjective character of an interpretation that goes against the one reached. In this way, the decision expressed in the judgement is presented as the proper and objective one and defined as *the* right solution to the case. Dissenting opinions—as opposed to the usual, impersonal voice of the court—are formulated in a personal tone, using 'I', which makes the judges' personal agency visible (Bladini, 2013). This was also how the dissenting opinion was expressed in the case, when the judge used the phrase 'in my opinion'. In such moments, it becomes clear that the judiciary relies on individuals whose work consists in *interpreting the law.*

In his book about the dilemma of the North American anti-slavery judges active during the slavery era, Robert Cover describes the dilemma of men caught between the demands of their role in the judiciary, which made them collaborate with the system of oppression, and their voice of conscience. He writes:

> In a static and simplistic model of law, the judge caught between law and morality has only four choices. He may apply the law against his conscience. He may apply conscience and be faithless to the law. He may resign. Or he may cheat: He may state that the law is not what he believes it to be and, thus, preserve an appearance (to others) of conformity of law and morality. Once we assume a more realistic model of law and the judicial process, these four positions become only poles setting limits to a complex field of action and motive. For in a dynamic model law is always becoming. And the judge has a legitimate role in determining what it is that the law will become.
>
> (1975, p. 6)

The context of my study is diametrically different. One of the basic principles underlying Swedish law today is that all people have equal value independent of their skin colour, ethnicity and religion. The Swedish laws that target racism build, albeit indirectly, on the heritage of the struggles against the forms of racial oppression that were legitimized by law in the same historical times that Cover analyses. Today, judges in Sweden can actually make use of legal tools to counter racism and do justice in cases involving racist violence, religious intolerance and discrimination.[2] And yet the ways in which they adjudicate in most cases I have analysed here fail to recognize a particular type of harm involved in such acts. Until now, my argument has been that this is due to the structure of legal reasoning about intent, subject, language, injury and responsibility. In this sense, I have been applying what Cover in the above quote calls a 'static model' of law.

While in the static model judges speak law through their interpretations and are never confronted with interpretative choices, let alone dilemmas, in a more dynamic model of law, judges are not mere legal technicians in the machinery of the judiciary, but rather those who actually make the law by exercising interpretation. It is through their decisions that the abstract and indeterminate language in which the rules are expressed is explicated and given an application. It is through the instances of adjudication that certain meanings of law gain authority, while other meanings are discredited. In this chapter, I would like to claim that the static model that I have been using so far needs to be expanded if we are to attend to all the dimensions of legal proceedings. The two cases against Ola Johansson suggest, I have been arguing, that it is difficult to understand the course of the trial and its outcome in the form of sentence and judgement without acknowledging the scope for agency of those involved in the cases. Furthermore, I want to suggest that by thinking of law through a dynamic model, in which judges are confronted with the task of interpreting a unique case, of framing the facts of the event on trial in a particular way and of giving a certain meaning to the rule to be applied, my analysis can bring some important insights.[3]

The two judgements and rhetorical justice

One of the main sites of the discretion of judges are verdicts,[4] another one is the form that the verdict is mediated through—the judgement (Lavén, 2013, p. 49). It is here that the judges execute their power of defining and explaining the case on trial. In the final part of this chapter, I will propose a reading of the judgements in the two cases, and will try to illuminate the ways in which the judges framed the crime in each—in the 2008 case as racist violence and in the 2009 case as an ordinary crime—thereby making visible their agency in the process of deciding the cases and interpreting the law.

As mentioned above, the judgements in the 2008 case and in the 2009 case differed considerably in their form. The length of the documents alone indicates some differences: the 2008 judgement is almost twice as long as the 2009 judgement. The difference in the extent to which the judges argued for the grounds of their decisions is striking. While the 2008 case has numerous references both to a precedent and to the legislative work, the 2009 case has almost no argument of this kind. For the sake of this analysis, however, the most significant difference lies in how the judges treated the possible racist nature of the violence performed by Ola Johansson.

In the 2008 case, the judge carefully crafted grounds for the court's decision by exposing, step by step, the rationale and providing the legal basis for the decision. By deconstructing the legal reasoning laid out in the

154 *On judging and responsibility*

judgement, we can see how a particular meaning of the law is established; one that makes it possible to interpret the act performed by Ola Johansson as racist violence.

When deciding on the issue of the defendant's responsibility for the crimes he had been charged with, the racist aspect of his acts was brought to the fore. The judge, when considering whether the act of name-calling performed by Ola Johansson should be classified as insult in legal terms, referred to a precedent and reasoned:

> To call a person of foreign extraction a 'fucking wog' has in the legal case NJA (1989 p. 374) been qualified as an insult according to Chapter 5 Section 3 of the Swedish Penal Code. The Supreme Court found that the utterance had referred to and aimed at offending the injured party's self-esteem. To call someone of foreign origin a terrorist or a Taliban, must in today's situation be regarded as having the same purpose and as offensive to the self-esteem. Ola Johansson is therefore also guilty of insult.
>
> (Judgement, Case 12)

By referring to a precedent, the court established that the insults uttered by Ola Johansson classified as a criminal offence. Hence, the court maintained the frameworks proposed by the prosecutor, where the particular character of the crime was linked to the fact that it was directed at a person with a minority background and that the insult itself was calculated to offend the injured party's self-esteem. To quote the relevant precedent, the decision of the Supreme Court that established that a certain racist expression—wog (*svartskalle*)—is to be considered a criminal offence of insult enabled the judge to give his decision the proper authority by inscribing it in the body of the existing jurisdiction. The judge applied the precedent's rationale to the case by comparing the two racist expressions. He did this by taking into consideration the new social context in which 'terrorist' or 'Taliban' can be used as racist insults. In this way, the judge contextualized the insult and evaluated its possible aim and potential impact.

Also in the next section of the judgement, the one concerning the sanction, the court maintained this framework. When weighing different circumstances that might influence the harshness of the penalty, the court, apart from the past record of the defendant, took the character of the crime into account. It stated: 'The fact that it [the violence] contained racist elements suggests that the penalty should be enhanced' (Judgement, Case 12).

In a similar way, the character of the crime appeared in the last section of the judgement, which concerned the question of damages. The court considered the amount of the damages separately: for the violence against a public servant and for the insult. While damages for the former are usually meted out by taking into account the quantity and the consequences of the physical violence, those for the latter reflect the idea that an offence against

On judging and responsibility 155

somebody's person, freedom, peace or good name should entail a reparation. The court once again referred to the Supreme Court's decision in the same case involving racist insult, in which damages were awarded based on the idea that:

> When deciding on the damages, it should be considered that the utterance goes against a fundamental societal value, that is, the equal value of every human being, regardless of race, colour and ethnic origin. It is thus in conflict with the efforts made by the Government authorities to counteract discrimination on ethnic grounds, efforts that, among other things, have manifested themselves in the introduction of the law (1986: 442) against ethnic discrimination.
>
> (The Supreme Court, case NJA, 1989, p. 374,
> quoted in the Judgement, Case 12)

The court decided on damages for the insult. This time the legal reasoning was built by the judge referring to one of the fundamental norms that is said to underpin the Swedish legal system, that is, 'the equal value of every human being, regardless of race, colour and ethnic origin' (Judgement). The norm is not only cited as a fundamental value in Swedish society, but is also described as promoted by the legislators in their efforts to counter discrimination.

The judgement in the 2008 case is an example of how the racist nature of an act can be underscored and made visible. It shows, furthermore, how this recognition impacted not only the sentence and the damages, but also the definition of the injury and the rhetoric of the judicial process. The reference to the racist nature of the crime appeared in all steps of the procedure: when defining the act as a crime, in this case an insult, when meting out the penalty, and when deciding on damages. The reference to a precedent and to the principle of equality regardless of race, ethnicity or religion provided the decision with the proper legal validity by inscribing it into the system of norms underlying Swedish law. The interpretation exercised in judging this particular case was presented as complying and coherent with the legal system as a whole, thus living up to the professional standards of a valid legal decision.

The grounds for the court's decision in the 2008 case suggest that how the acts on trial are understood by the judge, what rules are applied and what relevant sources are referred to in order to justify the legal decision can vary. The judge was here actively exercising his interpretative power to decide the case. At the same time, he was reading the law in a particular way, giving it a valid legal interpretation that might in the future contribute to the ways in which the regulations that deal with racist crimes will be interpreted and applied.

By contrast, in the judgement in the 2009 case, the possible racist nature of the crime was invisible. If it was not for Babak Rostami's account in

156 *On judging and responsibility*

court, in which he quotes Ola Johansson's insults and describes them as 'racist expressions' (Judgement, Case 13), nothing in the judgement would indicate that the case had anything to do with racist violence. The court, however, disregarded this part of Babak Rostami's story, so the possibility of the assault having a racist nature was not taken into consideration, and thus the penalty enhancement provision was not applied by the court.

The two judgements taken together show that there is scope for a judge to interpret the law in different ways: a similar act of violence performed by the same person was treated in court as a racist crime and as common violence. The courtroom may thus be understood as a place in which the law is given a meaning. The different judgements provide potential guidance for future cases involving racist violence and feed into the understanding of the legal provisions aimed at combating racism. As a result, the operation of the law is decided during the trials and in the judgements pronounced by judges.

As seen in the 2008 case, the discretion of judges is not unlimited. In order to make a valid judgement, the judge had to carefully craft his opinion and present legally persuasive grounds for the court's decision. In this sense, the discretion of judges is always confined by a specific legal reasoning that has to be accepted by the judicial system so that the decision cannot be overturned by a higher court. In other words, the assessment of the disputed facts and the interpretation of the law have to be performed within existing legal frames and in a language comprehensible to other practitioners of the law.

These cases also illustrate that the ways in which justice is dispensed are not confined to the imposed penalty. How the trial is framed and afterwards recounted in the judgement is part of the judicial process. In this document, the final decision on how the disputed event is interpreted by the legal authorities is rendered. In judges' rhetoric, a vision of the crime and of the injury is expressed. The power to describe, define and interpret the events is thereby realized. Moreover, by referring to the accounts given in the courtroom, judges sustain or discredit interpretations given by the parties involved in the trial.

Conclusions: the penalty enhancement provision—a law in progress

In this chapter, I have proposed that in order to understand the difference between the two ways of treating racist violence in court in the cases against Ola Johansson, I need to adopt a dynamic model of law and the judiciary; one in which law is made also in court by judges, other actors of the judicial system, such as prosecutors and solicitors, as well as other people involved in the trial, most importantly the defendant and the injured party. In this model, how the law is exercised depends not only on the scope and the limitations of the legal system—my argument in the two previous chapters—but also on the ways it is understood in trials, when deciding on cases

On judging and responsibility   157

involving persons who may act in a myriad of possible ways and thereby influence the course of the trial. I have also argued that different interpretations and visions of law, and of particular regulations, including the regulations against racism, are in competition in court. Furthermore, by applying different understandings of what these regulations mean, judges establish their meaning, thereby influencing the future reading of the law.

Such an understanding has helped me to see the differences between the two decisions as expressing two different readings of the law. The judgements then become a possible site of struggle over the meaning of the legal regulations that target racism. These regulations emerge as not yet completely decided and formed, but as developing: laws in progress. The impression of indeterminacy is strengthened by the relative novelty of the legislation against racism, and in particular of the penalty enhancement provision. By having been in use for only a couple of decades, this regulation has not yet a clearly established meaning and is not yet supported by a large body of precedents. What it means to pronounce that one of the motives for a crime is 'to aggrieve a person, ethnic group or some other similar group of people by reason of race, colour, national or ethnic origin, religious belief or other similar circumstance' (Swedish Penal Code Chapter 29 Section 2 (7)) has yet to be decided; during that process, distinct interpretations are in contest.

The image of the judge that has emerged in this chapter as actively contributing to the determination of the meaning of law raises yet another issue: that of responsibility. In the legal positivist doctrine, judges are accountable mainly in terms of their professional performance; they should be faithful to the law, objective, neutral and impartial. Thus, while the courts' ways of determining and identifying responsibility in cases that they adjudicate are strongly related to the idea of an individual subject, responsibility for the decisions made by the judges is dispersed and absolved in the system. Judges stand as representatives of the law, and their status as individuals taking decisions is limited to their professional role. As a consequence, their accountability exists only within the system and is reduced to their ability to follow the established rules. However, once we see judges as faced with different possible interpretations of the law, reflecting different ways in which society and justice can be imagined, their acts of judging start to involve another kind of responsibility. As such, in their exercising of jurisdiction—in telling the law—judges become political.

If we take the judges as agents who actually make the law through their practice of interpretation, also the vision of law as a coherent and self-contained system will be shattered. Instead, the law will emerge as an important site of contradictions and conflicts over the possible ways of deciding upon the facts on trial and, perhaps more importantly, upon the scope and the meaning of the legislation to be applied. From such a perspective, the ideal of a coherent and unitary nature of the law works through the concealment of the conflicts that underlie social life, including its institutionalized legal

158　On judging and responsibility

form, giving itself authority. Once the controversies and ambiguities are made visible, it is possible to conceive of 'a broad field of law as the expression of a system of principles and counter-principles whose actual or proper relation to each other can be represented in clashing ways' (Unger, 1986, p. 88). These principles can then be related to alternative visions of social life that are in contest in the law (Veitch et al., 2012, p. 143). Such an image of law makes visible the controversies and clashes that are inherent in each legal system. It also suggests that there is always a history of struggles over how law, and thereby also a social community, should be imagined. These struggles are necessarily present at the moment of enacting legislation, but they are also reflected in the ways in which every regulation has been read and interpreted in the past by the judiciary.

Thus, with the analysis of these two cases as a point of departure, I have suggested in this chapter that it is necessary to reformulate the understanding of the trial and the judgement, and to treat them as sites of a political struggle over the definitions and meanings of the law. Seen in this way, the courtroom becomes a space for socially relevant actions and a possible arena for engaging in anti-racist struggle.

Notes

1　The necessity of having a victim who is willing to press charges is reduced to a minimum in criminal law. This is due to a tradition of treating crimes as harmful not merely to the individual who falls victim to the particular criminal act, but to society as a whole. From this point of view, it is considered to be in the public interest to prosecute such crimes, as these cannot be reduced to private wrongs. This is why crimes are usually subject to public prosecution irrespective of whether the victim so wishes (Marshall & Duff, 1998, p. 13). However, unlike the majority of criminal offences, insult is, according to the Swedish Penal Code, a crime that is not covered by the public prosecution system. This means that the only person who can press charges is the injured party. Nevertheless, there are some exceptions to this rule: public prosecution is possible if it is in the public interest. One situation where it is considered to be so, according to the Penal Code, is when the 'insulting behaviour [is directed] towards a person with allusion to his or her race, colour, national or ethnic origin or religious belief' (Swedish Penal Code, Chapter 5, Section 5). Thus, racist insult is an offence that is considered a public wrong. Yet, even in such cases, the public prosecutor can only press charges if the injured party has reported the crime for legal action.

2　There are some important differences in how the role of judges is defined in these two legal traditions. While a vision of judges as law-makers is particularly prevalent in the common law tradition, in which precedent is an important source of law, in Sweden, as it pertains to the civil law tradition, case law is given less weight and the judges seem to have less scope for discretion (Banakar, 1998, p. 111). Yet, even in Sweden, precedents (*prejudikat*), in particular decisions of the Supreme Court and the courts of appeal, are actually an important source of law and are referred to frequently as the grounds for courts' decisions. Moreover, a tendency to regard judges as having discretion to make decisions and interpret the law has increased with the Europeanization and internationalization of the Swedish legal system in the last decades (Ställvik, 2009, p. 247). Hence, it is possible that a new way of thinking of the judge as actively practising law is emerging, bringing the Swedish judiciary closer to the systems in which judges are granted considerable discretion and regarded as law-makers. Without losing important contextual differences in how the role of judges is defined, I try, however, to formulate my argument on a more general level. I would suggest that even in a legal system in which the judge's role is concealed behind a positivist legal philosophy or a strongly bureaucratized professional culture, like the Swedish one, the ambiguity of legal language and the very nature of legal reasoning that requires judges to apply general rules to unique cases mean that the judges' work unavoidably consists in interpreting the meaning of the law. In this sense, also in Sweden, law is always produced and reproduced in the courtroom and in the justification of decisions taken in specific cases.

3 There is another interesting aspect that such a dynamic model of the judiciary makes more visible. It is actually that it helps us to see the 'judicial field', to use Bourdieu's term, as a part of society where a professional monopoly of certain services and certain power is created and sustained through a disqualification of those who do not belong to the field (Bourdieu, 1986). From this perspective, an analysis of the composition of the Swedish judiciary and of the underrepresentation of ethnic and religious minorities would be interesting to situate how judges' own social position in relation to ethnicity and religion, but also class, can actually be related to certain group interests.

4 What is important, according to the principle of immediateness that is central for the Swedish judiciary, is that the verdict is based mainly on what is said during the trial. This means that the judges usually do not study the files from the police investigation before the trial (Lavén, 2013, p. 47). The verdict is thus to some degree dependent on how the case is defined by the prosecution. However, when it comes to the decision on the penalty, including the application of the penalty enhancement provision, judges play a central role.

Bibliography

Ahmed, S. (2004). *The Cultural Politics of Emotion*. Edinburgh: Edinburgh University Press.

Banakar, R. (1997). *Doorkeepers of the Law: A Socio-Legal Study of Ethnic Discrimination in Sweden*. Aldershot: Ashgate.

Bladini, M. (2013). *I objektivitetens sken—en kritisk granskning av objektivitetsideal, objektivitetsanspråk och legitimeringsstrategier i diskurser om dömande i brottmål*. Göteborg: Makadam.

Blee, K. (2005). 'Racial Violence in the United States.' *Ethnic and Racial Studies*, 28(4), 599–619.

Bourdieu, P. (1986). 'The Force of Law: Toward a Sociology of the Juridical Field.' *Hastings Law Journal*, 38(5), 805–853.

Cover, R. (1975). *Justice Accused: Antislavery and the Judicial Process*. New Haven: Yale University Press.

Justitiedepartementet. (2013). *Nämndemannauppdraget—breddad rekrytering och kvalificerad medverkan (SOU 2013:49)*. Stockholm: Jutistiedepartementet.

Lacey, N. (1998). *Unspeakable Subjects: Feminist Essays in Legal and Social Theory*. Oxford: Hart.

Lavén, H. (2013). *Hur domstolar dömer i brottmål: om domare, rättegång, bevisning och påföljder* (1st edn.). Stockholm: Norstedts juridik.

160 On judging and responsibility

Marshall, S. & Duff, R. (1998). 'Criminalization and Sharing Wrongs.' *Canadian Journal of Law and Jurisprudance, 11*(1), 7–22.

Modéer, K. (1994). *Den svenska domarkulturen: europeiska och nationella förebilder.* Jönköping: Domstolsverket.

NJA. (1989). p. 374.

Ställvik, O. (2009). *Domarrollen: rättsregler, yrkeskultur och ideal.* Uppsala: Uppsala universitet.

Swedish Penal Code. Retrieved from: www.regeringen.se/rattsliga-dokument/departementsserien-och-promemorior/1999/01/ds-199936/

Unger, R. (1986). *The Critical Legal Studies Movement: Another Time, a Greater Task.* Cambridge, MA: Harvard University Press.

Veitch, S., Christodoulidis, E. & Farmer, L. (2012). *Jurisprudence: Themes and Concepts* (2nd edn.). Abingdon: Routledge.

Wennström, B. (2005). *Rättens individualisering: mot en ny juridisk antropologi.* Uppsala: Juridiska fakulteten, Uppsala universitet.

9   Conclusions

The analysis carried out in this book is the result of a kind of unsettlement. When studying court documents concerning cases of anti-Muslim violence, I discovered a silence around a particular nature of these acts of violence. The aspect that interested me of the acts, and that constituted the basic criterion for the cases to be classified as Islamophobic hate crimes, seemed invisible in most of the judgements. Exploring this silence became the core of this book. The underlying issue I have looked at was what happens when anti-Muslim racism is put on trial in Swedish courts.

In Chapters 4 and 5, I provided the historical context of this study. In broad outline, the image presented in these chapters was that the Swedish legal system today is equipped with several laws against racism. Moreover, in recent decades, countering what came to be called 'hate crime' has become a priority in Sweden, the implementation of which has included collecting statistics on such crimes. Through a historical account of the emergence of the legislation against racism in Sweden, I attempted to introduce the context of my study, one in which some forms of racism are considered to be a crime. At the same time, in these chapters, I demonstrated how this image was more complex, by showing that the process of criminalization of racism was far from unambiguous and that the dynamics underlying it could simultaneously lead to the introduction of progressive laws and to a denial of racism as a problem.

Chapter 2, while designed to introduce some important sites and contexts for an understanding of the development of anti-Muslim racism in recent decades in Sweden and more generally in Europe, became also an attempt at a first reading of parts of the material: police reports classified by Brå as Islamophobic hate crimes. My claim there was that it is not possible to fully comprehend the message, workings and effects of the acts reported to police without taking into consideration how they relate to certain tropes of anti-Muslim repertoires circulating in Europe.

It is against this background that the unsettlement provoked by the invisibility of the racist dimension of the violence adjudicated in court should be understood. If the racist nature of a crime was considered in law an aggravating circumstance, yet, in case after case, courts seemed not to notice this

162 *Conclusions*

nature of the violence, why was this happening and what did this mean for how justice was dispensed? It is from there that I started to ask questions. How is racism defined in law and in court? What is necessary for an act to be classified as racist? And, more indirectly: What kind of injury can be claimed in court? These questions guided my analysis of the cases I selected to explore the reasons why the possibility of an act being racist is not taken into consideration in the first place, or to understand the courts' rationale when deciding on whether an act is racist or not.

When analysing the case of the Manby mosque fire in Chapter 6, I claimed that the court's main focus when adjudicating the case was on the person who had performed the act, and especially on his intent. Intent is crucial in legal and judicial reasoning, since an act can be considered a crime provided that the defendant had a particular state of mind and that this has been proven by the prosecutor. Thus, in the Manby mosque case, the judgement revolved around the question of Sven Persson's intent to set the mosque on fire. I argued in Chapter 6 that whether a crime is racist or not is established in court in a similar way—through reference to a motive. At the same time, I claimed that both intent and motive are understood in a very specific way by the judiciary. By contrasting the Manby mosque fire case, in which the court did not consider the racist nature of the crime, with the Holmstad mosque fire case, in which the court did so, I concluded that the racist dimension of the crime was recognized only when the defendants' motives were openly stated or when they had a clear affiliation to a racist organization. It was difficult to find this type of motive in the Manby mosque case. Sven Persson explained his act in terms of jokes and denied any hostile views regarding Muslims or immigrants. I also claimed that in order to grasp the defendant's motives, the court needed to install a racist subject, conceived of in a particular way. Following the judicial understanding of motives, a racist subject was constructed as an individual cognizant of his motivations and able to provide an explanation of the reasons for his or her acts—ideologically open and explicit on racist opinions. Such a racist subject was lacking in this case. Although Sven Persson's statements were ambivalent, he was definitely not the conscious and ideologically open racist subject that the court would need in order to establish that the acts of throwing the Koran and other religious books around and setting a mosque on fire were acts of racism.

The case of the Manby mosque fire was not exceptional in this regard; the vast majority of crimes categorized by Brå as hate crimes lack any obvious links to extreme-right ideology, White Power movements or other forms of organized racism (Klingspor, Molarin & Brottsförebyggande rådet, 2009, p. 66; Klingspor, Molarin, Sporre & Brottsförebyggande rådet, 2008, p. 91; Molarin & Frenzel, 2010, p. 59; Sporre, Klingspor & Wigerholt, 2007, p. 76). Moreover, from the literature that explores the issue of motives in extreme manifestations of racism, such as the Holocaust, the Ku Klux Klan and the White Power movement, I learned that, even in cases that involved

Conclusions 163

explicit evidence of links to racist ideology or organizational affiliation, motives often remained obscure and complex (cf. Arendt, 2006; Blee, 2005). One conclusion from the analysis of the Manby mosque fire case was that the focus on motives actually makes it difficult to identify in court the racist nature of an act; moreover, it inhibits an understanding of the dynamics of racism.

Building on these and similar theories of racism (cf. Ahmed, 2004; Arendt, 2006; Blee, 2005; Butler, 1997; Rattansi, 2007), I proposed an understanding of racism that shifts attention from the motives and the person who performs racist acts to the meaning, message and effects of these acts. In cases where the subject's intentions are ambivalent and opaque and there seems to be no causal relation between a certain ideology or prejudice and the performed act, the racist nature of the act may manifest itself in this act carrying certain meanings and bringing about certain effects. This, of course, does not mean that there is no difference between a premeditated act performed by an individual affiliated with an openly racist organization or openly expressing racist ideas, and an ambivalent act performed by an individual whose motives are obscure and who is not fully cognizant of its potential impact. What I suggest is that both such acts can have similar effects and be similarly construed by those involved, the victims, and by society at large. This was clear in my analysis of the accounts of the representatives of the local Muslim community who felt threatened by the attack on their mosque. They understood these acts in the context of previous threats and incidents targeting them as a group and as an attempt to harm their religious identity. This suggests that the racist message sent by an act does not necessarily depend on intentions or ideological awareness of the person performing such an act.

In Chapter 7, I further explored the idea of racist acts as communicating a particular message. The case of insults addressed towards Fatima Ameen turned out to be suitable for this purpose as it disclosed the court's difficulties when adjudicating upon the insulting nature of the utterances directed at the injured party. My main point in Chapter 7 was that the court could not see racism in some of the utterances because it interpreted them extracted from their context, cut off from the histories that made them meaningful. I claimed that racist acts work through a reference to certain histories of oppression and that their harmfulness cannot be fully understood if this link is not considered.

In my analysis, I was influenced by theories of racism that are historically informed, that is, that draw on the analysis of the ways in which racism has expressed itself in the past. My focus on histories of oppression that were repeated in or referred to in racist acts, evinced particularly clearly in racist speech acts, was not limited to deciphering the meaning of such acts. Following Sara Ahmed, I instead argued that *these histories are actually acted out in racist practices* and that they do not belong to the past, but are a thing of the present: 'The past is living rather than dead; the past lives in

164 *Conclusions*

the very wounds that remain open in the present' (2004, p. 33). Hence, one effect of racist acts and a source of their harm is their enactment of certain forms of *categorization, debasement* and *oppression.* The violence performed in the cases that I analysed consisted thus not only in physical or verbal aggression, but also in an injury brought about by a reference to particular histories of racism. This dimension of the harm remains unintelligible unless understood in the context of these histories, I claimed. Only by understanding the insults as a kind of citation (Butler, 1997a, p. 34) and as 'sticky signs' (Ahmed, 2004, p. 92) was it possible to see them as bearing a particular message and hence carrying with them the potential of a special type of harm.

The case of insults against Fatima Ameen showed again that only blatant racism, this time in the form of a vulgar slur referring to her skin colour, was considered racist in court. This confirmed my claims from Chapter 6 that the courts experienced difficulties in identifying more subtle or coded forms of racism. In the case presented in Chapter 7, the court's identification of a racist slur almost exclusively in expressions drawing on classic racism, in which the injured party's physicality plays a crucial role, suggested that the court restricted its definition of racism to biological racism, leaving other expressions of racism aside and unpunished.

In all the cases analysed in this book, the defendants were found at least partly guilty of the crimes that the prosecutors charged them with. The violence they performed was identified as a crime and punished. Still, as I have claimed, a particular type of silence often hung over the racist character of these acts, resulting in a form of unrecognition. The laws against racism, such as the penalty enhancement provision, were rarely taken into consideration and, when they were, they were often found inapplicable by the courts. Thus, what happened was that the cases were named, interpreted and judged as cases of violence, but not as racist violence, as though the courts had difficulties in dealing with the racist nature of the violent acts. Or, as Reza Banakar argued in relation to cases of ethnic discrimination in Sweden, the courts relabelled such cases instead of attending to the core of the dispute, unwilling 'to deal with racism as racism, ethnic discrimination as ethnic discrimination' (Banakar, 1998, p. 88).

This silence was even more striking when considering the fact that, both in the case of the Manby mosque fire and the case of insults against Fatima Ameen, the injured parties claimed that the injury they suffered was related to the racist nature of the acts. This nature of the injury was central to their way of interpreting the violent acts and defining the harm that they had suffered. Yet, in both cases, the courts remained deaf to their claims.

This sort of unrecognition of injuries caused by racism manifested itself differently in different cases. In the case of the Manby mosque fire, the unrecognition was partly related to a strictly material way of treating harm, which I identify as one of the features of the secular nature of the judiciary. The insistence on expressing the losses suffered by the Muslim community in terms of money mirrored an incapacity to acknowledge anything other than the material dimensions of the injury. My argument here is that the harm done by the acts of throwing the Koran and other religious books around and setting the mosque on fire cannot be understood without recognizing their offensive meanings. By this I do not mean to claim that the material dimension of the injury was irrelevant, but that the materiality of the violence and the racist message conveyed in the acts of throwing the sacred books around and setting the mosque on fire were indeed inseparable. In this sense, the claim for recognition is not intended to *displace* other claims, most importantly claims for economic justice, as could follow from the critique of the idiom of recognition presented by Nancy Fraser (2000, p. 108). Rather I argue that it is impossible to attain justice by treating these two dimensions of the injury as clearly separate. Here I am inspired by Judith Butler when she questions the distinction between the economic and the cultural and thus between redistribution and recognition as two distinct forms of justice (Butler, 1997b).

However, in some ways the interpretation of the court in the case of the Manby mosque fire goes deeper, involving a more fundamental lack of recognition of the loss suffered by the Muslim community as a cultural loss. By defining the mosque as lacking 'any special significance in the sense that it is of cultural interest outside the Muslim community' (Judgement, Case 3), the court constructs Muslim culture as separate from Swedish culture and society. The court's denial of the cultural value of the mosque is not just an act of exclusion of Swedish Muslim communities, it is also constitutive of a normative Swedish identity. Thereby, a particular idea about what Swedish culture looks like is maintained and stabilized. The court, instead of remedying the racist violence and overturning its effects with the help of available laws against racism, perpetuates the debasement entailed by this act of anti-Muslim violence.

In the case of insults against Fatima Ameen, the unrecognition had to do with the court's reluctance or inability to read racist language. I have explained this inability by identifying a particular language doctrine that the court adopted, one of the consequences of which was that the court could recognize the harm claimed by the injured party only to a limited degree. Also, by focusing on the vulgarity and inappropriateness of the slander without referring to the racist imaginary that the slander mobilized, the court reframed the case as one of *general* rudeness and uncivility, shifting the focus from the ways in which racism involves a *particular* type of harm. In this sense, the unrecognition had to do with a type of denial of the harm entailed by racism.

When analysing the cases in Chapters 6 and 7, I suggested that there are several different reasons for these difficulties in attending to and redressing the injury caused by racism. The secular framework of the judiciary and the predominantly material ways of measuring injury make it difficult to recognize an injury targeting religious or cultural identity. The literal reading of a

166   *Conclusions*

racist slur and its disentanglement from histories of oppression obfuscate its injurious meaning. A procedure through which performed acts or racist slurs are treated as separate crimes diverts attention from the cumulative nature of racist violence or even prevents the court from noticing racism in the first place. Locating the origin of the injury in an individual makes the citational character of racist violence invisible.

One of the cases that I analysed in Chapter 8 suggested yet another possible reason for the difficulties in redressing the injury caused by racism in court. It seemed that, to make an act of racism visible in court, it was crucial that a certain kind of individual sense of harm needed to be expressed and contained in the available modes of giving an account of the injury. When such accounts were missing, so was the possibility of claiming that the act was of a racist nature. What was problematic in such an approach is that it based the possibility of reading some acts as racist only on the effects that such acts might have or might fail to have on an individual. Following Kathleen Blee (2005) and Sara Ahmed (2004), I argued that this makes it difficult to see individual acts of anti-Muslim racism as sending a message of vulnerability and disempowerment to communities beyond the actual scenes in which they occur.

As some scholars have pointed out, hate crime legislation often assumes that the crime is committed *because of*, or, as the translation of the Swedish law text says, *by reason of* the victim's group identity. They further argue that this presupposes that racism precedes the crime; rather than being an effect manifested in the violence, it is regarded merely as its cause (Ahmed, 2004, p. 55; Blee, 2005, p. 602). Following this argument, I have seen Muslim identities not as simply or exclusively taken up by Muslims through their belonging to particular communities of faith or tradition but also as, at least partly, imposed on Muslims through violent acts of the kind I have been concerned with here, placing them in particular histories of oppression. The Muslim subject is, in other words, constructed *through* the violent acts I analysed.

My conclusions in Chapters 6 and 7 were quite pessimistic. Once I had identified several obstacles to the application of legal provisions, it seemed almost impossible for a particular harm entailed by a racist act of violence to be recognized in court. I suggested that this had to do more with the fundamental ways in which law and the courts define subject, injury and responsibility in general that make it difficult to respond to such social injustices as racism, in which the workings of the injury are difficult to describe and understand if limited exclusively to the individuals directly involved in the crime. My critique of how the courts adjudicated in the cases analysed in this book echo the feminist critique of law and the state more generally (Brown, 1995; Smart, 2002) and scepticism about radical movements investing in legal reform as a tool in the fight for social justice (Butler, 1997a).

Moreover, following Carol Smart (2002), I identified a particular kind of power of the law, not only in the traditional sense of the word as a system

Conclusions   167

of coercion, but also in the ways the judiciary operates as a knowledge regime. According to this view, law and the judiciary fix the meaning and decide on the truth of a complex and often ambiguous reality. This model of the power of the judiciary has important consequences for understanding the potential and limits that the use of law for emancipatory purposes can have. Anti-racist strategies that engage in litigation and legal reform are forced to rely on the same knowledge regime: 'in order to have any impact on law one has to talk law's language, use legal methods, and accept legal procedures' (Smart, 2002, p. 160). Such strategies will always have to deal with the risks of using, and therefore reinforcing, the power embodied in the judiciary. In this sense, such emancipatory projects will run the risk that they may 'problematically mirror the mechanisms and configurations of power of which they are an effect and which they purport to oppose' (Brown, 1995, p. 3).

I have suggested yet another problem with using law in combating racism that has to do with the context in which racism is considered to be shameful. The criminalization of hate speech, racial discrimination and racist violence, as well as the opprobrium attached to manifestations of racism, contributed to a marginalization of overt expressions of classic, biological racism. This has meant, as I have discussed, that racist acts have taken on new forms, passing racist messages in more concealed ways. Such a transformation was apparent in the ways Sven Persson gave an account of himself in court. This account, I argued, seemed to avoid the accusation of racism. Moreover, such avoidance of the accusation of racism had seemed to be already present at the crime scene, in how he performed his acts. Similarly, the slurs cast by Lars Nilsson in his emails to Fatima Ameen were to some degree influenced by self-censorship. Lars Nilsson's awareness of the illegality, or at least inappropriateness, of the words used in his emails to Fatima Ameen had actually already shaped the utterance when he encrypted one of the words by omitting some letters and replacing them with two underscores: 'Go home to Africa, fast as hell, billboard n_gg_r!' This practice, quite widespread on the Internet, is intended to encrypt words regarded as improper or banned, making external censorship impossible. I suggest that, once morally condemned and proscribed by law, racism looks for new disguises, taking on new forms in order to escape accusation, not least a criminal charge. Based on the analysis of these cases, I argue that law becomes, in a way, implicated in how racist speech acts, and racist acts more generally, constantly adapt and transform themselves. Racist messages appear in a coded form and become unintelligible to the judiciary, which, in turn, strives to fix and freeze the changing forms of expression within its rigid frames. Hence, one of the most important conclusions of this book is that the same events and developments that led to the passing of laws against racism in Sweden and in other parts of the world have had an impact on how racism is articulated, making it difficult to use these laws in practice.

168 *Conclusions*

In contrast to my analyses in Chapters 6 and 7, where I focused on the workings of the judiciary and on the legal reasoning that made it difficult for the courts to address racism, in Chapter 8, I attempted to show how every case and every trial is also an effect of the agency of different actors. By contrasting two cases against the same person who performed similar acts of physical violence and verbal abuse against two taxi drivers, but whose acts were named, defined and interpreted differently by the courts, I was able to show how the way in which the cases unfolded throughout the judicial proceedings was influenced by those involved and, especially, by the discretion of the judges.

While one of these cases was similar to those analysed in previous chapters, in that the racist nature of the acts was almost completely invisible in the judgement, the other case constituted a counter-example. Here the judge placed the racist nature of the violence at the centre of his adjudication. This case enabled me to illustrate a possibility of the different understandings of racism and an alternative interpretation of legal provisions against racism within the framework of the same system. In a way, one consequence of my argument formulated in this chapter was that the understanding of law and the judiciary that I had constructed in the book up to that point, as a coherent and self-contained system, was questionable. I therefore introduced the idea that, in fact, judges are invested with agency and that laws are never totally predefined; rather, they are always rewritten and interpreted in court. The image of the judiciary that emerged in Chapter 8 was one in which different understandings of racism clash. On the theoretical level, this meant an introduction of judicial discretion into the model of the judiciary I had used thus far and, more generally, the introduction of agency into my analyses of the trials and judgements. Such a modified, dynamic model of the judiciary, I claim, suggests that the interpretation of the laws against racism is not set in stone, which opens up the possibility of attaining justice in cases involving racist violence.

Bibliography

Ahmed, S. (2004). *The Cultural Politics of Emotion*. Edinburgh: Edinburgh University Press.

Arendt, H. (2006). *Eichmann in Jerusalem: A Report on the Banality of Evil*. New York, NY: Penguin Books.

Banakar, R. (1998). *Doorkeepers of the Law: A Socio-Legal Study of Ethnic Discrimination in Sweden*. Aldershot: Ashgate.

Blee, K. (2005). 'Racial Violence in the United States.' *Ethnic and Racial Studies*, 28(4), 599–619.

Brown, W. (1995). *States of Injury: Power and Freedom in Late Modernity*. Princeton, NJ: Princeton University Press.

Butler, J. (1997a). *Excitable Speech: A Politics of the Performative*. New York; London: Routledge.

Butler, J. (1997b). 'Merely Cultural.' *Social Text*, 52/53, 265–277.

Conclusions 169

Fraser, N. (2000). 'Rethinking Recognition.' *New Left Review*, 3, 107–120.

Klingspor, K., Molarin, A. & Brottsförebyggande rådet. (2009). *Hatbrott 2008: polisanmälningar där det i motivbilden ingår etnisk bakgrund, religiös tro, sexuell läggning eller könsöverskridande identitet eller uttryck*. Stockholm: Brottsförebyggande rådet (BRÅ): Fritze.

Klingspor, K., Molarin, A., Sporre, T. & Brottsförebyggande rådet. (2008). *Hatbrott 2007: en sammanställning av anmälningar med främlingsfientliga, islamofobiska, antisemitiska och homofobiska motiv*. Stockholm: Brottsförebyggande rådet (BRÅ): Fritze.

Molarin, A. & Frenzel, A. (2010). *Hatbrott 2009: statistik över polisanmälningar där det i motivbilden ingår etnisk bakgrund, religiös tro, sexuell läggning eller könsöverskridande identitet eller uttryck*. Stockholm: Brottsförebyggande rådet (BRÅ): Fritze.

Rattansi, A. (2007). *Racism: A Very Short Introduction*. Oxford; New York: Oxford University Press.

Smart, C. (2002). *Feminism and the Power of Law*. London: Routledge.

Sporre, T., Klingspor, K. & Wigerholt, J. (2007). *Hatbrott 2006: en sammanställning av polisanmälningar med främlingsfientliga, islamofobiska, antisemitiska och homofobiska motiv*. Stockholm: Brottsförebyggande rådet (BRÅ): Fritze.

Index

agitation against a national or ethnic group: act on 54–60, 64, 68–70; freedom of speech 124, 134n5; hate crime 84, 92

Ahmed, Sara 2, 72, 88, 112, 118, 128, 135, 139, 149, 164, 166

anti-Muslim racism: definitions of 2, 95; discourses and imaginaries 15, 43–44; gendered nature of 16–19; migration 21–26, 117–118; nationalism 21–26; scales of 13, 13n3, 25, 26; *see also* Islamophobia; racism

anti-racism: anti-apartheid movement 61; anti-colonial struggles 54, 58–59, 63, 69; anti-racialism 71–72; Civil Rights movement 54, 58, 69, 71, 92; human rights 68; law 158, 167; research process 43

anti-Semitism: hate crime 80, 87–88, 90–91, 95; law 54–58, 69; *see also* race and religion; racism

Arendt, Hannah 46, 66, 118n8

arson 102–122

Asad, Talal 97, 128, 132

Blee, Kathleen 46, 85, 119 n9, 148–149, 166

Brottsförebyggande rådet 2, 13, 33–34, 80–97; *see also* hate-crime statistics

Butler, Judith 5, 20, 26, 46, 104, 116, 124, 134, 136, 139, 164–165

criminal law 55, 57, 65–67, 108n2, 119 n9, 147 n1

damage 1–2, 66, 103, 105, 108, 113–114, 148–149; *see also* injury

discrimination: act on unlawful discrimination 58–59, 70; anti-discrimination legislation 65–67; Committee on the Elimination of Racial Discrimination 61; discrimination of immigrants 6, 24; International Convention on the Elimination of all Forms of Racial Discrimination 58, 69; religious discrimination 69n20; veil 17

emotions: racist violence 91, 93, 133; research process 41–43

Europe 12–26, 40, 41, 44, 63, 65, 88, 107, 128, 131, 133, 137

evidence 1–2, 34–37, 48, 105, 113, 163

Fekete, Liz 2, 22

Felman, Shoshana 108–109

Foucault, Michel 4–5

Fredrickson, George M. 44, 44n4

freedom of religion 117

freedom of speech 15–16, 53, 112, 124–129, 133–134; *see also* Mohammed cartoons; racist humour

Goldberg, David 39, 58, 61, 71

hate crime 80–101, 103, 112, 148, 162; BRÅ's definition 86–88, 90–91; concept 91–95; Islamophobic hate crime 95–97; statistics 81–89, 89–91; *see also* racism

hate speech 15, 26, 123–140; *see also* agitation against a national or ethnic group; linguistic injury

hets mot folkgrupp see agitation against a national or ethnic group

Index 171

Holocaust 54–57, 63, 72, 162
human rights 18, 65, 88, 91; *see also* anti-racism

injury: injury caused by racism 2–5, 9, 36–37, 105–108, 109, 116, 135–136, 139; legal definitions 2–5, 46, 104, 105–108; linguistic injury/injurious speech 124–126, 128, 131, 139; materiality of 2–5, 105–108; sticky signs 135, 149, 164; *see also* damage; hate speech; insult
insult: anti-Muslim insult 14–16; legal understanding of 127–131, 133, 136–139, 147, 154–155; racist insult 136–139, 149, 164; *see also* accusation of terrorism; freedom of speech; injurious speech
intent 46, 63–64, 110, 112–116, 113n6, 118–119; *see also* motive
Islam 15, 18, 22, 25–26, 107, 112
Islamophobia *see* anti-Muslim racism
Islamophobic hate crime

judge: discretion of judges 47–48, 124, 149–153, 155–158, 168; evaluation of evidence 36; judges in Sweden 37, 42, 45, 149–153; lay judge 37, 37n1; responsibility 157
judgement 3–5, 42–43, 43–48, 45 n5, 125–126, 134, 139–140, 144, 153–156
judiciary: epistemology 4, 36; knowledge regime 4–5, 150, 167; language of the judiciary 2–3, 47, 156, 167; power of the judiciary 1–5, 42, 46–47, 167–168

Koran 105–106, 162–165

Mahmood, Saba 106, 133
migration: anti-Muslim racism 16, 21–26; migration regime 6, 23–25, 24n13, 59–60
Mohammed cartoons 20, 14–16, 14n4, 106, 112, 128; clash of civilizations 14–16
mosque 105–109, 113–114, 116–117, 118–119, 162–163
motive *see* racist motive
multiculturalism 61; backlash against 88–89, 95; freedom of choice 6, 24, 60–61; Swedish model of 6–7, 24

Muslims: in Sweden 22–23; construction of a Muslim subject 13n3, 16, 26, 122, 128

nation: anti-Muslim racism 21–26; construction of a Swedish national identity 6, 54; methodological nationalism 39–41; nationalism 25, 47–49

penalty enhancement provision 33, 53, 59–64, 115–116, 156–158, 164

race: biology 3, 21, 41, 70; concept 38, 70–71, 133; culture 41, 44n4; idea of racial progress 131; racial hygiene 68–69; Sweden 67–71; Swedish State Institute for Racial Biology 68
racism: class 133, 139; colour-blind racism 131; concept 38 n2; cultural racism 41, 44n4; everyday racism 13, 21, 26, 136; extremism 18, 65, 82–84, 133; language as a site of racism *see* linguistic injury/injurious speech, and injury caused by racism; racist subject 118–119, 150; racist humour 109–113, 162; racist motive 33, 43, 46, 53, 58, 63–64, 82–90, 93, 112–118, 118n8, 119 n9, 124, 162–163; racist slur *see* linguistic injury/injurious speech, and injury caused by racism; religion 3, 17–18, 21, 18n9, 44 n4, 90, 97, 106, 117; responsibility for 42, 104, 115–116, 135–136, 166; scientific racism 39, 44n4, 67–69, 130–131; vulnerability 20–21, 109, 121, 148–149, 166; White Power 6, 25, 46, 62, 70–71, 82, 83, 89–90, 121, 162; *see also* anti-Muslim racism
Rattansi, Ali 44, 118

Said, Edward 15, 63
Säpo 80–89
secularism 15, 18, 25–26, 97, 106–107, 128, 133, 164–165
slander *see* linguistic injury
Smart, Carol 5, 166–167
Sweden Democrats 6, 19, 25, 89
Swedish exceptionalism 5–7, 40

172 *Index*

terrorism: accusation of terrorism 12, 19–22, 125, 130, 143, 145, 154
trial: principle of oral proceedings 45; as a scene of address 46–47, 104

veil 16–19, 26, 87
victim 66, 84–87, 92–94, 109, 109 n4, 147n7, 148–149

xenophobia 38, 80–90, 96